100 CROCHET TILES

Charts and patterns for crochet motifs inspired by decorative tiles

EDITED BY SARAH CALLARD

DAVID & CHARLES

www.davidandcharles.com

CONTENTS

How to Use this Book	4
THE TILES	**6**
Hera 7.5"	8
Dig For Victory 7"	9
Talavera 1 4.75"	10
Autumn Glow 7"	11
Victoriana 4"	12
Secret Lotus 7"	13
Hebe 7.25"	14
Rainbows and Rays 8"	15
Orange Twist 6.75	17
Criss-cross 8"	18
Point to Point 8	19
Mind the Gap 6"	20
South-western Shells 5.75"	21
Moroccan Star 6.25"	21
Blue Hygge 6"	24
All of a Cluster 6"	26
Petunia 7"	27
Picot Fan 7"	28
Medusa 5.25"	29
Aphrodite 5.75"	30
Daisy Girl 8"	31
Delfina's Square 7.5	32
Blooming Pinwheel 7	34
Baby Wheels 7	36
Calypso 6 7/8	37
Compass Rose 8"	39
Laceflower 6	40

Artemis 8	41
Pandora	42
Spring Garden 6	43
Susana 8"	45
Rosemary Clusters 8"	46
Persephone 6	47
Hestia 5.8	49
Cobblestone 7	50
Estrella 8	52
Catalina 8	53
Mandalita 5.5	55
Wagon Wheel	56
Tessellation	58
Echo	59
Lotus Blossom 6	60
When Flowers Go Blue	61
Grow Your Garden	63
Bobble Burst	65
Blue Bobbles	67
Pebble Splash	68
Delft Blues 3.25	70
Mindful Mandala 8	72
Love in a Mist 6	74
Crescent Quarter 7	75
Indian Terracotta 4.75	77
Popcorn Fantasy	78
Frasera 8	80
Country Posy	82
Annie 5.75	84
Hand-painted	86

Snowflake Sweets	88	Iris	137
Playing with Cubes	91	Athena	139
Samuel	93	Talavera 2	140
Concentric Zigzags	96	Floral Hexagon	141
Zigzag Swirls	98	Crystal Ripple	142
Shining Star	100	Floral Burst	143
On a Slant	102	Starburst	144
Tiled Bricks	104	Clematis	145
Tunnel Vision	106	Octagonal Flower	146
Offset Squares	108	Marine Flower	147
Grecian	110	Popcorn Roundel	148
Wildflower	111	Flower Power	149
Iridescent	112	Classical Ogee	150
Deep Space	113		
Abstract Daisy	115	**THE PROJECTS**	**152**
Art Deco Sunset	116	Baby Wheels Blanket	154
Tottenham Court Road	117	Hand-painted Tiles Cushion	156
Kings Cross	120	Hebe Blanket	158
Russell Square	121	Partners Cushion	160
Northern and Central Lines	123	Petunia Bag	162
Porto Rooftops	124	Poinsettia Wall Panel	164
Port Drops	125	Offset Squares Pot Holder	166
Porto Train Station	127	Victoriana Bath Mat	167
Praça de Ribeira 1	128		
Praça de Ribeira 2	129		
Sao Bento	131	Crochet Techniques	168
Berry Hearts	132	The Designers	174
White and Yellow	134	Index	175
Paolozzi	135		
Circe	136		

HOW TO USE THIS BOOK

This collection of 100 beautiful crochet designs features patterns inspired by decorative ceramic tiles from around the world. You can mix and match the designs to create your own blankets and throws – or try one of the eight exciting projects, which show you other ways in which the tiles could be assembled. The projects can also be made using any other tiles that are the same shape from the book, so the possibilities are endless.

Each pattern also has a chart, either a stitch chart – which also shows the colour of each stitch – or a colour chart showing colour changes for tiles made in the mosaic, tapestry or intarsia techniques. You can work from the stitch charts instead of the written pattern, but since the colour charts do not show which stitch is being worked you will also need to follow the pattern. Some of the colour charts only show one segment of the design, so will need to be repeated several times around to make the complete tile.

BASIC KIT
All you will need to make these tiles is a crochet hook and some yarn, plus a yarn needle for weaving in ends or invisible joins. Most only need small amounts of each colour, so they are a great stash-buster. The projects specify the yarn amounts needed, and any other supplies required to complete the item.

US/UK TERMINOLOGY
All the patterns in this book are written using US crochet terms. See the table below for the equivalent UK stitch names.

US TERM	UK TERM
single crochet	double crochet
half double crochet	half treble
double crochet	treble crochet
treble crochet	double treble
double treble crochet	triple teble crochet

ABBREVIATIONS
approx, approximately
beg, beginning
BLO, back loop only
BPdc, back post double crochet
BPdtr, back post double treble
BPhdc, back post half double
BPsc, back post single crochet
ch, chain
ch-sp, chain space
cont, continue(d)
dc, double crochet
dc2tog, double crochet 2 stitches together
dc3tog, double crochet 3 stitches together
dc4tog, double crochet 4 stitches together
dtr, double treble
FPdc, front post double crochet
FPhdc, front post half double crochet
FPsc, front post single crochet
FPtr, front post treble
FLO, front loop only
foll, follow(ing)
hdc, half double crochet
prev, previous
rep, repeat
RS, right side
sc, single crochet
sc2tog, single crochet 2 stitches together
sc3tog, single crochet 3 stitches together
skip, miss
slst, slip stitch
sp, space
st(s), stitch(es)
stsc, standing single crochet
stdc, standing double crochet
sthdc, standing half double crochet
sttr, standing treble
tr, treble
tr3tog, treble 3 stitches together
tr4tog, treble 4 stitches together
WS, wrong side
yoh, yarn over hook
* – repeat instructions following asterisk as directed
[ ] – work instructions within brackets as many times stated

CROCHET CHART SYMBOLS

These symbols are used in the crochet stitch charts.

⟐	chain	⋏	dc3tog		5dc-bobble
•	slip stitch	⋏	dc4tog		4tr-bobble
+	single crochet	⋏	tr3tog		5tr-bobble
T	half double crochet	⋏	tr4tog		3dc-PC
T	double crochet		2dc-cl		4dc-PC
T	treble crochet		3dc-cl		5dc-PC
T	double treble crochet		4dc-cl		2ch-picot
			5dc-cl		3ch-picot
∪	front loop		2tr-cl		4ch-picot
∩	back loop		3tr-cl		3hdc-puff st
⌢	third loop		4tr-cl		4hdc-puff st
↺	front post		5tr-cl		spike sc
↻	back post		2dtr-cl		spike hdc
⋏	sc2tog		2dc-bobble		spike dc
⋏	sc3tog		3dc-bobble		V-st
Λ	dc2tog		4dc-bobble		W-st

THE TILES

HERA

DESIGNER: HATTIE RISDALE

YARN

Scheepjes Softfun Aquarel, light worsted (DK), in foll shade:
Floralscape (803)

HOOK

US size G/6 (4mm) hook

GAUGE (TENSION)

A single motif measures approx 7½in (19cm) using a US size G/6 (4mm) hook.

PATTERN

Using G/6 hook, make a magic ring.

Round 1: Working in ring, 2 ch (counts as 1 hdc), 2 hdc, 1 ch, [3 hdc, 1 ch] 3 times, slst in beg 2-ch to join. (12 hdc, 4 ch)

Round 2: 3 ch (counts as 1 dc throughout), 1 dc in same st, 1 dc, 2 dc in next st, 2 ch, *2 dc in next st, 1 dc, 2 dc in next st, 2 ch; rep from * twice more, slst in beg 3-ch to join. (20 dc, 4 x 2ch-sp corners)

Round 3: 3 ch, 1 dc in same st, 3 dc, 2 dc in next dc, 3 ch; *2 dc in next st, 3 dc, 2 dc in next st, 3 ch; rep from * twice more, slst in beg 3-ch to join. (28 dc, 4 x 3ch-sp corners)

Round 4: 3 ch, 1 dc in same st, [2 dc, 2 dc in next st] twice, 4 ch, *[2 dc in next st, 2 dc] twice, 2 dc in next st, 4 ch; rep from * twice more, slst in beg 3-ch to join. (40 dc, 4 x 4ch-sp corners)

Round 5: 3 ch, 1 dc in same st, 8 dc, 2 dc in next st, 5 ch, *2 dc in next st, 8 dc, 2 dc in next st, 5 ch; rep from * twice more, slst in beg 3-ch to join. (48 dc, 4 x 5ch-sp corners)

Round 6: 3 ch, 1 dc in same st, 10 dc, 2 dc in next st, 2 ch, [1 dc, 2 ch] twice in 3rd ch of 5-ch, *2 dc in next st, 10 dc, 2 dc in next st, 2 ch, [1 dc, 2 ch] twice in 3rd ch of beg 5-ch; rep from * twice more, slst in beg 3-ch to join. (64 dc, 12 x 2ch-sp)

Round 7: 3 ch, 1 dc in same st, 5 dc, 2 ch, skip 2 sts, 5 dc, 2 dc in next dc, 2 ch, 1 dc, 1 ch, (1 dc, 2 ch, 1 dc, 1 ch) in corner 2ch-sp, 1 dc, 2 ch, *2 dc in next st, 5 dc, 2 ch, skip 2 sts, 5 dc, 2 dc in next st, 2 ch, 1 dc, 1 ch, (1 dc, 2 ch, 1 dc, 1 ch) in corner 2ch-sp, 1 dc, 2 ch; rep from * twice more, slst in beg 3-ch to join. (72 dc, 12 x 2ch-sp, 8 ch, 4 x 2ch-sp corners)

Round 8: 3 ch, 1 dc in same st, 4 dc, 2 ch, skip 2 sts, 2 dc in 2ch-sp, 2 ch, skip 2 sts, 4 dc, 2 dc in next dc, [1 ch, 1 dc] twice, (1 dc, 2 ch, 1 dc) in 2ch-sp corner, [1 dc, 1 ch] twice, *2 dc in next dc, 4 dc, 2 ch, skip 2 sts, 2 dc in 2ch-sp, 2 ch, skip 2 sts, 4 dc, 2 dc in next dc, [1 ch, 1 dc] twice, (1 dc, 2 ch, 1 dc) in 2ch-sp corner, [1 dc, 1 ch] twice; rep from * twice more, slst in beg 3-ch to join. (80 dc, 8 x 2ch-sp, 16 ch, 4 x 2ch-sp corners)

Round 9: 3 ch, 1 dc in same st, 5 dc, 2 dc in 2ch-sp, 2 ch, skip 2 sts, 2 dc in 2ch-sp, 5 dc, 2 dc in next dc, (1 dc, 1 ch) in next dc, 2 dc, (2 dc, 2 ch, 2 dc) in 2ch-sp corner, 2 dc, 1 ch, 1 dc, *2 dc in next dc, 5 dc, 2 dc in 2ch-sp, 2 ch, skip 2 sts, 2 dc in 2ch-sp, 5 dc, 2 dc in next dc, (1 dc, 1 ch) in next dc, 2 dc, (2 dc, 2 ch, 2 dc) in 2ch-sp corner, 2 dc, 1 ch, 1 dc; rep from * twice more, slst in beg 3-ch to join. (112 dc, 4 x 2ch-sp, 8 ch, 4 x 2ch-sp corners)

Fasten off and weave in ends.

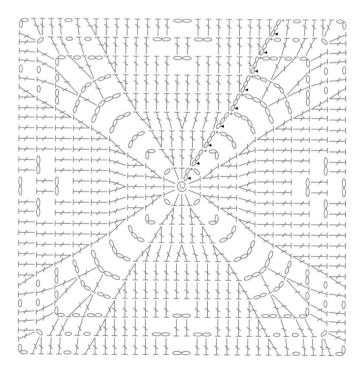

DIG FOR VICTORY

DESIGNER: ANNA NIKIPIROWICZ

YARN

Scheepjes Stone Washed, sport (4ply), in foll shades:
Colour 1: Lepidolite (830)
Colour 2: Enstatite (832)

HOOK

US size E/4 (3.5mm) hook.

GAUGE (TENSION)

A single motif measures approx 7in (18cm) using a US size E/4 (3.5mm) hook.

PATTERN

Using E/4 hook and colour 1, 5 ch, slst to join into a ring.

Round 1: Working into ring, 6 ch (counts as 1 dc and 3ch-sp throughout), [3 dc, 3 ch] 3 times, 2 dc, slst in 3rd of 6-ch to join. (12 dc, 4 x 3ch-sp corners)

Round 2: Slst in first 3ch-sp, 6 ch, 2 dc in same sp, *1 ch, skip next st, 1 dc, 1 ch, skip next st, (2 dc, 3 ch, 2 dc) in next corner 3ch-sp; rep from * to end, ending last rep with 1 dc in first 3ch-sp, slst in 3rd of 6-ch to join. (20 dc, 4 x 3ch-sp corners)

Change to colour 2.

Round 3: Slst in first 3ch-sp, 2 ch (counts as 2 ch-sp throughout), 2 sc in same sp, *2 sc, 1 dc in skipped st from Round 2 (making sure dc is placed in front of 1-ch), 1 sc, 1 dc in skipped st from Round 2, 2 sc, (2 sc, 2 ch, 2 sc) in next corner 3ch-sp; rep from * to end, ending last rep with 2 sc in first 3ch-sp, slst in first of 2-ch to join. (36 sc, 8 dc, 4 x 2ch-sp corners)

Change to colour 1.

Round 4: Slst in first 2ch-sp, 6 ch, 2 dc in same sp, *1 ch, skip next st, [1 dc, 1 ch, skip next st] 5 times, (2 dc, 3 ch, 2 dc) in next corner 3ch-sp; rep from * to end, ending last rep with 1 dc in first 3ch-sp, slst in 3rd ch of 6-ch to join. (36 dc, 4 x 3ch-sp corners)

Change to colour 2.

Round 5: Slst in first 3ch-sp, 2 ch, 2 sc in same sp, *2 sc, 1 dc in skipped st from Round 4 (making sure dc is placed in front of 1-ch), [1 sc, 1 dc in skipped st from Round 4] 5 times, 2 sc, (2 sc, 2 ch, 2 sc) in next corner 3ch-sp; rep from * to end, ending last rep with 2 sc in first 3ch-sp, slst in first ch of 2-ch to join. (52 sc, 24 dc, 4 x 2ch-sp corners)

Change to colour 1.

Round 6: Slst in first 2ch-sp, 6 ch, 2 dc in same sp, *1 ch, skip next st, [1 dc, 1 ch, skip next st] 9 times, (2 dc, 3 ch, 2 dc) in next corner 3ch-sp; rep from * to end, ending last rep with 1 dc in first 3ch-sp, slst in 3rd ch of 6-ch to join. (52 dc, 4 x 3ch-sp corners)

Change to colour 2.

Round 7: Slst in first 3ch-sp, 2 ch, 2 sc in same sp, *2 sc, 1 dc in skipped st from Round 6, [1 sc, 1 dc in skipped st from Round 6] 9 times, 2 sc, (2 sc, 2 ch, 2 sc) in next corner 3ch-sp; rep from * to end, ending last rep with 2 sc in first 3ch-sp, slst in first ch of 2-ch to join. (68 sc, 40 dc, 4 x 2ch-sp corners)

Change to colour 1.

continued on next page >

Round 8: Slst in first 2ch-sp, 6 ch, 2 dc in same sp, *1 ch, skip next st, [1 dc, 1 ch, skip next st] 13 times, (2 dc, 3 ch, 2 dc) in next corner 3ch-sp; rep from * to end, ending last rep with 1 dc in first 3ch-sp, slst in 3rd ch of 6-ch to join. (68 dc, 4 x 3ch-sp corners)

Change to colour 2.

Round 9: Slst in first 3ch-sp, 2 ch, 1 sc in same sp, *2 sc, 1 dc in skipped st from Round 8, [1 sc, 1 dc in skipped st from Round 8] 13 times, 2 sc, (1 sc, 2 ch, 1 sc) in next corner 3ch-sp; rep from * to end, ending last rep with 1 sc in first 3ch-sp, slst in first of 2-ch to join. (76 sc, 56 dc, 4 x 2ch-sp corners)

Change to colour 1.

Round 10: Slst in first 2ch-sp, 2 ch, 1 sc in same sp, *1 sc in each st to next corner sp, (1 sc, 2 ch, 1 sc) in next corner 3ch-sp; rep from * to end, ending last rep with 1 sc in first 2ch-sp, slst in first of 2-ch to join. (140 sc, 4 x 2ch-sp corners)

Round 11: As Round 10. (148 sc, 4 x 2ch-sp corners)

Fasten off and weave in ends.

TALAVERA 1

DESIGNER: EMMA POTTER

YARN

Sirdar Snuggly DK, light worsted (DK), in foll shade:
Treasure (516)

HOOK

US size G/6 (4mm) hook

GAUGE (TENSION)

A single motif measures approx 4¾in (12cm) using a US size G/6 (4mm) hook.

PATTERN

Using G/6 hook, 4 ch, slst to join into a ring.

Round 1: Working into ring, 2 ch (counts as 1 dc), 2 dc, [2 ch, 3 dc] 3 times, 2 ch, slst in top of beg 2-ch to join. (12 dc groups, 4 x 2ch-sp corners)

Round 2: 4 ch (counts as first 4ch-loop), 1 sc in middle dc, *4 ch, 1 sc in corner sp, 9 ch, 1 sc in same corner sp (corner loop made)**, 4 ch, 1 sc in middle dc; rep from * around ending last rep at **, slst in bottom of beg 4-ch to join. (4 x 9-ch corner loops, 8 x 4-ch loops)

Round 3: *Slst in first 4ch-sp, 5 ch, slst in next 4ch-sp, (5 dc, 3 ch, 5 dc) in 9-ch loop; rep from * around, slst in bottom of beg 5-ch to join. (4 corner wings, 4 x 5ch-sps)

Round 4: Slst in 5ch-sp, 5 ch (counts as first dtr), (2 dtr, 5 ch, 3 dtr) in 5ch-sp, slst in 5th dc, 3 sc in 3ch-sp, slst in next dc, *(3 dtr, 5 ch, 3 dtr) in 5ch-sp, slst in 5th dc, 3 sc in 3ch-sp, slst in next dc; rep from * around, slst in top of beg 5-ch to join. (24 dtr, 12 sc 4 x 5ch-sps)

Round 5: Slst in 2 dtr and first 5ch-sp (corner), 3 ch (counts as 1 dc), 3 dc, 3 ch, 4 dc in first corner, 5 ch, 1 sc in middle sc, (3 ch, slst in first ch, 1 sc) in same place (picot made), 5 ch, *(4 dc, 3 ch, 4 dc) in next corner, 5 ch, 1 sc in middle sc, (3 ch, slst in first ch, 1 sc) in same place, 5 ch; rep from * around, slst in top of beg 3-ch to join. (4 picot, 32 dc, 4 x 3ch-sp corners)

Fasten off and weave in ends.

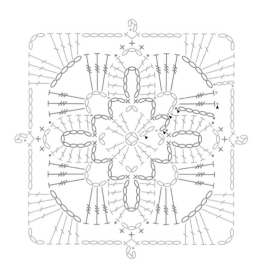

AUTUMN GLOW

DESIGNER: ANNA NIKIPIROWICZ

YARN

Scheepjes Stone Washed, sport (4ply), in foll shades:

Colour 1: New Jade (819)

Colour 2: Canada Jade (806)

Colour 3: Lemon Quartz (812)

Colour 4: Yellow Jasper (809)

Colour 5: Brown Agate (822)

HOOK

US size E/4 (3.5mm) hook

GAUGE (TENSION)

A single motif measures approx 7in (18cm) using a US size E/4 (3.5mm) hook.

NOTE

Join yarn with standing sts unless otherwise indicated, and join round with invisible join in standing st.

PATTERN

Using E/4 hook and colour 1, make a magic ring.

Round 1: 1 ch (does not count as st), [1 sc, 1 ch] 8 times in ring, enclosing yarn end as you work, pull on yarn end to close opening, slst in first sc to join. (8 sc, 8 ch)

Round 2: Join colour 2, 1 stsc in first 1ch-sp, 1 ch, skip next st, *1 sc in next 1ch-sp, 1 ch, skip next st; rep from * to end.

Fasten off colour 2.

Round 3: Join colour 1, 1 stdc in first 1ch-sp, 1 dc in same sp, 1 ch, skip next st, *2 dc in next 1ch-sp, 1 ch, skip next st; rep from * to end. (16 dc, 8 ch)

Fasten off colour 1.

Round 4: Join colour 3, 1 stsc in first dc, 1 sc in same st, 1 sc, 1 dc in skipped sc from prev round, *2 sc in next st, 1 sc, 1 dc in skipped sc from prev round (working in front of 1-ch); rep from * to end. (24 sc, 8 dc)

Fasten off colour 3.

Round 5: Join colour 2, 1 stsc in first st, 1 ch, skip next st, *1 sc, 1 ch, skip next st; rep from * to end. (16 sc, 16 ch)

Fasten off colour 2.

Round 6: Join colour 4, 1 stdc in first 1ch-sp, 1 dc in same sp, 1 ch, skip next st, *2 dc in next 1ch-sp, 1 ch, skip next st; rep from * to end. (32 dc, 16 ch)

Fasten off colour 4.

Round 7: Join colour 3, 1 stsc in first st, 1 sc in same st, 1 sc, 1 dc in skipped sc from prev round (working in front of 1-ch); *2 sc in next st, 1 sc, 1 dc in skipped sc from prev round (making sure to work dc in front of 1-ch); rep from * to end. (48 sc, 16 dc)

Fasten off colour 3.

Round 8: Join colour 5, 1 sthdc in first st, 1 hdc in each st to end. (64 hdc)

Fasten off colour 4.

Round 9: Join colour 4, 1 ch, 1 BPhdc around post of each st to end. (64 BPhdc)

Fasten off colour 5.

Round 10: Join colour 3, 1 sttr in first st , 3 ch, 1 tr in same st, 2 dc, 2 hdc, 7 sc, 2 hdc, 2 dc, *(1 tr, 3 ch, 1 tr) in next st, 2 dc, 2 hdc, 7 sc, 2 hdc, 2 dc; rep from * twice more. (68 sts, 4 x 3ch-sp corners)

continued on next page >

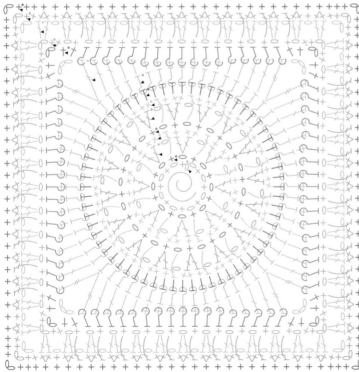

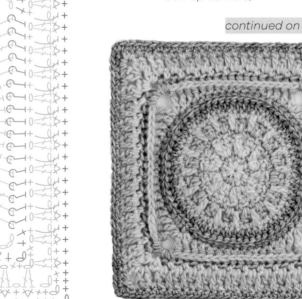

Fasten off colour 3.

Round 11: Join colour 2, 1 stsc in first corner 3ch-sp, 2 ch, 2 sc in same sp, 1 BPhdc around post of each st to next corner 3ch-sp, *(2 sc, 2 ch, 2 sc) in next 3ch-sp, 1 BPhdc around post of each st to next corner 3ch-sp; rep from * twice more, 1 sc in first corner sp. (84 sts, 4 x 2ch-sp corners)

Fasten off colour 2.

Round 12: Join colour 1, 1 stsc in first corner 2ch-sp, 2 ch, 2 sc in same sp, *[1 ch, skip next st, 1 sc] 10 times, 1 ch, skip next st, (2 sc, 2 ch, 2 sc) in next 2ch-sp; rep from * 3 more times, ending last rep with 1 sc in first corner 2ch-sp. (56 sc, 44 ch, 4 x 2ch-sp corners)

Fasten off colour 1.

Round 13: Join colour 3, 1 stdc in first corner 2ch-sp, 2 ch, 2 dc in same sp, *1 ch, skip next 2 sts, 2 dc in next 1ch-sp, [1 ch, skip next st, 2 dc in next 1ch-sp] 10 times, 1 ch, skip next 2 sts, (2 dc, 2 ch, 2 dc) in next corner 2ch-sp; rep from * to end, ending last rep with 1 dc in first corner 2ch-sp. (104 dc, 48 ch, 4 x 2ch-sp corners)

Fasten off colour 3.

Round 14: Join colour 4, 1 stsc in first corner 2ch-sp, 2 ch, 2 sc in same sp, *sc2tog, 1 sc in next 1ch-sp, sc2tog, [1 dc in skipped sc from prev round (working in front of 1-ch); sc2tog] 10 times, 1 sc in next 1ch-sp, sc2tog, (2 sc, 2 ch, 2 sc) in next corner 2ch-sp; rep from * to end, ending last rep with 1 sc in first corner 2ch-sp. (116 sts, 4 x 2ch-sp corners)

Fasten off colour 4.

Round 15: Join colour 5, 1 stsc in first corner 2ch-sp, 2 ch, 1 sc in same sp, *1 sc in each st to next corner 2ch-sp, (1 sc, 2 ch, 1 sc) in next corner 2ch-sp; rep from * to end. (124 dc, 4 x 2ch-sp corners)

Fasten off with invisible join, weave in all ends.

VICTORIANA

DESIGNER: EMMA POTTER

YARN

Drops Paris, worsted (aran), in foll shades:
Colour 1: White (16)
Colour 2: Black (15)

HOOK

US size H/8 (5mm) hook

GAUGE (TENSION)

A single motif measures approx 4in (10cm) using a US size H/8 (5mm) hook.

PATTERN

Using H/8 hook and colour 1, 4 ch, slst to join into a ring.

Round 1: 2 ch (counts as first dc), 11 dc in ring, slst in top of beg 2-ch to join. (12 dc)

Round 2: 2 ch (does not count as st), 1 dc in same place as 2-ch, 2 dc in each dc around, slst in to top of beg 2-ch to join. (24 dc)

Round 3: 8 ch (counts as 1 dc, 5 ch), skip 1 dc, 1 dc in next dc, *4 dc, 5 ch, skip 1 dc, 1 dc in next dc; rep from * twice more, 3 dc, slst in 3rd ch of beg 8-ch to join. (20 dc, 4 x 5ch-sp corners)

Fasten off colour 1.

Round 4: Join colour 2 in any dc immediately after a 5-ch, 1 ch (counts as first sc), 1 sc in each dc to 5-ch corner sp, *(3 dc, 3 ch, 3 dc) in skipped st below 5-ch, 5 sc; rep around, slst in beg 1-ch to join. (20 sc, 24 dc, 4 x 3ch-sp corners)

Fasten off and weave in ends.

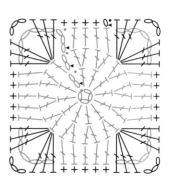

SECRET LOTUS

DESIGNER: JOHANNA LINDAHL

YARN

Drops Cotton Light, light worsted (DK), in foll shades:

Colour 1: Yellow (28)

Colour 2: Khaki (12)

Colour 3: Pink (18)

Colour 4: Dark Red (17)

HOOK

US size G/6 (4mm) hook.

GAUGE (TENSION)

A single motif measures approx 7in (18cm) using a US size G/6 (4mm) hook.

PATTERN

Using G/6 hook and colour 1, make a magic ring.

Round 1 (RS): Working into ring, 5 ch (counts as 1 dc, 2ch-sp), [3 dc, 2 ch] 3 times, 2 dc, slst in 3rd ch of beg 5-ch to join. (12 dc, 4 x 2ch-sp corners)

Fasten off colour 1.

Round 2: Join colour 2 in any corner 2ch-sp, 7 ch (counts as 1 dc, 4ch-sp), 1 dc in same ch-sp, *1 ch, 1 sc, 1 ch, 1 dc, 1 ch, 1 sc, 1 ch, (1 dc, 4 ch, 1 dc) in next 2ch-sp; rep from * twice more, 1 ch, 1 sc, 1 ch, 1 dc, 1 ch, 1 sc, 1 ch, slst in 3rd ch of beg 7-ch to join. (12 dc, 8 sc, 16 ch, 4 x 2ch-sp corners)

Fasten off colour 2.

Round 3: Join colour 3 in any corner 4ch-sp, 4 ch (counts as 1 dc, 1 ch), (1 dc, 2 ch, 1 dc, 1 ch, 1 dc) in same 4ch-sp, *1 ch, skip 4 sts, (1 dc, 1 ch, 1 dc) in next st, 1 ch, skip 4 sts, (1 dc, 1 ch, 1 dc, 2 ch, 1 dc, 1 ch, 1 dc) in next 4ch-sp; rep from * twice more, 1 ch, skip 4 sts, (1 dc, 1 ch, 1 dc) in next dc, 1 ch, skip 4 sts, slst in 3rd ch of beg 4-ch to join. (24 dc, 20 ch, 4 x 2ch-sp corners)

Fasten off colour 3.

Round 4: Join colour 4 in middle 1ch-sp on any side, 4 ch (counts as 1 dc, 1 ch), 1 sc in next 1ch-sp, 1 ch, 2 dc in next 1ch-sp, 1 dc, (2 dc, 2 ch, 2 dc) in corner 2ch-sp, *1 dc, 2 dc in next 1ch-sp, 1 ch, 1 sc in next 1ch-sp, 1 ch, (1 dc, 1 ch, 1 dc) in next 1ch-sp, 1 ch, 1 sc in next 1ch-sp, 1 ch, 2 dc in next 1ch-sp, 1 dc, (2 dc, 2 ch, 2 dc) in next 2ch-sp; rep from * twice more, 1 dc, 2 dc in next 1ch-sp, 1 ch, 1 sc in next 1ch-sp, 1 ch, 1 dc in 1ch-sp at base of beg ch, 1 ch, slst in 3rd ch of beg 4-ch to join. (48 dc, 8 sc, 20 ch, 4 x 2ch-sp corners)

Fasten off colour 4.

Round 5: Join colour 2 in any corner 2ch-sp, 4 ch (counts as 1 hdc, 2 ch), 1 hdc in same 2ch-sp, *5 BPdc, 2 ch, skip 4 sts, 1 hdc in next 1ch-sp, 2 ch, skip 4 sts, 5 BPdc, (1 hdc, 2 ch, 1 hdc) in next 2ch-sp; rep from * twice more, 5 BPdc, 2 ch, skip 4 sts, 1 hdc in next 1ch-sp, 2 ch, skip 4 sts, 5 BPdc, slst in 2nd ch of beg 4 ch to join. (40 BPdc, 12 hdc, 12 x 2ch-sp)

Fasten off colour 2.

Round 6: Join colour 1 in any corner 2ch-sp, 3 ch (counts as 1 sc, 2ch-sp), 1 sc in same 2ch-sp, *6 sc, 2 sc in next 2ch-sp, 1 ch, 2 sc in next 2ch-sp, 6 sc, (1 sc, 2 ch, 1 sc) in next 2ch-sp; rep from * twice more, 6 sc, 2 sc in next 2ch-sp, 1 ch, 2 sc in next 2ch-sp, 6 sc, slst in first ch of beg 3-ch to join. (72 sc, 4 ch, 4 x 2ch-sp corners)

continued on next page >

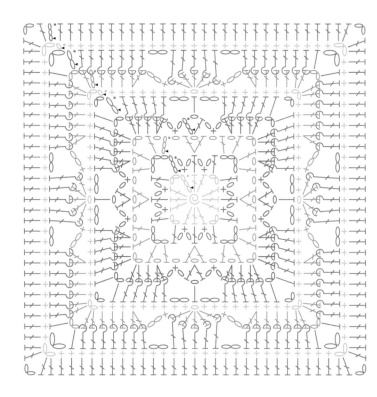

Fasten off colour 1.

Round 7: Join colour 3 in any corner 2ch-sp, 3 ch (counts as 1 dc), (1 dc, 2 ch, 2 dc) in same 2ch-sp, *3 dc, 2 dc in next sc, 2 ch, skip 2 sts, 1 sc, skip 2 sts, 5 dc in next 1ch-sp, skip 2 sts, 1 sc, 2 ch, skip 2 sts, 2 dc in next sc, 3 dc, (2 dc, 2 ch, 2 dc) in next 2ch-sp; rep from * twice more, 3 dc, 2 dc in next sc, 2 ch, skip 2 sts, 1 sc, skip 2 sts, 5 dc in next 1ch-sp, skip 2 sts, 1 sc, 2 ch, skip 2 sts, 2 dc in next sc, 3 dc, slst in top of beg 3-ch to join. (76 dc, 8 sc, 12 x 2ch-sp)

Fasten off colour 3.

Round 8: Join colour 2 in any corner 2ch-sp, 4 ch (counts as 1 hdc, 2 ch), 1 hdc in same ch-sp, *7 BPdc, 2 ch, skip 3 sts, 5 BPdc, 2 ch, skip 3 sts, 7 BPdc, (1 hdc, 2 ch, 1 hdc) in next 2ch-sp; rep from * twice more, 7 BPdc, 2 ch, skip 3 sts, 5 BPdc, 2 ch, skip 3 sts, 7 BPdc, slst in 2nd ch of beg 4-ch to join. (76 BPdc, 8 hdc, 12 x 2ch-sp)

Fasten off colour 2.

Round 9: Join colour 1 in any corner 2ch-sp, 3 ch (counts as 1 sc, 2ch-sp), 1 sc in same ch-sp, *8 sc, 2 sc in next 2ch-sp, 5 sc, 2 sc in next 2ch-sp, 8 sc, (1 sc, 2 ch, 1 sc) in next 2ch-sp; rep from * twice more, 8 sc, 2 sc in next 2ch-sp, 5 sc, 2 sc in next 2ch-sp, 8 sc, slst in first ch of beg 3-ch to join. (108 sc, 4 x 2ch-sp corners)

Fasten off colour 1.

Round 10: Join colour 2 in any corner 2ch-sp, 3 ch (counts as 1 dc), (1 dc, 2 ch, 2 dc) in 2ch-sp at base of beg ch, *27 dc, (2 dc, 2 ch, 2 dc) in next 2ch-sp; rep from * twice more, 27 dc, slst in top of beg 3-ch to join. (124 dc, 4 x 2ch-sp corners)

Fasten off and weave in ends.

HEBE

DESIGNER: HATTIE RISDALE

YARN

Paintbox Yarns Cotton DK, light worsted (DK), in foll shades:
Colour 1: Champagne White (403)
Colour 3: Candyfloss Pink (450)
Colour 4: Marine Blue (434)
Colour 5: Washed Teal (433)
Sirdar Happy Cotton DK, light worsted (DK), in foll shade:
Colour 2: Tea Time (751)

HOOK

US size G/6 (4mm) hook

GAUGE (TENSION)

A single motif measures approx 7¼in (18.5cm) using a US size G/6 (4mm) hook.

PATTERN

Using G/6 hook and colour 1, make a magic ring.

Round 1: 3 ch (counts 1 dc), 15 dc in ring, slst in top of beg 3-ch to join. (16 dc)

Fasten off colour 1.

Round 2: Join colour 2 with slst in top of any dc, 4 ch (counts as 1 dc, 1 ch), (1 dc, 1 ch) in each space between dc around, slst in 3rd ch of beg 4-ch to join. (16 dc, 16 ch)

Fasten off colour 2.

Round 3: Join colour 3 with slst in any 1ch-sp, 3 ch (counts as 1 dc), 2 dc in same sp, 3 dc in each sp around, slst in top of beg 3-ch. (48 dc)

Fasten off colour 3.

Round 4: Join colour 4 with slst in any st, 1 ch (counts as 1 sc), 1 sc in each st around, slst in beg 1-ch to join. (48 sc)

Fasten off colour 4.

Round 5: Join colour 1 with slst in BLO of any sc in first dc of 3-dc group, 6 ch (counts as 1 dc, 3 ch), *[skip 2 sts (1 hdcBLO, 3 ch) in next st] twice, skip 2 sts, (1 dcBLO, 5 ch) in next st, skip 2 sts (1 dcBLO, 3 ch) in next st; rep from * 3 more times omitting final (1 dcBLO, 3 ch), slst in 3rd ch of beg 6-ch to join, do not fasten off. (8 dc, 8 hdc, 12 x 3ch-sp, 4 x 5ch-sp corners)

Round 6: Slst in next 3ch-sp, 3 ch (counts as 1 dc), 3 dc in same sp, 4 dc in next two sps, *(4 dc, 2 ch, 4 dc) in 5ch-sp, 4 dc in next 3ch-sp; rep from * twice, (4 dc, 2 ch, 4 dc) in final 5ch-sp, slst in top of beg 3-ch to join. (80 dc, 4 x 2ch-sp corners)

Fasten off colour 1.

Round 7: Join colour 3 with slst in any st, 3 ch (counts as 1 dc) 1 dc in each st around and (2 dc, 2 ch, 2 dc) in each corner 2ch-sp, slst in top of beg 3-ch to join. (96 dc, 4 x 2ch-sp corners)

Fasten off colour 3.

Round 8: Join colour 5 with slst in 2nd dc after 2ch-sp, 4 ch (counts as 1 dc, 1 ch), (1 dc, 1 ch) in every other st and (2 dc, 2 ch, 2 dc, 1 ch) in each corner 2ch-sp, slst in 3rd ch of beg 4-ch to join. (64 dc, 52 ch, 4 x 2ch-sp corners)

Fasten off colour 5.

Round 9: Join colour 1 with slst in any 1ch-sp, 2 ch (counts as 1 hdc), 1 hdc in same sp, 2 hdc in each 1ch-sp and (2 dc, 2 ch, 2 dc) in each corner 2ch-sp, slst in top of beg 2-ch to join, do not fasten off. (104 hdc, 16 dc, 4 x 2ch-sp corners)

Round 10: 1 ch (counts as 1 sc), 1 sc in each st around and (2 sc, 2 ch, 2 sc) in each corner 2ch-sp, slst in beg 1-ch to join. (136 sc, 4 x 2ch-sp corners)

Fasten off and weave in ends.

RAINBOWS AND RAYS

DESIGNER: JULIE YEAGER

YARN

Scheepjes Stone Washed, sport (4ply), in foll shades:
Colour 1: Pink Quartzite (821)
Colour 3: Coral (816)
Colour 4: Rhodochrosite (835)
Scheepjes River Washed, sport (4ply), in foll shades:
Colour 2: Mekong (943)
Colour 5: Steenbras (942)
Colour 6: Yarra (949)

HOOK

US size G/6 (4mm) hook

GAUGE (TENSION)

A single motif measures approx 8in (20cm) using a US size G/6 (5mm) hook.

NOTES

In st counts, a ch counts as one st.
To join with single crochet, yoh, insert in designated st, yoh and pull through (2 loops on hook), yoh and pull through both loops.

PATTERN

Using G/6 hook and colour 1, 5 ch, slst to join into a ring.

Round 1: 3 ch (counts as 1 dc throughout), 15 dc in ring, slst in top of beg 3-ch to join. (16 dc)

Fasten off colour 1.

Round 2: Join colour 2 with slst in any st, 4 ch (counts as 1 dc, 1 ch), [(1 dc, 1 ch) in next st] 15 times, slst in 3rd ch of beg 4-ch to join. (16 dc, 16 ch)

Fasten off colour 2.

continued on next page >

Round 3: Join colour 3 with sc in any dc, [1 sc in 1ch-sp, 1 FPtr around post of dc in Round 1, 1 sc in next dc in Round 2] 16 times omitting last st, slst in first st to join. (16 FPtr, 32 sc)

Fasten off colour 3.

Round 4: Join colour 4 with slst in any FPtr, 3 ch, 4 dc in same st, [skip 2 sts, 1 sc in FPtr, skip 2 sts, 5 dc in FPtr] 8 times omitting last 5 sts, slst in top of beg 3-ch to join. (40 dc, 8 sc)

Fasten off colour 4.

Round 5: Join colour 2 with sc in 2nd dc of any 5-dc group, [(1 sc, 2 ch, 1 sc) in next st, 1 sc, skip 1 st, 1 sc in sc, 1 FPtr in dc in Round 2 (same colour and slightly to right), 2 ch, 1 FPtr in next dc in Round 2 (same colour), return to Round 4, 1 sc in same sc as last sc, skip 1 st, 1 sc] 8 times omitting last st, slst in first st to join. (16 FPtr, 48 sc, 16 x 2ch-sp)

Fasten off colour 2.

Round 6: Join colour 5 with slst in first 2ch-sp of last round, 3 ch, 4 dc in same sp, [3 dc in next 2ch-sp, 5 dc in next 2ch-sp] 8 times omitting last 5 sts, slst in top of beg 3-ch to join. (64 dc)

Fasten off colour 5.

Round 7: Join colour 2 with sc in first dc of any 5-dc group, 1 sc in next st, [(1 sc, 2 ch, 1 sc) in next st, 2 sc, skip 1 st, 1 sc in dc, 1 FPtr in FPtr below, 2 ch, 1 FPtr in next FPtr below, return to Round 6, 1 sc in same dc as last sc, skip 1 st, 2 sc] 8 times omitting last 2 sts, slst in first st to join. (16 FPtr, 64 sc, 16 x 2ch-sp)

Fasten off colour 2.

Round 8: Join colour 6 with slst in first 2ch-sp of last round, 3 ch, 6 dc in same sp, [5 dc in next 2ch-sp, 7 dc in next 2ch-sp] 8 times omitting last 7 sts, slst in top of beg 3-ch to join. (96 dc)

Fasten off colour 6.

Round 9: Join colour 2 with sc in first dc of any 7-dc group, 6 sc, [1 FPtr in FPtr below, skip 2 sts, 1 sc, 1 FPtr in next FPtr below, skip 2 sts, 7 sc] 8 times omitting last 7 sts, slst in first st to join. (16 FPtr, 64 sc)

Fasten off colour 2.

Round 10: Join colour 4 with scBLO in first st of last round, 4 scBLO, [1 hdcBLO, 1 dcBLO, 1 trBLO, 3 trBLO in next st, 1 trBLO, 1 dcBLO, 1 hdcBLO, 13 scBLO] 4 times omitting last 5 sts, slst in first sc to join. (88 sts)

Round 11: 1 ch, 1 sc in same st, 2 sc, [2 hdc, 4 dc, (2 dc, 1 ch, 2 dc) in next st, 4 dc, 2 hdc, 9 sc] 4 times omitting last 3 sts, slst in first sc to join. (104 sts)

Fasten off colour 4.

Round 12: Join colour 5 with sc in any 1ch-sp, (2 ch, 1 sc) in same sp, [1 FPdtr in FPtr below in Round 9, skip 1 st, 10 sc, 1 FPdc in FPtr below in Round 9, skip 1 st, 1 sc, 1 FPdc in FPtr below in Round 9, skip 1 st, 10 sc, 1 FPdtr in FPtr below in Round 9, skip 1 st, (1 sc, 2 ch, 1 sc) in 1ch-sp for corner] 4 times omitting last corner, slst in first sc to join. (108 sts, 4 x 2ch-sp corners)

Fasten off and weave in ends.

ORANGE TWIST

DESIGNER: LYNNE ROWE

YARN

Ricorumi DK Cotton, light worsted (DK), in foll shades:

Colour 1: Tangerine (026)
Colour 2: Black (060)
Colour 3: White (001)

HOOK

US size E/4 (3.5mm) hook

GAUGE (TENSION)

A single motif measures approx 6¾in (17cm) using a US size E/4 (3.5mm) hook.

NOTES

Each petal in Round 1 is worked separately and consists of 2 rows. Round 2 is worked in 3ch-sps behind petals.

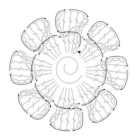

ROUND 1

PATTERN

Using E/4 hook and colour 1, make a magic ring.

Round 1 (RS): Working into ring, 3 ch (counts as 1 dc), 3 dc, turn, 3 ch (counts as 1 dc), 1 dc in dc at base of 3-ch, 3 dc, turn (first petal made), 3 ch, *take 3-ch just made across back of petal just worked, 4 dc in original ring, turn, 3 ch, 1 dc in dc at base of 3-ch, 3 dc, turn (2nd petal made), 3 ch; rep from * 6 more times (8 petals made), slst in top of beg 3-ch to join. (8 petals, 8 x 3ch-sp)

Fasten off colour 1.

Round 2: Join colour 2 with slst in any 3ch-sp behind petal, 3 ch (counts as 1 dc), (2 dc, 2 ch, 3 dc) in same 3ch-sp (first corner), *3 dc in next 3ch-sp behind next petal, (3 dc, 2 ch, 3 dc) in next 3-ch sp behind petal (2nd corner); rep from * twice more, 3 dc in last 3ch-sp behind last petal, slst in top of beg 3-ch to join. (36 dc, 4 x 2ch-sp corners)

Fasten off colour 2.

Round 3: Join colour 3 with slst in any 2ch-sp corner, 3 ch (counts as 1 dc), (2 dc, 2 ch, 3 dc) in same sp (first corner), 3 dc in each sp between 3-dc groups to next corner, *(3 dc, 2 ch, 3 dc) in corner 2ch-sp, 3 dc in sp between 3-dc groups to next corner; rep from * twice more, slst in top of beg 3-ch to join. (48 dc, 4 x 2ch-sp corners)

Fasten off colour 3.

Round 4: Join colour 2 with slst in any 2ch-sp corner, 3 ch (counts as 1 dc), (2 dc, 2 ch, 3 dc) in same sp (first corner), 3 dc in each sp between 3-dc groups to next corner, *(3 dc, 2 ch, 3 dc) in corner 2ch-sp, 3 dc in each sp between 3-dc groups to next corner; rep from * twice more, slst in top of beg 3-ch to join. (60 dc, 4 x 2ch-sp corners)

Fasten off colour 2.

Rounds 5 to 7: Rep Rounds 3 and 4 once then Round 3 once more, using colours as set for each round. (96 dc, 4 x 2ch-sp corners)

Fasten off and weave in ends.

ROUNDS 2-7

CRISS-CROSS

DESIGNER: RACHELE CARMONA

YARN

Scheepjes Softfun, light worsted (DK), in foll shades:

Colour 1: Periwinkle (2619)
Colour 2: Crepe (2612)

HOOK

US size G/6 (4mm) hook

GAUGE (TENSION)

A single motif measures approx 8in (20cm) using a US size G/6 (4mm) hook.

PATTERN

SECTION 1

Using G/6 hook and colour 1, 3 ch, slst to join into a ring.

Row 1 (WS): Working in ring, 1 sc, 1 ch, 1 sc, turn. (2 sc, 1 ch)

Row 2: 1 ch, (1 sc, 1 ch, 1 sc) in ch-sp, turn. (2 sc, 2 ch)

Fasten off colour 1.

Row 3: Join colour 2 with slst in first ch-sp, (1 sc, 1 ch, 1 sc) in same sp, 1 ch, 1 sc in final ch-sp, turn. (3 sc, 2 ch)

Row 4: 1 ch, 1 sc in first ch-sp, 1 ch, (1 sc, 1 ch, 1 sc) in final ch-sp, turn. (3 sc, 3 ch)

Fasten off colour 2.

Row 5: Join colour 1 with slst in first ch-sp, (1 sc, 1 ch, 1 sc) in same sp, (1 ch, 1 sc in next sp) across to final ch-sp, 1 sc in final ch-sp, turn. (4 sc, 3 ch)

Row 6: (1 ch, 1 sc in ch-sp) across to final ch-sp, 1 ch, (1 sc, 1 ch, 1 sc) in final ch-sp, turn. (4 sc, 4 ch)

Fasten off colour 1.

Rows 7 to 22: Rep Rows 5 and 6, changing colours every two rows to maintain stripe pattern, ending with colour 1.

Fasten off colour 1.

Rows 23 to 34: Using colour 2; rep Rows 5 and 6. (18 sc, 18 ch)

Fasten off colour 2.

SECTION 2

Row 1: With RS facing, join colour 1 with slst in final sc of Row 34 on Section 1, 1 sc in same st, working down diagonal edge of Section 1, (1 ch, 1 sc) 24 times evenly, placing final sc in sc of Row 1 on Section 1, turn. (25 sc, 24 ch)

Rows 2 to 4: 1 sc in first ch-sp, (1 ch, 1 sc in next ch-sp) across to end, turn. (22 sc, 21 ch)

Fasten off colour 1.

Rows 5 to 8: Join colour 2 in first ch-sp and work in patt. (18 sc, 17 ch)

Fasten off colour 2.

Rows 9 to 24: Join colour 1 and maintain patt, changing to colour 2 on Row 13, colour 1 on Row 17 and colour 2 on Row 21. (2 sc, 1 ch-sp)

Row 25: 1 sc in ch-sp.

Finish off and weave in ends.

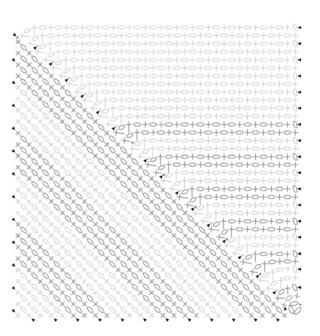

POINT
TO POINT

DESIGNER: RACHELE CARMONA

YARN

Scheepjes Softfun, light worsted (DK), in foll shades:
Colour 1: Latte (2622)
Colour 2: Slate Blue (2602)
Colour 3: Sea Mist (2625)

HOOK

US size G/6 (4mm) hook

GAUGE (TENSION)

A single motif measures approx 8in (20cm) using a US size G/6 (4mm) hook.

PATTERN

SECTION 1

Using G/6 hook and colour 1, 3 ch, slst to join into a ring.

Row 1 (RS): 1 sc, [1 ch, 1 sc] twice, turn. (3 sc, 2 ch)

Row 2: (1 sc, 1 ch, 1 sc) in first ch-sp, 1 ch, (1 sc, 1 ch, 1 sc) in final ch-sp, turn. (4 sc, 3 ch)

Rows 3 to 6: (1 sc, 1 ch, 1 sc) in first ch-sp, [1 ch, 1 sc in next ch-sp] across to final ch-sp, 1 ch, (1 sc, 1 ch, 1 sc) in final ch-sp, turn. (8 sc, 7 ch)

Rows 7 to 44: [1 ch, 1 sc in next ch-sp] across, turn. (7 sc, 7 ch)

Rows 45 to 50: [1 sc in next ch-sp, 1 ch] across to final ch-sp, 1 sc in final ch-sp, turn. (2 sc, 1 ch)

Row 51: 1 sc in ch-sp.

Fasten off colour 1.

SECTION 2

Row 1: Join colour 2 with slst in first st of Row 45, 1 sc in same st, working down long side of Section 1, [1 ch, 1 sc in next ch-sp] 19 times, turn. (20 sc, 19 ch)

Rows 2 to 12: 1 sc in first ch-sp, [1 ch, 1 sc in next ch-sp] across to end, turn. (9 sc, 8 ch)

Fasten off colour 2.

Row 13: Join colour 1 with slst in first ch-sp, 1 sc in same sp and finish row in patt, turn. (8 sc, 7 ch)

Fasten off colour 1.

Rows 14 to 19: Join colour 2 with slst in first ch-sp and work in patt, turn. (2 sc, 1 ch-sp)

Row 20: 1 sc in ch-sp.

Fasten off colour 2.

SECTION 3

Rows 1 to 20: Using colour 3, work as for Section 2, changing to colour 1 for Row 13 as before.

Fasten off and weave in ends.

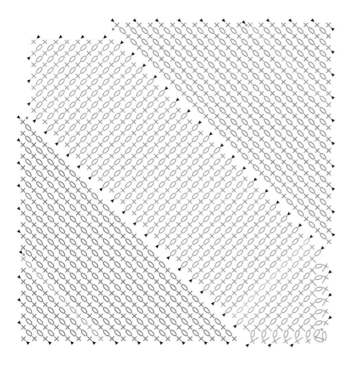

MIND THE GAP

DESIGNER: STEFFI GLAVES

YARN

Cygnet DK, light worsted (DK), in foll shades:
Colour 1: Light Grey (195)
Colour 2: Sunshine (184)
Colour 3: White (208)
Colour 4: Apple (6711)

HOOK

US size D/3 (3mm) hook

GAUGE (TENSION)

A single motif measures approx 6in (15cm) using a US size D/3 (3mm) hook.

NOTE

Change to next colour on last yoh of last st in old colour.

PATTERN

Using size D hook and colour 1, 31 ch.

Row 1: 1 sc in 2nd ch from hook, 1 sc in each ch to end. (30 sc)

Rows 2 and 3: 1 ch (does not count as st throughout), 30 sc.

Row 4: 1 ch [using colour 1, 1 sc, using colour 2, 1 sc] 15 times.

Row 5: Using colour 1, as Row 2.

Rows 6 and 7: Using colour 3, as Row 2.

Row 8: Using colour 1, as Row 2.

Rows 9 to 11: Using colour 2, as Row 2.

Row 12: Using colour 1, as Row 2.

Rows 13 and 14: Using colour 3, as Row 2.

Row 15 (RS): Using colour 4, slst, 1 ch, 2 sc, [1 FPsc loosely in next st in Row 12, 5 sc in Row 14] 4 times, 1 FPsc, 3 sc.

Row 16 (RS): Using colour 3, 1 slstBLO, 1 ch, 30 scBLO.

Row 17: Using colour 3, as Row 2.

Row 18 (RS): Using colour 4, slst, 1 ch, [5 sc, 1 FPsc in Row 15 colour 4 st] 5 times, slst in last colour 3 st in Row 18 to secure last FPsc (creates staggered brick effect).

Rows 19 and 20: Using colour 1, as Rows 16 and 17.

Row 21 (RS): Using colour 4, slst, 1 ch, 5 sc, using colour 3, 2 sc, using colour 4, 16 sc, using colour 3, 2 sc, using colour 4, 5 sc, change to colour 3 on last st.

Row 22: 1 ch, 30 sc (carrying colour 4 and working over).

Row 23: Using colour 3, 1 ch, 4 sc, using colour 4, 1 FPsc in colour 4 st of Row 21, using colour 3, 2 sc, using colour 4, 1 FPsc in colour 4 st of Row 21, using colour 3, 14 sc, using colour 4, 1 FPsc in colour 4 st of Row 21, using colour 3, 2 sc, using colour 4, 1 FPsc in colour 4 st of Row 21, using colour 3, 4 sc.

Row 24: Using colour 3, as Row 22.

Row 25: Using colour 4, 1 ch, 4 sc, 1 FPsc in Row 23 FPsc, using colour 3, 2 sc, using colour 4, 1 FPsc, 14 sc, 1 FPsc, using colour 3, 2 sc, using colour 4, 1 FPsc, 4 sc.

Rows 26 and 27 (RS): Using colour 1, rep Rows 2 and 3.

Row 28: Using colour 4, as Row 2.

Row 29 (RS): Using colour 3, slst, [using colour 2, 1 sc, using colour 3, 1 sc] 15 times.

Row 30: Using colour 4, with RS facing, slst, 1 ch, 30 sc.

Fasten off and weave in ends.

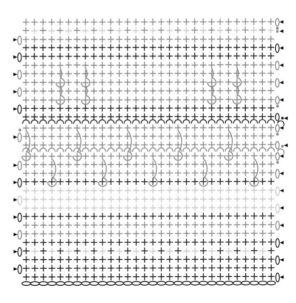

SOUTH-WESTERN SHELLS

DESIGNER: SARAH SHRIMPTON

YARN

Scheepjes Stone Washed, sport (4ply), in foll shades:
Colour 1: Brown Agate (822)
Colour 3: Yellow Jasper (809)
Colour 4: Coral (816)
Colour 5: Axinite (831)
Scheepjes River Washed, sport (4ply), in foll shade:
Colour 2: Tiber (958)

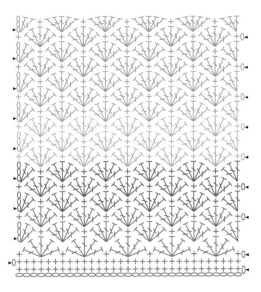

HOOK

US size G/6 (4mm) hook

GAUGE (TENSION)

A single motif measures approx 5¾in (14.5cm) using a US size G/6 (4mm) hook.

PATTERN

Using G/6 hook and colour 1, 31 ch.

Rows 1 and 2: 1 ch, 1 sc in each st to end, turn. (31 sc)

Row 3: 1 ch, 1 sc, *skip 2 sts, 5 dc in next st, skip 2 sts, 1 sc in next st; rep from * to end, turn. (25 dc, 6 sc)

Row 4: 3 ch, 2 dc in same st as 3 ch, skip 2 sts, 1 sc in next st, *skip 2 sts, 5 dc in next st, skip 2 sts, 1 sc in next st; rep from * to last 3 sts, skip 2 sts, 3 dc in last st, turn. (25 dc, 6 sc)

Row 5: As Row 3.

Fasten off colour 1.

Rows 6 to 8: Using colour 2, rep Rows 3 to 5.

Fasten off colour 2.

Rows 9 to 11: Using colour 3, rep Rows 3 to 5.

Fasten off colour 3.

Rows 12 to 14: Using colour 4, rep Rows 3 to 5.

Fasten off colour 4.

Rows 15 to 17: Using colour 5, rep Rows 3 to 5.

Row 18: Using colour 5, as Row 4.

Fasten off and weave in ends.

MOROCCAN STAR

DESIGNER: CAITIE MOORE

YARN

Nurturing Fibres Eco-Cotton, light worsted (DK), in foll shades:
Colour 1: Bessie
Colour 2: Vanilla
Colour 3: Denim
Colour 4: Lime
Colour 5: Aventurine

HOOK

US size G/6 (4mm) hook

OTHER TOOLS AND MATERIALS

4 stitch markers

GAUGE (TENSION)

A single motif measures approx 6¼in (16cm) using a US size G/6 (4mm) hook.

SPECIAL ABBREVIATION

2ch-picot, picot with 2 ch

NOTE

Join yarn with standing sts unless otherwise indicated, and join round with invisible join in standing st.

PATTERN

Using G/6 hook and colour 1, make a magic ring

Round 1: 8 sc in ring. (8 sc)

Fasten off colour 1.

continued on next page >

Round 2: Join colour 1 in any st, *(1 slstFLO, 1 hdcFLO, 1 slstFLO) in same st; rep from * to end. (8 hdc, 16 slsts)

Fasten off colour 1.

Round 3: Join colour 2 in any BLO; 3 dcBLO in each st to end. Mark 4 sts equally around. (24 dc)

Fasten off colour 2.

Round 4: Join colour 3 in any BLO; *2 dc, 2 dc in same st; rep from * to end. (32 dc)

Fasten off colour 3.

Round 5: Join colour 4 in dc falling above st marker, *(1 sc, 1 FPtr around marked st in row below, 1 sc) in same st, 7 ch, skip 7 sts to st above next st marker; rep from * to end, slst in first st of round to join. (4 tr, 8 sc, 4 x 7ch-sp)

Fasten off colour 4.

Round 6: Join colour 5 to Round 4 in dc to left of Round 5 sc (on left of FPtr), *2 sc, 1 FPhdc, 2 FPdc around same st, 1 FPhdc, 2 sc, 2 ch, skip (1 sc, 1 FPtr, 1 sc from Round 5), cont working in Round 4; rep from * to end. (16 sc, 8 hdc, 8 dc, 4 x 2ch-sp)

Fasten off colour 5.

Round 7: Join colour 4 in any FPtr from Round 5 making sure not to work in 2-ch from prev round rather keeping it to back, *(1 sc, 1 hdc, 1 dc, 2 ch, 1 dc, 1 hdc, 1 sc) in FPtr (petal made), 7 ch, work in next FPtr; rep from * to end. (4 petals, 4 x 7ch-sp, 4 x 2ch-sp)

Fasten off colour 4.

Round 8: Join colour 2 directly behind any petal in 2 ch-sp from Round 6, *(1 sc, 1 hdc, 2 dc, 1 tr, 2 ch, 1 tr, 2 dc, 1 hdc, 1 sc) in 2ch-sp, 8 ch, work in next 2 ch-sp; rep from * to end. (40 sts, 4 x 8ch-sp, 4 x 2ch-sp)

Fasten off colour 2.

Round 9: Join colour 5 to Round 6 in first sc to left of colour 4 petal (this st may be hidden, so look carefully!), keeping long ch (from Rounds 7 and 8) at back of work for entire round, *2 sc in same st, 6 hdc, 2 sc in next st, sc in first sc of Round 8 (colour 2) petal, cont working around petal as follows, 2 hdcBLO, 2 dcBLO, (2 hdc, 2 ch, 2 hdc) in 2ch-sp, 2 dcBLO, 2 hdcBLO, 1 sc, cont working in Round 6; rep from * to end. (104 sts)

Fasten off colour 5.

Round 10: Join colour 2 in any st, *1 sc in each st to 2ch-sp, 2 ch, skip 2ch-sp; rep from * around. (96 sc, 4 x 2ch-sp)

Fasten off colour 2.

Round 11: Join colour 1 in 7ch-sp from Round 7, making sure to keep all other long ch to back, *(5 sc, 1 hdc, 3 dc, 1 hdc, 5 sc) in 7ch-sp, 4 ch; rep from * to end. (40 sc, 8 hdc, 12 dc, 4 x 4ch-sp)

Fasten off colour 1.

Round 12: Join colour 3 in first sc after 4-ch from prev round, *4 sc, 3 hdc, (1 hdc, 2ch-picot, 1 hdc) in same st, 3 hdc, 4 sc, 4 ch, cont working in next Round 11 petal; rep from * to end. (32 sc, 32 hdc, 4 x 4ch-sp, 4 picot)

Fasten off colour 3.

Round 13: Join colour 2 in first sc after 4-ch, *8 sc, 2ch-picot, skip picot, 8 sc, 4 ch, skip 4 ch; rep from * to end. (64 sc, 4 x 4ch-sp, 4 picot)

Fasten off colour 2.

ROUNDS 1-10

ROUNDS 11-13

Round 14: Join colour 4 in 8ch-sp from Round 8 at back of work RS facing, *11 tr, 5 hdc in 4ch-sp from Round 13; rep from * to end. (44 tr, 20 hdc)

Fasten off colour 4.

Round 15: Join colour 4 in any st from prev round, *1 dc, 1 FPdc; rep from * to end. (64 dc)

Fasten off colour 4.

Round 16: Join colour 4 in any dc, *1 dc, 1 FPdc around FPdc; rep from * to end. (64 dc)

Fasten off colour 4.

Round 17: Join colour 2 in any st, *7 hdc, 2 hdc in same st; rep from * to end. (72 dc)

Fasten off colour 2.

Place marker in hdc aligned with picot from Round 13 (colour 3 and colour 1 petal), *count 17 sts, place marker in next st (should be lined up with next Round 13 picot); rep from * to place 2 more markers.

Round 18: Join colour 3 in any marked st, *(2 dc, 1 ch, 2 dc) in same st, 1 dc in 3rd loop of hdc, 1 hdc in 3rd loop of next 3 hdc, 1 sc in 3rd loop of next 9 hdc, 3 hdc in 3rd loop of next 3 hdc, 1 dc in 3rd loop of next hdc; rep from * to end. (24 dc, 24 hdc, 36 sc, 4 x 1ch-sp corners)

Fasten off colour 3. (88 sts)

Round 19: Join colour 5 in 1ch-sp, *(2 hdc, 1 ch, 2 hdc) in 1ch-sp, 2 FPdc, 17 hdc, 2 FPdc; rep from * to end. (84 hdc, 16 dc, 4 x 1ch-sp corners)

Fasten off, remove st markers and weave in ends.

ROUNDS 14–19

BLUE HYGGE

DESIGNER: CAITIE MOORE

YARN

Nurturing Fibres Eco-Cotton, light
worsted (DK), in foll shades:
Colour 1: Pecan
Colour 2: Vanilla
Colour 3: Old Gold
Colour 4: Denim
Colour 5: Watershed

HOOK

US size G/6 (4mm) hook

OTHER TOOLS AND MATERIALS

4 stitch markers

GAUGE (TENSION)

A single motif measures approx 6in
(15cm) using a US size G/6 (4mm) hook.

SPECIAL ABBREVIATION

2ch-picot, picot with 2 ch

NOTE

*Join yarn with standing sts unless
otherwise indicated, and join round with
invisible join in standing st.*

PATTERN

Using G/6 hook and colour 1, make a
magic ring.

Round 1: 2 ch (counts as 1 hdc),
7 hdc, pull on tail to close ring.
(8 hdc)

Fasten off colour 1.

Round 2: Join colour 2 in any st, 1 sc
in each st around. (8 sc)

Fasten off colour 2.

Round 3: Join colour 3 in any st, *(1
scFLO, 1 hdcFLO, 1 dcFLO, 2ch-picot,
1 dcFLO, 1 hdcFLO, 1 scFLO) in same
st (petal made), slst in next st; rep
from * to end. (4 petals, 4 picot)

Fasten off colour 3.

Round 4 (WS): Join colour 4 in any
BLO from Round 2, *(1 hdcBLO, 1 ch,
1 hdcBO) in same st; rep from * to
end. (24 sts)

Fasten off colour 4.

Round 5 (RS): Join colour 4 in any
1ch-sp, *(1 sc, 1 hdc, 1 dc, 2ch-picot,
1 dc, 1 hdc, 1 sc) in 1ch-sp (petal
made), skip next st, slst in next st;
rep from * to end. (8 petals, 8 picot)

Fasten off colour 4.

Round 6 (WS): Join colour 5 in any
hdc from Round 4, *1 FPdc around
hdc, 1 ch; rep from * to end. (16 dc,
16 ch)

Fasten off colour 5.

Round 7 (RS): Join colour 5 in 1ch-sp
aligned between petals from Round
5, *(2 hdc, 1 dc, 2ch-picot, 1 dc, 2 hdc)
in 1ch-sp (petal made), 1 sc in next
hdc, 1 sc in 1ch-sp, 1 sc in next hdc;
rep from * to end. (8 petals, 8 picot)

Fasten off colour 5.

Round 8 (WS): Join colour 4 in any
FPdc from Round 6, *1 FPdc around
FPdc, 1 ch; rep from * to end. (16 dc,
16 ch)

Fasten off colour 4.

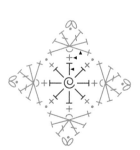

ROUNDS 1-3

ROUNDS 4-5

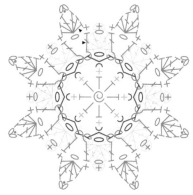

ROUNDS 6-7

Round 9 (RS): Join colour 4 in any 1ch-sp aligned between two petals from Round 7, *(2 hdc, 1 dc, 2ch-picot, 1 dc, 2 hdc) in 1ch-sp (petal made), 1 sc in next hdc, 1 sc in 1ch-sp, 1 sc in next hdc; rep from * to end. (8 petals, 8 picot)

Fasten off colour 4.

Round 10 (WS): Join colour 5 in any FPdc from Round 6, *1 FPdc around FPdc, 2 ch; rep from * to end. (16 dc, 16 x 2ch-sp)

Fasten off colour 5.

Round 11 (RS): Join colour 5 in 2ch-sp aligned between two petals from Round 9, *(2 hdc, 1 dc, 2ch-picot, 1 dc, 2 hdc) in 2ch-sp (petal made), 1 sc in next hdc, 1 sc in 2ch-sp, 1 sc in next hdc; rep from * to end. (8 petals, 8 picot)

Fasten off colour 5.

Round 12: Join colour 1 in first dc to left of any picot, *9 scBLO, 1 ch, skip picot; rep from * to end. (72 sc, 8 ch)

Fasten off colour 1.

Round 13: Join colour 2 in any 1ch-sp, *1 sc in 1ch-sp, 3 scBLO, 3 hdcBLO, 3 scBLO; rep from * to end. (56 sc, 24 hdc)

Fasten off colour 2.

Round 14: Join colour 2 in any st, 1 sc in each around. (80 sc)

Fasten off colour 2.

Round 15: Join colour 3 in any st, 1 hdcBLO in each st around. (80 hdc)

Fasten off colour 3.

Line up motif so petals from Round 1 are in North, South, East, West positions. Clockwise from top, these are petals 1, 2, 3 and 4. Place st marker in hdc (from prev round) directly above petal from Round 9 that lies between petal 1 and petal 2. Count 19 sts (excluding one with marker) and place another marker in next st. This st should be above a petal that lies between petal 2 and 3. Rep around to mark out 4 corners.

Round 16: Join colour 4 at any st marker, *(1 tr, 1 ch, 1 tr) in same st, 3 dcBLO, 3 hdcBLO, 7 scBLO, 3 hdcBLO, 3 dcBLO; rep from * to end. (84 sts, 4 x 1ch-sp corners)

Fasten off colour 4.

Round 17: Join colour 5 in any 1ch-sp, *(2 dc, 1 ch, 2 dc) in 1ch-sp, skip next st, 3 FPdc, 3 FPhdc, skip next st, 6 scBLO, 3 FPhdc, 3 FPdc; rep from * around. (88 sts, 4 ch)

Fasten off, remove st markers, and weave in ends.

ROUNDS 8-9

ROUNDS 10-17

ALL OF A CLUSTER

DESIGNER: RACHELE CARMONA

YARN

Scheepjes Stone Washed, sport (4ply), in foll shades:
Colour 1: Citrine (817)
Colour 2: Beryl (833)
Colour 3: Morganite (834)
Colour 4: Turquoise (824)

HOOK

US size G/6 (4mm) hook

GAUGE (TENSION)

A single motif measures approx 6in (15cm) using a US size G/6 (4mm) hook.

SPECIAL ABBREVIATIONS

2dc-cl, cluster of 2 dc
3dc-cl, cluster of 3 dc

PATTERN

Using G/6 hook and colour 1, 3 ch, slst to join into a ring.

Round 1: (1 sc, 2 ch) in ring (counts as first tr), 15 tr in ring, slst in first tr to join. (16 tr)

Round 2: (1 sc, 1 ch), complete 3dc-cl in same st, [3 ch, 3dc-cl in next st] 15 times, 3 ch, slst in first 3dc-cl to join. (16 x 3dc-cl, 16 x 3ch-sp)

Fasten off colour 1.

Round 3: Join colour 2 with slst in any 3ch-sp, (1 sc, 5 ch, 1 sc) in same sp, *3 ch, 1 sc in next ch-sp, 7 dc in next ch-sp, 1 sc in next ch-sp, 3 ch, (1 sc, 5 ch, 1 sc) in next ch-sp; rep from * 3 more times omitting final (1 sc, 5 ch, 1 sc), slst in first sc to join. (28 dc, 16 sc, 8 x 3ch-sp, 4 x 5ch-sp)

Fasten off colour 2.

Round 4: Join colour 3 with slst in first ch-3 sp of Round 3, 1 sc in same sp, *1 ch, (1 dc, 1 ch) in next 7 dc, 1 sc in next 3ch-sp, 5 ch, skip 5ch-sp, 1 sc in next 3ch-sp; rep from * 3 more times omitting final sc, slst in first sc to join. (28 dc, 8 sc, 8 ch-sp, 4 x 5ch-sp)

Fasten off colour 3.

Round 5: Join colour 4 with slst in both ch-5 sps from Rounds 3 and 4, treating them as one ch-sp, (1 sc, 5 ch, 1 sc) all in same sp, *2 ch, skip one 1ch-sp, (3tr-cl, 2 ch) in each of next 6 ch-sps, (1 sc, 5 ch, 1 sc) in both ch-5 sps from Rounds 3 and 4, treating them as one ch-sp; rep from * 3 more times omitting final (1 sc, 5 ch, 1 sc), slst in first sc to join. (24 x 3dc-cl, 8 sc, 28 x 2ch-sp, 4 x 5ch-sp)

Fasten off colour 4.

Round 6: Join colour 1 with slst in first ch-2 sp of Round 5, 1 sc in same sp, *[3 ch, 1 sc in next 2ch-sp] twice, 3 ch, (3dc-cl, 3 ch, 3dc-cl) in next 2ch-sp, (3 ch, 1 sc in next 2ch-sp) 3 times, 5 ch, 1 sc in next 2ch-sp, rep from * 3 more times omitting final sc, slst in first sc to join. (8 x 3dc-cl, 24 sc, 28 x 3ch-sp, 4 x 5ch-sp)

Round 7: Slst in first 3ch-sp, 1 sc in same sp, *[3 ch, 1 sc in next ch-sp] twice, 3 ch, (1 sc, 3 ch, 1 sc) in next ch-sp, [3 ch, 1 sc in next ch-sp] 3 times, 3 ch, 1 sc in both ch-5 sps from Rounds 5 and 6, treating them as one ch-sp, 3 ch, 1 sc in next ch-sp; rep from * 3 more times omitting final sc, slst in first sc to join. (36 sc, 36 x 3ch-sp)

Fasten off and weave in ends.

PETUNIA

DESIGNER: ANA MORAIS SOARES

YARN

Rosários4 Damasco, 10-ply (aran), in foll shades:

Colour 1: Cream (03)
Colour 2: Yellow (33)
Colour 3: Blue (35)

HOOK

US size E/4 (3.5mm) hook

GAUGE (TENSION)

A single motif measures approx 7in (18cm) using a US size E/4 (3.5mm) hook.

SPECIAL ABBREVIATIONS

3dc-cl, cluster of 3 dc

spike sc, single crochet worked in st two or more rows below

PATTERN

Using E/4 hook and colour 1, make a magic ring.

Round 1: 1 ch (does not count as st), 8 sc in ring, slst in first sc to join. (8 sc)

Fasten off colour 1.

Round 2: Join colour 2, (3dc-cl, 3 ch) in each st around, slst in first 3dc-cl to join. (8 clusters, 8 x 3ch-sp)

Fasten off colour 2.

Round 3: Join colour 3, (2 dc, 2 ch, 2 dc) in every 3ch-sp, slst in first dc to join. (32 dc, 8 x 2ch-sp)

Fasten off colour 3.

Round 4: Join colour 2, *1 spike sc in 3dc-cl from Round 2, 5 ch, skip (2 dc, 2 ch, 2 dc) from Round 3; rep from * to end, slst in first spike sc to join. Do not cut yarn. (8 spike sc, 8 x 5ch-sp)

Round 5: Slst in 5ch-sp, 3 ch (counts as 1 dc), 1 dc in same 5ch-sp, *1 dc in 2ch-sp from Round 3 working around 5ch-sp, 2 dc in same 5ch-sp, 1 FPdc around spike sc from Round

4, 5 dc in next 5ch-sp, 1 FPdc around next spike sc from Round 4, 2 dc in next 5ch-sp; rep from * 3 times omitting last 2 dc, slst in top of beg 3-ch to join. (48 dc)

Fasten off colour 2.

Round 6: Join colour 1, 3 dc in any dc worked in 2ch-sp from Round 3 (first corner made), *1 dc, 3 hdc, 1 sc, 1 dc in 2ch-sp from Round 3 immediately below, working in front of Round 5 sts, skip st behind dc, 1 sc, 3 hdc, 1 dc, 3 dc in dc worked in 2ch-sp from Round 3 (corner); rep from * 3 times omitting last 3 dc corner, slst in first dc to join. (24 dc, 24 hdc, 8 sc)

Fasten off colour 1.

Round 7: Join colour 3 in middle dc of 3-dc corner, *(2 dc, 2 ch, 2 dc) in middle dc, 6 dc, 1 FPdc around next st, skip st behind FPdc, 6 dc; rep from * 3 times, slst in first dc to join. (68 dc, 4 x 2ch-sp corners)

Fasten off colour 3.

Round 8: Join colour 1 in 2ch-sp corner, *(2 hdc, 2 ch, 2 hdc) in corner sp, 17 hdc; rep from * 3 times, slst in first hdc to join. (84 hdc, 4 x 2ch-sp corners)

Fasten off colour 1.

continued on next page >

Round 9: Join colour 2 in 2ch-sp corner, *(2 dc, 2 ch, 2 dc) in corner sp, 3 dc, [1 ch, skip next st, 3dc-cl in next st] 7 times, 1 ch, skip next st, 3 dc; rep from * 3 times, slst in first dc to join. (40 dc, 28 clusters, 32 ch, 4 x 2ch-sp corners)

Fasten off colour 2.

Round 10: Join colour 1 in 2ch-sp corner, *(1 sc, 2 ch, 1 sc) in corner sp, 5 sc, [1 sc in next ch-sp, FPsc around next 3dc-cl] 7 times, 1 sc in next ch-sp, 5 sc; rep from * 3 times, slst in first sc to join. (108 sc, 4 x 2ch-sp corners)

Fasten off colour 1.

Round 11: Join colour 3 in 2ch-sp corner, *(2 dc, 2 ch, 2 dc) in corner sp, 3 dc, [1 ch, skip next st, 3dc-cl in next st] 10 times, 1 ch, skip next st, 3 dc; rep from * 3 times, slst in first dc to join. (40 dc, 40 clusters, 44 ch, 4 x 2ch-sp corners)

Fasten off colour 3.

Round 12: Join colour 1 in 2ch-sp corner, *(1 sc, 2 ch, 1 sc) in corner sp, 5 sc, [1 sc in next ch-sp, FPsc around next 3dc-cl] 10 times, 1 sc in next ch-sp, 5 sc; rep from * 3 times, slst in first sc to join. (132 sc, 4 x 2ch-sp corners)

Fasten off and weave in ends.

PICOT FAN

DESIGNER: MEGHAN BALLMER

YARN

Bernat Softee Cotton, light worsted (DK), in foll shade:
Feather Gray

HOOK

US size F/5 (3.75mm) hook

GAUGE (TENSION)

A single motif measures approx 7in (18cm) using a US size F/5 (3.75mm) hook.

SPECIAL ABBREVIATION

dc-picot, 1 dc in st, 3 ch, slst in top of dc

PATTERN

Using F/5 hook, make a magic ring.

Round 1: 2 ch (does not count as st throughout), 12 dc in ring, pull on tail to close ring, slst in first dc to join, turn. (12 sts)

Round 2: 1 ch, 1 sc in first st, *6 ch, skip 2 sts, 1 sc; rep from * twice more, 6 ch, skip 2 sts, slst in first sc to join, turn. (4 sc, 4 x 6ch-sp)

Round 3: 2 ch, *8dc in 6ch-sp, 2 ch, skip sc; rep from * 3 more times, slst in first dc to join, turn. (32 dc, 4 x 2ch-sp)

Round 4: 6 ch (counts as 1 dc, 3 ch), *skip 2ch-sp, 7 dc-picot, 1 dc, 3 ch; rep from * twice more, skip 2ch-sp, 7 dc-picot, slst in 3rd of beg 6-ch, slst in 3ch-sp, turn. (28 dc-picot, 4 dc, 4 x 3ch-sp)

Round 5: 8 ch (counts as 1 dc, 5 ch), *skip 2 picots, 1 sc in next picot, 5 ch, skip 1 picot, 1 sc in next picot, 5 ch, skip 2 picots, 1 dc in 3ch-sp, 5 ch; rep from * twice more, skip 2 picots, 1 sc in next picot, 5 ch, skip 1 picot, 1 sc in next picot, 5 ch, skip 2 picots, slst in 3rd of beg 8-ch, turn. (8 sc, 4 dc, 12 x 5ch-sp)

Round 6: 2 ch, *3dc in 5ch-sp, 2 ch, 8dc in next 5ch-sp (corner), 2 ch, 3dc in 5ch-sp, 2 ch; rep from * 3 more times, slst in first dc to join, turn. (56 dc, 12 x 2ch-sp)

Round 7: 3 ch (counts as 1 dc), *2dc in 2ch-sp, 3 dc, 2dc in 2ch-sp, 7 dc-picot, 1 dc, 2dc in 2ch-sp, 3 dc; rep from * twice more, 2dc in 2ch-sp, 3 dc, 2dc in 2ch-sp, 7 dc-picot, 1 dc, 2 dc in 2ch-sp, 2 dc, slst in top of beg 3-ch to join. (28 dc-picot, 52 dc)

Fasten off and weave in ends.

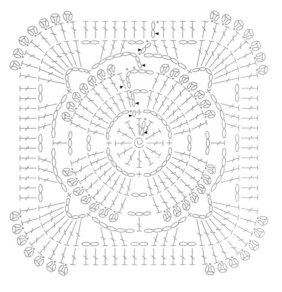

MEDUSA

DESIGNER: HATTIE RISDALE

YARN

Phildar Phil Coton 4, light worsted (DK), in foll shades:
Colour 1: Piscine (1298)
Colour 2: Rosee (1149)
Colour 3: Craie (1937)

HOOK

US size G/6 (4mm) hook

GAUGE (TENSION)

A single motif measures approx 5¼in (13.5cm) using a US size G/6 (4mm) hook.

SPECIAL ABBREVIATIONS

3dc-cl, cluster of 3 dc
spike dc, dc worked in st two or more rows below

PATTERN

Using G/6 hook and colour 1, make a magic ring.

Round 1: 3 ch (counts as 1 dc), 11 dc in ring, slst in top of beg 3-ch to join. (12 dc)

Fasten off colour 1.

Round 2: Join colour 2 with sl st in any sp between two dc, 3 ch (counts as 1 dc), 1 dc in same sp, 2 dc in each sp around, slst in top of beg 3-ch to join. (24 dc)

Fasten off colour 2.

Round 3: Join colour 3 with slst in any sp between two sets of 2-dc, 2 ch (counts as first part of 3dc-cl), (complete 3dc-cl, 3 ch) in same sp, (3dc-cl, 3 ch) in each sp around, slst in top of beg 3dc-cl to join. (12 clusters, 12 x 3ch-sp)

Fasten off colour 3.

Round 4: Work spike sts in this round loosely. Join colour 1 with slst in top of 3dc-cl, 2 ch (counts as 1 sc, 1 ch), *(1 spike, 1 ch) in middle of 2-dc from Round 2, (1 sc, 1 ch) in top of 3dc-cl; rep from * around, (1 spike dc, 1 ch) in middle of the final 2-dc from Round 2, slst in first ch of beg 2-ch to join. (12 spike dc, 12 sc, 24 ch)

Fasten off colour 1.

Round 5: Join colour 2 with slst in any 1ch-sp to left of spike dc, *[(1 ch, 1 hdc, 1 dc, 1 ch) in same sp, (1 dc, 1 hdc, 1 ch) in next sp, join to same sp with slst, move to next sp with a slst] twice, (1 ch, 1 dc, 1 tr, 2 ch) in same sp, (1 tr, 1 dc, 1 ch) in next sp, join to same sp with a slst, move to next sp with a slst; rep from * 3 more times, slst in beg slst to join. (24 dc, 16 hdc, 8 tr, 32 ch, 4 x 2ch-sp corners)

Fasten off colour 2.

Round 6: Join colour 1 with slst in 1ch-sp at top of first small petal after large corner petal, 3 ch (counts as 1 hdc, 1 ch), (1 dc, 1 ch) in slst between two petals, (1 hdc, 2 ch) in 1ch-sp (in petal), (1 tr, 1 ch) in slst between two petals, (1 dc, 1 ch, 1 dc, 2 ch, 1 dc, 1 ch, 1 dc, 1 ch) in 2ch-sp (in larger corner petal), *(1 tr, 2 ch) in slst, (1 hdc, 1 ch) in ch sp, (1 dc, 1 ch) in slst, (1 hdc, 2 ch) in ch sp, (1 tr, 1 ch) in slst, (1 dc, 1 ch, 1 dc, 2 ch, 1 dc, 1 ch, 1 dc, 1 ch) in 2ch-sp; rep from * twice more, (1 tr, 2 ch) in slst between two petals, join with slst in 2nd ch of beg 3-ch, do not fasten off. (8 hdc, 20 dc, 8 tr, 40 ch, 4 x 2ch-sp corners)

Round 7: 2 ch (counts as 1 hdc), 1 hdc in same sp, [2 hdc in next ch-sp] twice, 1 ch, [2 hdc in next ch-sp] twice, (2hdc, 2 ch, 2hdc) in 2ch-sp, [2 hdc in next ch-sp] twice, *[1 ch, 2 hdc in next ch-sp] 4 times, 1 ch, [2 hdc in next ch-sp] twice, (2hdc, 2 ch, 2hdc) in 2ch-sp, [2 hdc in next ch-sp] twice, rep from * twice more, 2 hdc in next ch-sp, 1 ch, slst in second ch of 2-ch to join. (80 hdc, 8 ch, 4 x 2ch-sp corners)

Fasten off colour 1.

Round 8: Join colour 3 to BLO of any st, 1 ch (counts as 1 sc), 1 scBLO in each st and 1 sc in each ch-sp around working (2 hdc, 2 ch, 2 hdc) in 2ch-sp corners, slst in beg 1-ch to join. (88 sc, 16 hdc, 4 x 2ch-sp corners)

Fasten off and weave in ends.

APHRODITE

DESIGNER: HATTIE RISDALE

YARN

Paintbox Yarns Cotton DK, light worsted (DK), in foll shades:

Colour 1: Light Caramel (409)
Colour 2: Ballet Pink (453)
Colour 3: Champagne White (403)
Colour 4: Blush Pink (454)

HOOK

US size G/6 (4mm) hook

GAUGE (TENSION)

A single motif measures approx 5¾in (14.5cm) using a US size G/6 (4mm) hook.

SPECIAL ABBREVIATIONS

4tr-cl, cluster of 4 tr
5tr-cl, cluster of 5 tr
5dc-cl, cluster of 5 dc
3dc-cl, cluster of 3 dc

PATTERN

Using G/6 hook and colour 1, make a magic ring.

Round 1: 3 ch (counts as 1 dc), 15 dc in ring, slst in 3rd ch of beg 3-ch to join. (16 dc)

Fasten off colour 1.

Round 2: Join colour 2 with slst between any two dc, 4 ch (counts as 1 dc, 1 ch), (1 dc, 1 ch) in each sp around, slst in 3rd of beg 3-ch to join. (16 dc, 16 ch)

Fasten off colour 2.

Round 3: Join colour 3 with slst in 1ch-sp, 3 ch (counts as first part of 4tr-cl), complete 4tr-cl in same sp, 2 ch, (4tr-cl, 2 ch) in each ch-sp around, slst in 3rd ch of 3-ch at top of 4tr-cl to join. (16 x 4tr-cl, 16 x 2ch-sp)

Fasten off colour 3.

Round 4: Join colour 4 with slst in any 2ch-sp, 1 ch (counts as 1 sc), 4 sc in same sp, 5 sc in each 2ch-sp around, slst in beg ch-1 to join, do not fasten off. (80 sc)

Round 5: 5 ch, slst in sp between two 5-sc groups, *6 ch, (5tr-cl, 2 ch, 5tr-cl) in next sp, 6 ch, slst in next sp, [5 ch, slst in sp between two 5-sc groups] twice; rep from * 3 times omitting last 5-ch, slst in first ch of beg 5-ch to join. (8 x 5tr-cl, 8 x 5ch-sp, 8 x 6ch-sp, 4 x 2ch-sp)

Fasten off colour 4.

Round 6: Join colour 2 with slst in any 5ch-sp to left of corner group, *6 ch, slst in 5ch-sp, 6 ch, slst in 6ch-sp, 4 ch, (5dc-cl, 3 ch, 5dc-cl) in 2ch-sp, 4 ch, slst in 6ch-sp, 6 ch, slst in 5ch-sp; rep from * 3 times, slst in beg slst to join, do not fasten off. (8 x 5dc-cl, 12 x 6ch-sp, 8 x 4ch-sp, 4 x 3ch-sp)

Round 7: Slst in first two ch, slst in ch-sp, *6 ch, slst in 6ch-sp, 8 ch, slst in 3ch-sp, (3 ch, 3dc-cl, 3 ch, 3dc-cl, 3 ch, slst) in same sp, 8 ch, slst in 6ch-sp, 6 ch, slst in 6ch-sp; rep from * 3 times, slst in beg slst to join, do not fasten off. (8 x 3dc-cl, 8 x 6ch-sp, 8 x 8ch-sp, 12 x 3ch-sp)

Round 8: Slst in next three ch, slst in ch-sp, *7 ch, slst in 8ch-sp, 6 ch, (2 sc, 2 ch, 2 sc) in 2ch-sp, 6 ch, slst in 8ch-sp, [7 ch, slst in 6ch-sp] twice, rep from * 3 times, slst in beg slst to join. (16 sc, 12 x 7ch-sp, 8 x 6ch-sp, 4 x 2ch-sp)

Fasten off and weave in ends.

DAISY GIRL

DESIGNER: JULIE YEAGER

YARN

Scheepjes Stone Washed, sport (4ply), in foll shades:
Colour 1: Blue Apatite (805)
Colour 2: Beryl (833)
Colour 3: Moon Stone (801)

HOOK

US size G/6 (4mm) hook

GAUGE (TENSION)

A single motif measures approx 8in (20cm) using a US size G/6 (4mm) hook.

SPECIAL ABBREVIATIONS

spike sc, sc worked in st two or more rows below
V-st, (1 dc, 3 ch, 1 dc) in same st

NOTE

In Round 8 space between 5-sc groups is not a ch sp.

PATTERN

Using G/6 hook and colour 1, 5 ch, slst to join into a ring.

Round 1: 3 ch (counts as 1 dc throughout), 15 dc in ring, slst in top of beg 3-ch to join. (16 dc)

Fasten off colour 1.

Round 2: Join colour 2 with slst in any st, 6 ch (counts as 1 dc, 3 ch), 1 dc in same st, [skip 1 st, V-st in next st] 7 times, skip 1 st, slst in 3rd ch of beg 6-ch to join. (8 V-sts)

Fasten off colour 2.

Round 3: Join colour 1 with slst in any 3ch-sp, 2 ch (counts as 1 hdc throughout), 3 hdc in same sp, [4 hdc in next 3ch-sp] 7 times, slst in top of beg 2-ch to join. (32 hdc)

Fasten off colour 1.

Round 4: Join colour 3 with slst in any st, 5 ch (counts as 1 dc, 2 ch), [skip 1 st, (1 dc, 2 ch) in next st] 15 times, slst in 3rd ch of beg 5-ch to join. (16 dc, 16 ch-2 sp)

Fasten off colour 3.

Round 5: Join colour 1 with slst in any skipped hdc from Round 3, 3 ch, working around and enclosing 2ch-sp, 2 dc in same st, [working around and enclosing 2ch-sp, 3 dc in next skipped st from Round 3] 15 times, slst in top of beg 3-ch to join. (48 dc)

Fasten off colour 1.

Round 6: Join colour 2 with sc in 3rd dc of any 3-dc group, 2 sc, [2 ch, 3 sc] 15 times, 2 ch, slst in first sc to join. (48 sc, 16 ch-2 sp)

Fasten off colour 2.

Round 7: Join colour 1 with sc in any ch-2 sp, 4 sc in same sp, [5 sc in next ch-2 sp] 15 times, slst in first st to join. (80 sc)

Fasten off colour 1.

Round 8: Work each st in space between 5-sc groups. Join colour 3 with sc in any space between 5-sc groups, [1 ch, 7 dc in space between next group, 1 ch, 1 sc in space between next group] 7 times, 1 ch, 7 dc in space between next group, 1 ch, slst in first sc to join. (56 dc, 8 sc, 16 ch)

continued on next page >

Fasten off colour 3.

Round 9: Join colour 1 with sc in first dc of any group, 6 sc, [spike sc in 4th sc of 5-sc group from Round 7, skip (1 ch, 1 sc, 1 ch) of Round 8, spike sc in 2nd sc of 5-sc group from Round 7, 7 sc] 7 times, spike sc in 4th sc of 5-sc group from Round 7, skip (1 ch, 1 sc, 1 ch) of Round 8, spike sc in 2nd sc of 5-sc group from Round 7, slst in first st to join. (72 sc)

Fasten off colour 1.

Round 10: Join colour 2 with slstBLO in first sc after any spike sc, 3 ch, 1 dcBLO in same st, *1 hdcBLO, 4 scBLO, 2 scBLO in next st, dc2togBLO, 2 scBLO in next st, 4 scBLO, 1 hdcBLO, 2 dcBLO in next st, [2 trBLO in next st] twice, 2 dcBLO in next st; rep from * twice more, 1 hdcBLO, 4 scBLO, 2 scBLO in next st, dc2togBLO, 2 scBLO in next st, 4 scBLO, 1 hdcBLO, 2 dcBLO in next st, [2 trBLO in next st] twice, slst in top of beg 3-ch to join. (92 sts)

Round 11: 3 ch, 1 dc, [1 hdc, 14 sc, 1 hdc, 3 dc, (2 dc, 1 ch, 2 dc) in next st for corner, 3 dc] 3 times, 1 hdc, 14 sc, 1 hdc, 3 dc, (2 dc, 1 ch, 2 dc) in next st, 1 dc, slst in top of beg 3-ch to join. (104 sts, 4 x 1ch-sp corners)

Fasten off colour 2.

Round 12: Join colour 1 with sc in any ch-1 sp, 2 ch, 1 sc in same sp, [1 sc, 1 FPdc, 22 sc, 1 FPdc, 1 sc, (1 sc, 2 ch, 1 sc) in 1ch-sp] 3 times, 1 sc, 1 FPdc, 22 sc, 1 FPdc, 1 sc, slst in first sc to join. (112 sts, 4 x 2ch-sp corners)

Fasten off and weave in ends.

DELFINA'S SQUARE

DESIGNER: ANA MORAIS SOARES

YARN

Rosários4 Glória, worsted (aran), in foll shades:
Colour 1: Coral (45)
Colour 2: Aqua (49)
Colour 3: Blue (47)
Colour 4: White Pearl (41)

HOOK

US size G/6 (4mm) hook

GAUGE (TENSION)

A single motif measures approx 7½in (19cm) using a US size G/6 (4mm) hook.

SPECIAL ABBREVIATION

4ch-picot, picot with 4 ch

PATTERN

Using G/6 hook and colour 1, make a magic ring.

Round 1: 3 ch (counts as 1 dc), 3 dc, 5 ch, [4 dc, 5 ch] 3 times into ring, slst in first dc to join. (16 dc, 4 x 5ch-sp)

Round 2: 3 ch (counts as first dc of dc4tog), dc3tog (first dc4tog made), *5 ch, sc in next 5ch-sp, 5 ch, dc4tog; rep from * 3 more times omitting last dc4tog, slst in top of beg 3-ch to join. (4 dc4tog, 4 sc, 8 x 5ch-sp)

Round 3: 1 ch (does not count as st), *(3 sc, 4ch-picot, 3 sc) in next 5ch-sp, skip to next 5ch-sp; rep from * 7 more times, slst in first sc to join. (48 sc, 8 picot)

Fasten off colour 1.

Round 4: Join colour 2, 1 sc in 2nd sc after a picot, 3 sc, 3 ch, skip (1 sc, 4ch-picot, 1 sc), *4 sc, 3 ch, skip (1 sc, 4ch-picot, 1 sc); rep from * 6 more times, slst in first sc to join. (32 sc, 8 x 3ch-sp)

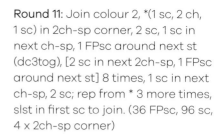

Round 5: Slst in next sc, 3 ch (counts as 1 dc), 1 dc, *1 ch, skip next st, 4 dc in next 3ch-sp, 1 ch, skip next st, 2 dc; rep from * 7 more times omitting last 2 dc, slst in first dc to join. (48 dc, 16 ch)

Fasten off colour 2.

Round 6: Join colour 3, 1 sc in first dc of a 4-dc group of Round 5, 3 sc, *1 tr in next skipped st of Round 4 working in front of ch-sp from prev round, 1 sc in ch-sp behind tr, 2 sc, 1 sc in next ch-sp, 1 tr in next skipped st from Round 4 working in front of ch-sp from prev round, 4 sc; rep from * 7 more times omitting last 4 sc, slst in first sc to join. (16 tr, 48 sc)

Fasten off colour 3.

Round 7: Join colour 4, (1 tr, 2 ch, 1 tr) in tr from prev round worked before picot from Round 3 to left of first dc4tog from Round 2 (first corner made), *1 ch, 1 tr, 1 ch, skip next st, 1 dc, 1 ch, skip next st, [1 hdc, 1 ch, skip next st] twice, [1 sc, 1 ch, skip next st] twice, [1 hdc, 1 ch, skip next st] twice, 1 dc, 1 ch, skip next st, 1 tr,

1 ch, [1 tr, 2 ch, 1 tr] in next st (corner made); rep from * 3 more times omitting last corner sts, slst in first tr to join. (16 tr, 8 dc, 16 hdc, 8 sc, 44 ch, 4 x 2ch-sp corners)

Round 8: 1 ch (does not count as st), 1 sc in same st, *(1 sc, 1 ch, 1 sc) in next 2ch-sp corner, [1 sc in next st, 1 sc in next ch-sp] 11 times, 1 sc in last st of side; rep from * 3 more times omitting last sc, slst in first sc to join. (100 sc, 4 x 2ch-sp corners)

Fasten off colour 4.

Round 9: Join colour 2, *(1 sc, 2 ch, 1 sc) in 2ch-sp corner, 1 scBLO in every st to the next 2ch-sp corner; rep from * 3 more times, slst in first sc to join. (108 sc, 4 x 2ch-sp corners)

Fasten off colour 2.

Round 10: Join colour 1, *(2 dc, 2 ch, 2 dc) in 2ch-sp corner, 1 ch, dc3tog, [2 ch, dc3tog] 8 times, 1 ch; rep from * 3 more times, slst in first dc to join. (36 dc3tog, 16 dc, 8 ch, 36 x 2ch-sp)

Fasten off colour 1.

Round 11: Join colour 2, *(1 sc, 2 ch, 1 sc) in 2ch-sp corner, 2 sc, 1 sc in next ch-sp, 1 FPsc around next st (dc3tog), [2 sc in next 2ch-sp, 1 FPsc around next st] 8 times, 1 sc in next ch-sp, 2 sc; rep from * 3 more times, slst in first sc to join. (36 FPsc, 96 sc, 4 x 2ch-sp corner)

Fasten off colour 2.

Round 12: Join colour 4, *(1 sc, 2 ch, 1 sc) in 2ch-sp corner, [1 ch, skip next st, 1 scBLO in next st] 16 times, 1 ch, skip last st before corner; rep from * 3 more times, slst in first sc to join. (72 sc, 68 ch, 4 x 2ch-sp corners)

Fasten off colour 4.

Round 13: Join colour 1, *(1 sc, 2 ch, 1 sc) in 2ch-sp corner, [1 ch, skip next st, 1 sc in next ch-sp] 17 times, 1 ch, skip last st before corner; rep from * 3 more times, slst in first sc to join. (76 sc, 72 ch, 4 x 2ch-sp corners)

Fasten off colour 1.

Round 14: Join colour 3, *(1 sc, 2 ch, 1 sc) in 2ch-sp corner, [1 sc in next st, 1 sc in next ch-sp] 18 times, 1 sc in last st before corner; rep from * 3 more times, slst in first sc to join. (156 sc, 4 x 2ch-sp corners)

Fasten off and weave in ends.

BLOOMING PINWHEEL

DESIGNER: ANA MORAIS SOARES

YARN

Rosários4 Regata, light worsted (DK), in foll shades:
Colour 1: Yellow (31)
Colour 2: Green (26)
Colour 3: Light Blush Pink (23)
Colour 4: Blush Pink (21)
Colour 5: White Pearl (01)

HOOK

US size E/4 (3.5mm) hook

GAUGE (TENSION)

A single motif measures approx 7in (18cm) using a US size E/4 (3.5mm) hook.

SPECIAL ABBREVIATIONS

V-st, (1 dc, 2 ch, 1 dc) in same st
4dc-cl, cluster of 4 dc

PATTERN

Using E/4 hook and colour 1, make a magic ring.

Round 1: 1 ch (does not count as st throughout), 6 sc in ring, slst in first sc to join. Do not close ring. (6 sc)

Round 2: 1 ch, 12 hdc in ring, working over sc from Round 1, sl st in first hdc to join. Close ring. (12 hdc)

Round 3: 1 ch, 1 scFLO in each st around, slst in first sc to join or make invisible join. (12 sc)

Fasten off colour 1.

Round 4: Join colour 2, working in Round 2 sts, [1 scBLO, 2 scBLO in next st] around, slst in first sc to join. (18 sc)

Round 5: 5 ch (counts as 1 dc, 2 ch), 1 dc in same st (first V-st made), *skip one st, V-st in next st; rep from * to end, slst in 3rd ch of beg 5-ch to join. (9 V-sts)

Fasten off colour 2.

Round 6: Join colour 3, [1 sc in sp between 2 V-sts, 3 ch, 4dc-cl in next 2ch-sp, 3 ch] 9 times, slst in first sc to join. (9 sc, 9 clusters, 18 x 3ch-sp)

Fasten off colour 3.

Round 7: Join colour 4, [1 FPsc around 4dc-cl, slst in next 3ch-sp, 3 ch (counts as 1 dc), 5 dc in same 3ch-sp, skip sc, sl st in next 3ch-sp] 9 times, slst in first FPsc to join. (9 FPsc, 54 dc, 18 slsts)

Fasten off colour 4. Turn work.

Round 8 (WS): Join colour 5, [1 slst catching back legs of sc from Round 6, 5 ch] 9 times, slst in first slst to join. Turn work. (9 slsts, 9 x 5ch-sp)

Round 9 (RS): Sl st in 5ch-sp, 3 ch (counts as 1 dc throughout), 5 dc in same 5ch-sp, *[5 dc in next 5ch-sp] twice, 6 dc in next 5ch-sp; rep from * twice more omitting last 6-dc group, slst in top of beg 3-ch to join. (48 dc)

Round 10: 3 ch, (1 dc, 2 ch, 2 dc) in same st (first corner made), *1 dc, 9 hdc, 1 dc, (2 dc, 2 ch, 2 dc) in next st (corner made); rep from * 3 more times omitting last corner sts, slst in top of beg 3-ch to join. (24 dc, 36 hdc, 4 x 2ch-sp corners)

Round 11: 2 ch (counts as 1 hdc), hdcBLO in next st, *(2 hdc, 2 ch, 2 hdc) in next 2ch-sp corner, 15 hdcBLO; rep from * 3 more times omitting last 2 hdcBLO, slst in top of beg 2-ch to join. (76 hdc, 4 x 2ch-sp corners)

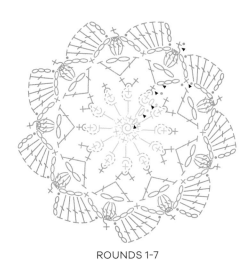

ROUNDS 1-7

Fasten off colour 5.

Round 12: Join colour 2, *1 dc in 2ch-sp corner, 1 tr in 2ch-sp corner of Round 10 in middle of 4-hdc worked there, working in front of current 2ch-sp, (1 dc, 2 ch, 1 dc) in 2ch-sp of current round (corner made), 1 tr in 2ch-sp corner of Round 10 in middle of 4-hdc worked there, working in front of current 2ch-sp, 1 dc in current 2ch-sp, skip first st (is a bit hidden), 1 dc in next st, 1 trFLO in first st from Round 10, skip next st (behind trFLO), 6 dc, 2 trFLO in corresponding sts of Round 10, skip next 2 sts (behind 2 trFLO), 6 dc, 1 trFLO in last st of Round 10, skip next st (behind trFLO), 1 dc in last st before 2ch-sp corner; rep from * 3 more times, slst in first dc to join. (24 tr, 76 dc, 4 x 2ch-sp corners)

Fasten off colour 2.

Round 13: Join colour 5, *(1 sc, 2 ch, 1 sc) in 2ch-sp corner, 1 scBLO, 1 FPhdc, 2 scBLO, 1 FPhdc, 6 scBLO, 2 FPhdc, 6 scBLO, 1 FPhdc, 2 scBLO, 1 FPhdc, 1 scBLO; rep from * 3 more times, slst in beg sc to join. (24 FPhdc, 80 sc, 4 x 2ch-sp corner)

Fasten off colour 5.

Round 14: Join colour 4, *(1 hdc, 2 ch, 1 hdc) in 2ch-sp corner, 26 hdcBLO; rep from * 3 more times, slst in first hdc to join. (112 hdc, 4 x 2ch-sp corners)

Fasten off colour 4.

Round 15: Join colour 3 working entire round in 3rd loop of hdc from prev round (loop behind "v" of st), *(2 hdc, 2 ch, 2 hdc) in 2ch-sp corner, 28 hdc; rep from * 3 more times, slst in first hdc to join. (128 hdc, 4 x 2ch-sp corners)

Fasten off colour 3.

Round 16: Join colour 1, *(2 dc, 2 ch, 2 dc) in 2ch-sp corner, [skip next 2 sts, V-st in next st] 10 times, skip last 2 sts; rep from * 3 more times, slst in first dc to join. (40 V-sts, 16 dc, 4 x 2ch-sp corners)

Fasten off colour 1.

Round 17: Join colour 3, *(2 hdc, 2 ch, 2 hdc) in 2ch-sp corner, skip first st, 1 hdc in next st, 1 hdc in space between 2nd corner dc and first V-st from previous round, 2 hdc in 2ch-sp of next V-st, [1 hdc in next sp between V-sts, 2 hdc in 2 ch-sp of next V-st] 9 times, 1 hdc in sp between last V-st and first corner dc from previous round, 2 hdc; rep from * 3 more times, slst in first hdc to join. (152 hdc, 4 x 2ch-sp corners)

Fasten off colour 3.

Round 18: Join colour 4 in corner, *(1 sc, 2 ch, 1 sc) in same sp, skip first st, [1 scBLO, 1 sc in both loops of next st] 18 times, 1 scBLO in next st; rep from * 3 more times, slst in first sc to join. (156 sc, 4 x 2ch-sp corners)

Round 19: 1 ch (does not count as st), sc in same st, *(1 sc, 1 hdc, 1 sc) in 2ch-sp corner, 39 sc; rep from * 3 more times, omitting last sc, slst in first sc to join. (164 sc, 4 hdc corner sts)

Fasten off and weave in ends.

ROUNDS 8-19

BABY WHEELS

DESIGNER: ANA MORAIS SOARES

YARN

Rosários4 Bio Love, sport (4ply), in foll shade:
Blue (10)

HOOK

US size C/2 or D/3 (3mm) hook

GAUGE (TENSION)

A single motif measures approx 7in (18cm) using US size C/2 or D/3 (3mm) hook.

SPECIAL ABBREVIATION

5dc-cl, cluster of 5 dc

PATTERN

Using C/2 or D/3 hook, make a magic ring.

Round 1: Working into ring, 5 ch (counts as 1 dc, 2 ch), [1 dc, 2 ch] 5 times, slst in 3rd ch of beg 5-ch to join. (6 dc, 6 x 2ch-sp)

Round 2: 1 ch, (does not count as st throughout), [1 sc, 3 sc in 2ch-sp] 6 times, slst in first st to join. (24 sc)

Round 3: 6-ch (counts as 1 dc, 3 ch), skip next st, 5dc-cl in next st, 3 ch, skip next st, [1 dc in next st, 3 ch, skip next st, 5dc-cl in next st, 3 ch, skip next st] 5 times, slst in 3rd ch of beg 6 ch to join. (6 dc, 6 clusters, 12 x 3ch-sp)

Round 4: 1 ch, [1 sc, 3 sc in 3ch-sp, 1 FPsc around cluster, 3 sc in next 3ch-sp] 6 times, slst in first st to join. (48 sc)

Round 5: 3 ch, (counts as 1 dc), 1 dcBLO in same st, *3 dcBLO, 2 dcBLO in next st; rep from * all around omitting last 2 dc, slst in top of beg 3-ch to join. (60 dc)

Round 6: 1 ch, skip beg 3-ch, *1 trFLO in sc from Round 4 (sc worked in dc from Round 3), 5 scBLO (do not skip dc after beg 3-ch, behind tr), 1 trFLO in FPsc from Round 4, 5 scBLO (do not skip dc behind tr); rep from * 5 more times (last sc of final 5-scBLO will fall in beg 3-ch), slst in first st to join. (12 tr, 60 sc)

Round 7: 1 ch, 1 sc in same st, *5 ch, skip next 2 sts, 1 sc in next st; rep from * all around omitting last sc, slst in first st to join. (24 sc, 24 x 5ch-sp)

Round 8: Slst in next 2 ch from next 5ch-sp, 1 ch, 1 sc in same 5ch-sp, *5 ch, 1 sc in next 5ch-sp; rep from * all around omitting last sc, slst in first st to join. (24 sc, 24 x 5ch-sp)

Round 9: 1 ch, 1 hdc in same st, *4 sc in next 5ch-sp, 1 hdc in next st; rep from * all around omitting last hdc, slst in first st to join. (24 hdc, 96 sc)

Round 10: 3 ch (counts as 1 dc), 1 dcBLO in each st around, slst in top of beg 3-ch to join. (120 dc)

Round 11: 1 ch, 1 trFLO in hdc from Round 9, skip next st (beg 3-ch), 4 scBLO, *1 trFLO in next hdc from Round 9, skip next st, 4 scBLO; rep from * all around, slst in first st to join. (24 tr, 96 sc)

Round 12: 4 ch (counts as 1 tr), [1 tr, 2 ch, 2 tr] in same st (first corner made), *2 trBLO, 3 dcBLO, 6 hdcBLO, 7 scBLO, 6 hdcBLO, 3 dcBLO, 2 trBLO, (2 tr, 2 ch, 2 tr) in next st (corner made); rep from * 3 more times omitting last corner sts, slst in top of beg 4-ch to join. (32 tr, 24 dc, 48 hdc, 29 sc, 4 x 2ch-sp corners)

Round 13: Slst in next st and next 2ch-sp corner, 4 ch, (counts as 1 tr), [1 tr, 2 ch, 2 tr] in same 2ch-sp corner (first corner made), *1 trBLO, 6 dcBLO, 4 hdcBLO, 11 scBLO, 4 hdcBLO, 6 dcBLO, 1 trBLO, (2 tr, 2 ch, 2 tr) in next 2ch-sp (corner made); rep from * 3 more times omitting last corner sts, slst in top of beg 4-ch to join. (8 tr, 48 dc, 32 hdc, 44 sc, 4 x 2ch-sp corners)

Round 14: 3 ch (counts as 1 hdc, 1 ch), skip next st, [2 hdc, 2 ch, 2 hdc] in next 2ch-sp corner (first corner made), *1 ch, skip next st, [1 hdc in next st, 1 ch, skip next st] 18 times, (2 hdc, 2 ch, 2 hdc) in next 2ch-sp (corner made); rep from * 3 more times, omitting last hdc, last 1 ch and last corner sts, slst in 2nd ch of beg 3-ch to join. (88 hdc, 76 ch, 4 x 2ch-sp corners)

Round 15: 1 ch, 1 sc in same st, 1 sc in next ch-sp, 2 sc, *[1 sc, 2 ch, 1 sc] in next 2 ch-sp corner (first corner made), 2 sc, 1 sc in next ch-sp, [1 sc, 1 sc in next ch-sp] 18 times, 2 sc; rep from * 3 more times omitting last 4 sc and last corner sts, slst in first st to join. (172 sc, 4 x 2ch-sp corners)

Fasten off and weave in ends.

CALYPSO

DESIGNER: HATTIE RISDALE

YARN

Phildar Phil Coton 4, light worsted (DK), in foll shades:
Colour 1: Craie (1937)
Colour 2: Oeillet (1044)
Colour 3: Rosee (1149)
Colour 4: Soleil (1019)
Colour 5: Cyan (1362)
Colour 6: Pomme (1435)
Colour 7: Pistache (1298)

HOOK

US size G/6 (4mm) hook

GAUGE (TENSION)

A single motif measures approx 6⅞in (17.5cm) using a US size G/6 (4mm) hook.

SPECIAL ABBREVIATIONS

4dc-cl, cluster of 4 dc
4tr-cl, cluster of 4 tr

PATTERN

Using G/6 hook and colour 1, make a magic ring.

Round 1: 3 ch (counts as 1 dc), 11 dc in ring, slst in 3rd of beg 3-ch to join. (12 dc)

Fasten off colour 1.

Round 2: Join colour 2 with slst between any two dc, 1 ch (counts as 1 sc), 1 sc in same sp, 2 sc in each sp around, slst in beg 1-ch to join. (24 sc)

Fasten off colour 2.

Round 3: Join colour 3 with slst in any sp between two 2-sc groups, 2 ch (counts as first part of 4dc-cl), complete 4dc-cl in same sp, 2 ch, (4dc-cl, 2 ch) in each sp around, slst in 2nd of beg 2-ch to join. (12 x 4dc-cl, 12 x 2ch-sp)

Fasten off colour 3.

continued on next page >

Round 4: Join colour 4 with slst between two dc of Round 1, crochet a round of slst surface crochet around dc of Round 1.

Fasten off colour 4.

Round 5: Join colour 5 with slst between pair of sc in Round 2, crochet a round of slst surface crochet around sc of Round 2.

Fasten off colour 5.

Round 6: Join colour 2 with slst in 2ch-sp, 3 ch (counts as first part of 4tr-cl), (complete 4tr-cl, 4tr-cl, 3 ch) in same sp, (4tr-cl, 4tr-cl, 3 ch) in each 2ch-sp around, sl st in 3rd of beg 3-ch to join. (24 x 4tr-cl, 12 x 3ch-sp)

Fasten off colour 2.

Round 7: Join colour 5 with slst in any 3ch-sp, 1 ch (counts as 1 sc), (5 sc, 1 ch) in same sp, (6 sc, 1 ch) in each sp around, slst in beg 1-ch to join. (72 sc, 12 ch)

Fasten off colour 5.

Round 8: Join colour 6 with slst through loops that join two 4tr-cl of any petal in Round 6, 3 ch (counts as 1 dc) 2 dc in same sp, 3 hdc in 3ch-sp in Round 6 (over 6-sc in Round 7), 3 dc through top loops of next petal, (4 tr, 2 ch, 4 tr) at top of next petal (corner), *3 dc through loops of next petal, 3 hdc in 3ch-sp in Round 6, 3 dc through loops of next petal, (4 tr, 2 ch, 4 tr) to make corner; rep from * twice, slst in 3rd of beg 3-ch to join. (12 hdc, 24 dc, 32 tr, 4 x 2ch-sp corners)

Fasten off colour 6.

Round 9: Join colour 7 with slst in first tr after 2ch-sp corner, 2 ch (counts as 1 hdc), 1 hdc in each st around and (2 hdc, 2 ch, 2 hdc) in each 2ch-sp corner, slst in 2nd of beg 2-ch to join, do not fasten off. (84 hdc, 4 x 2ch-sp corners)

Round 10: 1 ch (counts as 1 sc), 1 sc in top loops of each st around and (1 sc, 2 ch, 1 sc) in each corner sp, slst in beg 1-ch to join. (92 sc, 4 x 2ch-sp corners)

Fasten off colour 7.

Round 11: Join colour 5 with slst in first sc after any corner group of sts, 2 ch (counts as 1 hdc), 1 hdc in same sp, 2 hdc in every other st along each side working (2 hdc, 1 ch, 2 hdc) at corners, slst in 2nd of beg 2-ch to join. (104 hdc, 4 x 1ch-sp corners)

Fasten off colour 5.

Round 12 (WS): Turn to work on WS, join colour 2 with slst in first sp after corner group, 2 ch (counts as 1 hdc), 1 hdc in same sp, 2 hdc in each sp around working (2 hdc, 1 ch, 2 hdc) in corner 1ch-sps, slst in 2nd of beg 2-ch to join, do not fasten off. (112 hdc, 4 x 1ch-sp corners)

Round 13 (RS): Turn to work on RS, 1 ch (counts as 1 sc), (2 sc, 1 ch, 2 sc) in corner sp, 2 sc in each sp around, 1 sc in beg sp, slst in beg 1-ch to join. (120 sc, 4 x 1ch-sp corners)

Fasten off and weave in ends.

COMPASS ROSE

DESIGNER: JULIE YEAGER

YARN

Scheepjes Stone Washed, sport (4ply), in foll shades:
Colour 1: Beryl (833)
Colour 3: Coral (816)
Colour 4: Turquoise (824)
Colour 5: Yellow Jasper (809)
Scheepjes River Washed, sport (4ply), in foll shade:
Colour 2: Danube (948)

HOOK

US size G/6 (4mm) hook

GAUGE (TENSION)

A single motif measures approx 8in (20cm) using a US size G/6 (4mm) hook.

SPECIAL ABBREVIATION

3tr-cl, cluster of 3 tr

PATTERN

Using G/6 hook and colour 1, 4 ch, slst to join into a ring.

Round 1: Working in ring, 3 ch (counts as tr throughout), complete 3tr-cl in same place, [5 ch, 3tr-cl] 3 times, 5 ch, slst in top of beg 3tr-cl to join. (4 x 3tr-cl, 4 x 5ch-sp)

Fasten off colour 1.

Round 2: Join colour 2 with sc in any 5ch-sp, 2 sc in same sp, [3tr-cl in beg ring, 3 sc in 5ch-sp, 1 FPsc around top of next 3tr-cl, 3 sc in 5ch-sp] 4 times omitting last 3 sc, slst in first sc to join. (28 sc, 4 x 3tr-cl)

Fasten off colour 2.

Round 3: Join colour 3 with sc in any FPsc, 1 sc, [1 hdc, 1 dc, 3 dc in next st (corner), 1 dc, 1 hdc, 3 sc] 4 times omitting last 2 sc, slst in first sc to join. (40 sts)

Fasten off colour 3.

Round 4: Join colour 4 with slst in 2nd dc of any corner, 3 ch, (1 dc, 1 ch, 2 dc) in same st (corner), [9 dc, (2 dc, 1 ch, 2 dc) in next st for corner] 4 times omitting last corner, slst in top of beg 3-ch to join. (52 dc, 4 x 1ch-sp corners)

Fasten off colour 4.

Round 5: Join colour 5 with sc in 2nd dc of any corner, *3 ch (corner), skip 1 ch, 1 sc, [skip 1 st, 1 ch, 1 sc] 6 times; rep from * 3 times omitting last st, slst in first sc to join. (28 sc, 4 x 3ch-sp corners)

Round 6: [(1 sc, 1 hdc, 1 dc, 1 ch, 1 dc, 1 hdc, 1 sc) in 3ch-sp, 1 sc in 1ch-sp, 7 dc in ch-sp, 1 sc in next two ch-sp, 7 dc in ch-sp, 1 sc in ch-sp] 4 times, slst in first sc to join. (96 sts)

Fasten off colour 5.

Round 7: Join colour 2 with sc in any 1ch-sp corner, 3 ch (corner), 1 sc in same sp, [3 sc, skip 1 st, 3 sc, 3 sc in next st, 3 sc, skip 2 sts, 3 sc, 3 sc in next st, 3 sc, skip 1 st, 3 sc, (1 sc, 3 ch, 1 sc) in 1ch-sp] 4 times omitting last corner, slst in first sc to join. (104 sc, 4 x 3ch-sp corners)

Fasten off colour 2.

Round 8: Join colour 3 with sc in any 3ch-sp corner, 3 ch (corner), 1 sc in same sp, [3 sc, skip 1 st, 4 sc, 3 sc in next st, 3 sc, skip 2 sts, 3 sc, 3 sc in next st, 4 sc, skip 1 st, 3 sc, (1 sc, 3 ch, 1 sc) in 1ch-sp] 4 times omitting last corner, slst in first sc to join. (112 sc, 4 x 3ch-sp corners)

continued on next page >

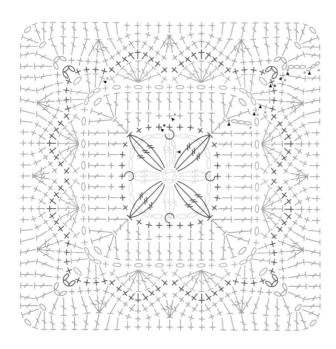

Fasten off colour 3.

Round 9: Join colour 4 with slst in any 3ch-sp, (3 ch, dc, 1 ch, 2 dc) in same sp (corner), [2 dc, dc4tog, 1 hdc, 5 sc, dc4tog, 5 sc, 1 hdc, dc4tog, 2 dc, (2 dc, 1 ch, 2dc) in 3ch-sp] 4 times omitting last corner, slst in top of beg 3-ch to join. (92 sts, 4 x 1ch-sp corners)

Round 10: 3 ch, 1 dc, [(2dc, 1 ch, 2 dc) in 1ch-sp (corner), 5 dc, 2 hdc, 9 sc, 2 hdc, 5 dc] 4 times omitting last 2 dc, slst in top of beg 3-ch to join. (108 sts, 4 x 1ch-sp corners)

Fasten off and weave in ends.

LACEFLOWER

DESIGNER: RACHELE CARMONA

YARN

Scheepjes Softfun, light worsted (DK), in foll shade:
Lace (2426)

HOOK

US size G/6 (4mm) hook

GAUGE (TENSION)

A single motif measures approx 6in (15cm) using a US size G/6 (4mm) hook.

SPECIAL ABBREVIATIONS

2dc-cl, cluster of 2 dc
3dc-cl, cluster of 3 dc
3tr-cl, cluster of 3 tr

PATTERN

Using G/6 hook, 3 ch, slst to join into a ring.

Round 1: (1 sc, 2 ch) in ring (counts as first tr), [1 ch, 1 tr in ring] 11 times, 1 ch, slst in first tr to join. (12 tr, 12 ch)

Round 2: (1 sc, 1 ch, 2dc-cl) all in first ch-sp (counts as first 3dc-cl), [3 ch, 3dc-cl in next ch-sp] 11 times, 3 ch, slst in first 3dc-cl to join. (12 x 3dc-cl, 12 x 3ch-sp)

Round 3: 4 sc in each ch-sp, slst in first sc to join. (48 sc)

Round 4: 1 sc in next st, [3 ch, skip 1 st, 1 sc in next st] 23 times, 3 ch, slst in first sc to join. (24 sc, 24 x 3ch-sp)

Round 5: Slst in first ch, 1 sc in 3ch-sp, *5 ch, [3tr-cl in next 3ch-sp, 2 ch] 4 times, 3tr-cl in next 3ch-sp, 5 ch, 1 sc in next 3ch-sp; rep from * 3 more times omitting final sc, slst in first sc to join. (20 x 3tr-cl, 4 sc, 16 x 2ch-sp, 8 x 5ch-sp)

Round 6: Slst in first 3 ch, 1 sc in 5ch-sp, *[3 ch, 1 sc in next 2ch-sp] 4 times, 3 ch, 1 sc in 5ch-sp, 5 ch, 1 sc in next 5ch-sp; rep from * 3 more times omitting final sc, slst in first sc to join. (24 sc, 20 x 3ch-sp, 4 x 5ch-sp)

Fasten off and weave in ends.

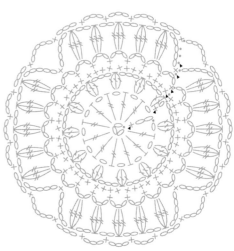

ARTEMIS

DESIGNER: HATTIE RISDALE

YARN

Sirdar Happy Cotton DK, light worsted (DK), in foll shades:
Colour 1: Tea Time (751)
Colour 2: Dolly (761)

HOOK

US size G/6 (4mm) hook

GAUGE (TENSION)

A single motif measures approx 5in (12.5cm) using a US size G/6 (4mm) hook.

SPECIAL ABBREVIATION

2dc-cl, cluster of 2 dc

PATTERN

(make 4 motifs of Rounds 1 and 2)

Using G/6 hook and colour 1, make a magic ring.

Round 1: Working in ring, 2 ch (counts as first part of 2dc-cl), complete 2dc-cl, 2dc-cl, 2 ch, *[2dc-cl] twice, 2 ch; rep from * 2 more times, slst in top of 2-ch to join. (8 clusters, 4 x 2ch-sp)

Fasten off colour 1.

Round 2: Join colour 2 with a slst in any space between pair of clusters, *(4 dc, 2 ch, 4 dc) in 2ch-sp, slst between pair of clusters; rep from * 3 more times, slst in beg slst to join. (32 dc, 4 x 2ch-sp)

Fasten off colour 2.

JOIN MOTIFS

Take Motif 1, slst to join colour 1 between pair of clusters in Round 1, [slstBLO in next 4 dc, (2 sc, 2 ch, 2 sc) in 2ch-sp, slstBLO in next 4 dc, slst between pair of clusters in Round 1] 4 times omitting final slst in beg sp, slst in beg slst to join.

Take Motif 2, slst to join colour 1 between 2 pairs of clusters in Round 1, rep section between [ ] twice, *slstBLO in next 4 dc, (2 sc, 1 ch, join to 2-ch sp in Motif 1 with slst, 1 ch, 2sc) in 2ch-sp, slstBLO in next 4dc, slst between two pairs of clusters in Round 1, rep from * joining to next 2ch-sp of Motif 1, omit final slst between two clusters, slst in beg sl st to join.

Take Motif 3, rep as for Motif 2, but join to Motif 2.

Take Motif 4, slst to join colour 1 between 2 pairs of clusters in Round 1, work section between [ ] once, slstBLO in next 4 dc, (2 sc, 1 ch, join to Motif 1 with slst, 1 ch, 2 sc) in 2ch-sp, slstBLO in next 4 dc, slst between 2 pairs of clusters of Round1, slstBLO in next 4 dc, (2 sc, 1 ch, join to Motif 1 with slst, join to Motif 3 with slst, 1 ch, 2 sc) in 2ch-sp, slstBLO in next 4 dc, slst between 2 pairs of clusters, slstBLO in next 4 dc, (2sc, 1ch, join to Motif 3 with slst, 1 ch, 2 sc) in 2ch-sp, slstBLO in next 4 dc, join to beg slst with a slst.

Fasten off colour 1.

BORDER

Join colour 1 with slst in any outside corner 2ch-sp, 2 ch (counts as 1 hdc), *[miss first sc, 4 scBLO, 1 hdcBLO, miss slst between petals, 1 hdcBLO, 4 scBLO], 1 sc in two corner sp, miss first sc, 4 scBLO, 1 hdcBLO, miss slst between petals, 1 hdcBLO, 4 scBLO, (1 hdc, 2 ch, 1 hdc) in corner 2 ch sp; rep from * 3 more times omitting final hdc, slst in 2nd ch of beg 2-ch to join. (68 sc, 24 hdc, 4 x 2ch-sp corners)

Fasten off and weave in ends.

MOTIF

JOINING MOTIFS

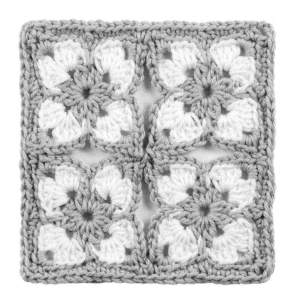

PANDORA

DESIGNER: HATTIE RISDALE

YARN

Yarn and Colors Charming, light worsted (DK), in foll shades:

Colour 1: Pesto (085)
Colour 2: Girly Pink (035)
Colour 3: Pistachio (084)
Colour 4: Green Ice (075)
Colour 5: Peony Pink (038)
Colour 6: Mint (076)
Colour 7: Cream (002)

HOOK

US size G/6 (4mm) hook

GAUGE (TENSION)

A single motif measures approx 7½in (19cm) using a US size G/6 (4mm) hook.

NOTE

Make one square in each of foll colour combinations.
Square 1: Round 1 = colour 1; Round 2 = colour 2
Square 2: Round 1 = colour 2; Round 2 = colour 3
Square 3: Round 1 = colour 4; Round 2 = colour 5
Square 4: Round 1 = colour 5; Round 2 = colour 6
Square 5: Round 1 = colour 3; Round 2 = colour 4
Square 6: Round 1 = colour 1; Round 2 = colour 6
Square 7: Round 1 = colour 4; Round 2 = colour 1
Square 8: Round 1 = colour 6; Round 2 = colour 5
Square 9: Round 1 = colour 5; Round 2 = colour 3

PATTERN

FIRST SQUARE

Using G/6 hook and first colour, make a magic ring.

Round 1: 3 ch (counts as 1 dc), 2 dc, 2 ch, *3 dc, 2 ch; rep from * twice more, slst in top of beg 3-ch to join. (12 dc)

Fasten off first colour.

Round 2: Join 2nd colour with slst in any 2ch-sp, 2 ch (counts as 1 hdc) 1 hdc, 2 ch, 2 hdc in same sp, *3 hdc, (2 hdc, 2 ch, 2 hdc) in 2ch-sp; rep from * twice more, 3 hdc, slst in top of beg 2-ch to join. (7 hdc, 4 x 2ch-sp corners)

Fasten off 2nd colour.

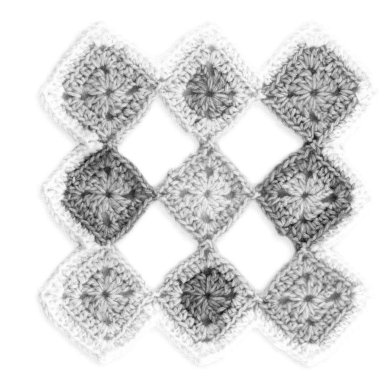

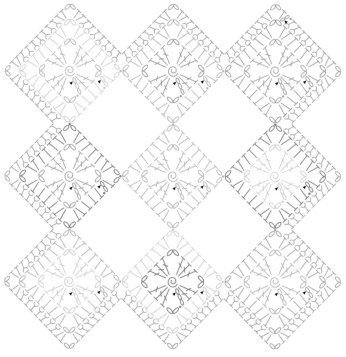

MAKE AND JOIN SQUARES

Squares are added using join-as-you-go method, joining at corners only.

Make Square 2 up to end of 3rd side, (2 hdc, 1 ch, slst to join to Square 1 corner sp, 1 ch, 2 hdc) to work 3rd corner and join, 3 hdc to complete last side, slst in top of beg 2-ch to join.

Make and join remaining squares in same way, foll assembly diagram. Squares 3, 4 and 7 are worked to end of 3rd side and join in one corner, Squares 5, 6, 8 and 9 are worked to end of 2nd side and join in two corners.

BORDER

Join colour 7 with slst in any outside corner sp, 2 ch (counts as 1 hdc), (1 hdc, 2 ch, 2 hdc) in same sp, *1 hdcBLO in each hdc to next outside corner, (2 hdc, 2 ch, 2 hdc) in outside corner sp; rep from * around omitting (2 hdc, 2 ch, 2 hdc) on last rep, slst in top of beg 2-ch to join.

Fasten off and weave in all ends.

SPRING GARDEN
....
DESIGNER: ANA MORAIS SOARES

YARN

Rosários4 Regata, light worsted (DK), in foll shades:
Colour 1: Green (27)
Colour 2: White Pearl (01)
Colour 3: Pale Lilac (68)
Colour 4: Pink (45)

HOOK

US size E/4 (3.5mm) hook

GAUGE (TENSION)

A single motif measures approx 7in (18cm) using a US size E/4 (3.5mm) hook.

SPECIAL ABBREVIATIONS

3dc-cl, cluster of 3 dc
4dc-cl, cluster of 4 dc
3tr-cl, cluster of 3 tr
2dtr-cl, cluster of 2 dtr

PATTERN

Using E/4 hook and colour 1, make a magic ring.

Round 1: 1 ch (does not count as st throughout), 8 sc in ring, slst in first sc to join. (8 sc)

Round 2: 1 ch, 1 sc in same st, [4 ch, 1 sc in next st] 7 times, 4 ch, slst in first sc to join. (8 sc, 8 x 4ch-sp)

Fasten off colour 1.

Round 3: Join colour 2, [1 hdc in 4ch-sp, 4 ch] 8 times, slst in first hdc to join. (8 hdc, 8 x 4ch-sp)

Fasten off colour 2.

Round 4: Join colour 3, [4dc-cl in 4ch-sp, 5 ch] 8 times, slst in first 4dc-cl to join. (8 clusters, 8 x 5ch-sp)

Fasten off colour 3.

Round 5: Join colour 4, [1 FPhdc around 4dc-cl, 3 sc in 5ch-sp, 3tr-cl around hdc from Round 3 working in front of 5ch-sp, 3 sc in same 5ch-sp] 8 times, slst in first FPhdc to join. (8 clusters, 8 hdc, 48 sc)

Fasten off colour 4.

Round 6: Join colour 1, 1 scBLO in each st around, slst in first sc to join. (64 sc)

Fasten off colour 1.

Round 7: Join colour 2, *(1 dc, 2 ch, 1 tr, 2 ch, 1 dc) in sc worked in a 3tr-cl from Round 5 (first corner made), 3 ch, skip next 3 sts, 1 hdc in next st, 3 ch, skip next 3 sts, 1 sc in next st, 3 ch, skip next 3 sts, 1 hdc in next st, 3 ch, skip next 3 sts; rep from * 3 more times, slst in first dc to join. (4 tr, 8 dc, 8 hdc, 4 sc, 16 x 3ch-sp, 8 x 2ch-sp)

Round 8: 1 ch, 1 FPhdc around same st, 2 hdc in next 2ch-sp, *(1 FPdc, 2 ch, 1 FPdc) around next st (corner made), 2 hdc in next 2ch-sp, 1 FPhdc around next st, [3 hdc in next 3ch-sp, 1 FPhdc around next st] 4 times, 2 hdc in next 2ch-sp; rep from * 3 more times omitting last FPhdc and 2 hdc, slst in first FPhdc to join. (8 FPdc, 20 FPhdc, 64 hdc, 4 x 2ch-sp corners)

Fasten off colour 2.

Round 9: Join colour 1, *(1 hdc, 2 ch, 1 hdc) in 2ch-sp corner, 23 hdc; rep from * 3 more times, slst in first hdc to join. (100 hdc, 4 x 2ch-sp corners)

Fasten off colour 1.

Round 10: Join colour 2, working entire round in 3rd loop of hdc from prev round (loop behind "v" of st), *(2 hdc, 2 ch, 2 hdc) in 2ch-sp corner, 25 hdc; rep from * 3 more times, slst in first hdc to join. (116 hdc, 4 x 2ch-sp corners)

continued on next page >

Fasten off colour 2.

Round 11: Join colour 4, working entire round in 3rd loop of hdc from prev round, *(2 hdc, 2 ch, 2 hdc) in 2ch-sp corner, 29 hdc; rep from * 3 more times, slst in first hdc to join. (132 hdc, 4 x 2ch-sp corners)

Fasten off colour 4.

Round 12: Join colour 3, *(3dc-cl, 4 ch, 3dc-cl) in 2ch-sp corner, skip first st, [2 ch, skip 2 sts, 3dc-cl in next st] 10 times, 2 ch, skip 2 last sts; rep from * 3 more times, slst in first 3dc-cl to join. (48 clusters, 44 x 2ch-sp, 4 x 4ch-sp corners)

Fasten off colour 3.

Round 13: Join colour 1, *(3 hdc, 2dtr-cl in 2ch-sp from Round 11 working between 3dc-cl already made there and in front of 4ch-sp, 3 hdc) in 4ch-sp corner, [1 FPhdc around next st, 2 hdc in 2ch-sp] 11 times, 1 FPhdc around next st; rep from * 3 more times, slst in first hdc to join. (4 x 2dtr-cl, 48 FPhdc, 112 hdc, 4 x 2dtr-cl corners)

Fasten off colour 1.

Round 14: Join colour 2, working entire round in 3rd loop of hdc from prev round, *(1 FPhdc, 2 ch, 1 FPhdc) around 2dtr-cl, 40 hdc; rep from * 3 more times, slst in first FPhdc to join. (8 FPhdc, 160 hdc, 4 x 2ch-sp corners)

Fasten off colour 2.

Round 15: Join colour 4, *3 sc in 2ch-sp corner, slstBLO in each st around; rep from * 3 more times, slst in first sc to join. (168 slsts, 4 x 3-sc corners)

Fasten off and weave in ends.

SUSANA

DESIGNER: JULIE YEAGER

YARN

Scheepjes River Washed, sport (4ply), in foll shades:

Colour 1: Rhine (952)
Colour 2: Nile (944)
Colour 3: Yarra (949)

Scheepjes Stone Washed, sport (4ply), in foll shade:
Colour 4: Enstatite (832)

HOOK

US size G/6 (4mm) hook

GAUGE (TENSION)

A single motif measures approx 8in (20cm) using a US size G/6 (4mm) hook.

SPECIAL ABBREVIATIONS

2dc-cl, cluster of 2 dc
2tr-cl, 2-tr cluster
2dc-cl 5-group, ([2dc-cl, 1 ch] 4 times, 2dc-cl) in same sp

NOTES

Ch-3 at beg of a round counts as 1 dc; ch-2 counts as 1 hdc.
In st counts, a ch counts as one st.
To join with single crochet, yoh, insert in designated st, yoh and pull through (2 loops on hook), yoh and pull through both loops.
In Round 6 space between 5-dc groups is not a ch-sp.

PATTERN

Using G/6 hook and colour 1, 5 ch, slst to join into a ring.

Round 1: 3 ch, 1 tr in same sp to complete 2tr-cl, [1 ch, 2tr-cl] 11 times, 1 ch, slst in top of beg 2tr-cl to join. (12 x 2tr-cl, 12 ch)

Fasten off colour 1.

Round 2: Join colour 2 with FPsc around top of any 2tr-cl, [2 sc in next 1ch-sp, FPsc around top of 2tr-cl] 11 times, 2 sc in next 1ch-sp, slst in first FPsc to join. (36 sts)

Round 3: 4 ch, 2 tr in same st, [2 ch, skip 2 sts, 3 tr in next FPsc] 11 times, 2 ch, slst in top of beg 4-ch to join. (36 tr, 12 x 2ch-sp)

Round 4: 2 ch, dc2tog, [5 ch, skip 2ch-sp, dc3tog] 11 times, 5 ch, slst in top of beg ch to join. (12 x dc3tog, 12 x ch-5 sp)

Fasten off colour 2.

Round 5: Join colour 3 with slstBLO in 4th ch of any 5-ch sp, working around and enclosing 2ch-sp of Round 3 and 5ch-sp of Round 4, 5 dc in 2ch-sp from Round 3, [5 dc in next 2ch-sp from Round 3] 11 times, slst in first dc to join. (60 dc)

Round 6: Slst in space between 5-dc groups, 4 ch, 3 tr, 1 ch, 4 tr in same space, [2 ch, skip 5 dc, 1 hdc in next space, 5 ch, skip 5 dc, 1 hdc in next space, 2 ch, skip 5 dc, (4 tr, 1 ch, 4 tr) in next space for corner] 4 times omitting last corner, slst in top of beg 4-ch to join. (32 tr, 8 hdc, 8 x 2ch-sp, 4 x 5ch-sp, 4 x 1ch-sp corners)

Fasten off colour 3.

Round 7: Join colour 4 with slst in any 1ch-sp, (3 ch, 1 dc, 1 ch, 2dc) in same sp, [4 dc, 2 dc in 2ch-sp, 1 dc in hdc, 5 hdc in 5ch-sp, 1 dc in hdc, 2 dc in 2ch-sp, 4 dc, (2 dc, 1 ch, 2 dc) in 1ch-sp for corner] 4 times omitting last corner, slst in top of beg ch-3 to join. (72 dc, 20 hdc, 4 x 1ch-sp corners)

Fasten off colour 4.

continued on next page >

Round 8: Join colour 2 with slst in any 1ch-sp corner, 2 ch (counts as first dc of first 2dc-cl), complete 2dc-cl 5-group in same sp, *skip 2 sts, [1 tr in next st, 2 ch, skip 2 sts] 6 times, 1 tr, skip 2 sts, 2dc-cl 5-group in 1ch-sp for corner; rep from * 3 more times omitting last corner, slst in top of beg 2dc-cl to join. (4 x 2dc-cl 5-groups, 28 tr, 24 x 2ch-sp)

Fasten off colour 2.

Round 9: Join colour 4 with sc in first 1ch-sp of any corner 2dc-cl 5-group, [1 FPsc around top of next cluster, 1 sc in 1ch-sp] 3 times, FPsc around top of next cluster, *working around and enclosing Round 8, skip 1 st from Round 7, 1 dc in next st from Round 7, [1 sc in tr from Round 8, 1 dc in next 2 sts from Round 7] 6 times, 1 sc in tr from Round 8, 1 dc in next st from Round 7, skip next st from Round 7, cont in Round 8, [1 FPsc around top of cluster, 1 sc in 1ch-sp] 4 times, 1 FPsc around top of next cluster; rep from * 3 more times omitting last 8 sts, slst in first st to join. Push tr st of Round 8 to front. (120 sts)

Fasten off and weave in ends.

ROSEMARY CLUSTERS

DESIGNER: JULIE YEAGER

YARN

Scheepjes Stone Washed, sport (4ply), in foll shades:

Colour 1: Pink Quartzite (821)

Colour 3: Coral (816)

Colour 5: Larimar (828)

Colour 7: Malachite (825)

Scheepjes River Washed, sport (4ply), in foll shades:

Colour 2: Nile (944)

Colour 4: Yarra (949)

Colour 6: Ganges (945)

HOOK

US size G/6 (4mm) hook

GAUGE (TENSION)

A single motif measures approx 8in (20cm) using a US size G/6 (4mm) hook.

SPECIAL ABBREVIATIONS

2dc-cl, cluster of 2 dc

3dc-cl, cluster of 3 dc

spike dc, double crochet worked in st two or more rows below

NOTE

Keep a loose hand with front post trebles and with spike sts.

PATTERN

Using G/6 hook and colour 1, 4 ch, slst to join into a ring.

Round 1: Working into ring, 3 ch, 1 dc in same place to complete first 2dc-cl, [2 ch, 2dc-cl] 7 times, 2 ch, slst in top of first 2dc-cl. (8 x 2dc-cl, 8 x 2ch-sp)

Fasten off colour 1.

Round 2: Join colour 2 with slst in any 2ch-sp, 3 ch (counts as 1 dc throughout), 2 dc in same sp, [1 FPdc around top of next 2dc-cl, 3 dc in 2ch-sp] 8 times omitting last 3 sts, slst in top of beg 3-ch to join. (32 dc)

Fasten off colour 2.

Round 3: Join colour 3 with slst in any FPdc, 3 ch, (counts as first dc of 3dc-cl), complete first 3dc-cl in same st, [3 ch, 3dc-cl] twice in same st for corner, *skip 3 sts, 1 sc, 1 FPtr around top of 2dc-cl in Round 1, 1 sc in same st as prev sc, skip 3 sts, ([3dc-cl, 3 ch] twice, 3dc-cl) in next st for corner; rep from * around omitting last corner, slst in top of first 3dc-cl to join. (12 x 3dc-cl, 8 x 3ch-sp, 4 FPtr, 8 sc)

Fasten off colour 3.

Round 4: Join colour 4 with FPsc around top of middle cluster of any three 3dc-cl group, 3 sc in next 3ch-sp, 1 FPsc around top of next cluster, *spike dc in dc from Round 2, 1 ch, spike dc in dc from Round 2, cont in Round 3, [1 FPsc around top of next 3dc-cl, 3 sc in next 3ch-sp] twice, 1 FPsc around top of next 3dc-cl; rep from * around omitting last 5 sts, slst in first FPsc to join. (44 sts, 4 ch)

Round 5: 3 ch, 4 dc in same st, [5 dc, 1 dc in 1ch-sp, 5 dc, 5 dc in next st] around omitting last 5 sts, slst in top of beg 3-ch to join. (64 dc)

Fasten off colour 4.

Round 6: Join colour 5 with slst in 3rd dc of any 5-dc corner, 3 ch, complete first 3dc-cl in same st, [3 ch, 3dc-cl] twice in same st for corner, *skip 3 sts, (3dc-cl, 3 ch, 3dc-cl) in next st, skip 3 sts, 1 sc, FPtr in FPtr from Round 3, 1 sc in same st as prev sc, skip 3 sts, (3dc-cl, 3 ch, 3dc-cl) in next st, skip 3 sts, ([3dc-cl, 3 ch] twice, 3dc-cl) in next st for corner; rep from * around omitting last corner, slst in first 3dc-cl to join. (28 x 3dc-cl, 16 x 3ch-sp, 8 sc, 4 FPtr)

Fasten off colour 5.

Round 7: Join colour 6 with FPsc around top of middle cluster of any three 3dc-cl groups, *3 sc in next 3ch-sp, FPsc around top of next 2 clusters, 3 sc in next 3ch-sp, FPsc around top of next cluster, spike dc in dc in Round 5, 1 ch, spike dc in dc in Round 5, cont in Round 6, FPsc around top of next 3dc-cl, 3 sc in next 3ch-sp, FPsc around top of next two 3dc-cl, 3 sc in next 3ch-sp, FPsc around top of next 3dc-cl; rep from * around omitting last st, slst in first FPsc to join. (84 sts, 4 ch)

Round 8: 3 ch, 4 dc in same st, [10 dc, 1 dc in 1ch-sp, 10 dc, 5 dc in next st] around omitting last 5 sts, slst in top of beg 3-ch to join. (104 dc)

Fasten off colour 6.

Round 9: Join colour 7 with sc in 3rd dc of any 5-dc corner, 1 sc in same st, *12 sc, 1 FPtr in FPtr in Round 6, skip 1 st, cont in Round 8, 12 sc, 3 sc in next st for corner; rep from * around omitting last 2 sts and ending with 1 sc in same st as beg sc, slst in first st to join. (108 sc, 4 tr)

Fasten off and weave in ends.

PERSEPHONE

DESIGNER: HATTIE RISDALE

YARN

Paintbox Yarns Cotton DK, light worsted (DK), in foll shades:
Colour 1: Banana Cream (421)
Colour 2: Spearmint Green (426)
Colour 3: Lime Green (429)
Colour 4: Candyfloss Pink (450)

HOOK

US size G/6 (4mm) hook

GAUGE (TENSION)

A single motif measures approx 6⅛in (15.5cm) using a US size G/6 (4mm) hook.

SPECIAL ABBREVIATIONS

2dc-cl, cluster of 2 dc
3tr-cl, cluster of 3 tr
4dc-bobble, bobble of 4 dc
4tr-bobble, bobble of 4 tr

PATTERN

Using G/6 hook and colour 1, make a magic ring.

Round 1: 3 ch (counts as 1 dc), 15 dc in ring, pull on tail to close ring, slst in top of beg 3-ch to join. (16 dc)

Fasten off colour 1.

Round 2 (bobble): Join colour 2 with slst in any dc, 1 ch (counts as 1 sc), *4dc-bobble in next st, 1 sc in next st; rep from * around omitting final sc, slst in beg 1-ch to join. (8 bobbles, 8 sc)

Fasten off colour 2.

continued on next page >

Round 3: Join colour 3 with slst in any sc, 2 ch (counts as first part of 2dc-cl), (complete 2dc-cl, 3 ch, 2dc-cl) in same sp, *(2dc-cl, 3 ch, 2dc-cl) in sc; rep from * around, slst in top of beg cluster to join. (16 x 2dc-cl, 8 x 3-ch)

Fasten off colour 3.

Round 4: Join colour 4 with slst in sp between two sets of (2dc-cl, 3 ch, 2dc-cl), *2 ch, (2 dc, 1 tr, 1 ch, 1 tr, 2 dc, 2 ch) in 3ch-sp, slst in sp between two sets of (2dc-cl, 3 ch, 2dc-cl); rep from * around, slst in beg slst to join. (16 tr, 32 dc, 40 ch)

Fasten off colour 4.

Round 5: Join colour 3 with slst in any 1ch-sp, (7 ch (counts as 1 tr, 3 ch), 3tr-cl, 3 ch, 3tr-cl, 3 ch, 1 tr) in same sp, *(3tr-cl, 2 ch, 1 hdc, 2 ch, 3tr-cl) in next 1 ch sp, (1 tr, 3 ch, 3tr-cl, 3 ch, 3tr-cl, 3 ch, 1 tr) in next sp; rep from * twice more, (3tr-cl, 2 ch, 1 hdc, 2 ch, 3tr-cl) in final sp, slst in 4th ch of beg 7-ch to join. (16 x 3tr-cl, 8 tr, 4 hdc, 8 x 2ch-sp, 12 x 3ch-sp)

Fasten off colour 3.

Round 6 (bobble): Work in colour 4, using colour 2 for bobble. Work over bobble yarn when not using. Join colour 4 with slst in top of 2nd 3tr-cl of any corner group, 2 ch (counts as 1 hdc), 4 hdc in 3ch-sp, join colour 2 with slst in top of tr, 3 ch (counts as first part of 4tr-bobble), complete 4tr-bobble, *1 hdc in next 3tr-cl working over colour 2, 3 hdc in 2ch-sp, pick up colour 2, 4tr-bobble in next hdc, 3 hdc in 2ch-sp, 1 hdc in top of 3tr-cl, 4tr-bobble in next tr, 4 hdc in 3ch-sp, 1 hdc in top of 3tr-cl, (2 dc, 4tr-bobble, 2 dc) in corner, [1 hdc in top of 3tr-cl, 4 hdc in 3ch-sp, 4tr-bobble in next tr]; rep from * 3 times omitting section in [ ] on 3rd rep, slst in top of beg 2-ch, fasten off colour 2 only. (16 bobbles, 72 hdc, 16 dc)

Round 7: 2 ch (counts as 1 hdc), *1 hdc in each st to corner, (2 dc, 2 ch) in top of corner bobble st, 2 dc in next dc; rep from * 3 more times, 1 hdc, slst in top of beg 2-ch to join. (96 hdc, 16 dc, 4 x 2ch-sp corners)

Round 8: 1 ch (counts as 1 sc), *1 sc in each st to corner, (2sc, 2 ch, 2sc) in corner; rep from * 3 more times, 3 sc, slst in beg 1-ch to join. (128 sc, 4 x 2ch-sp corners)

Fasten off and weave in ends

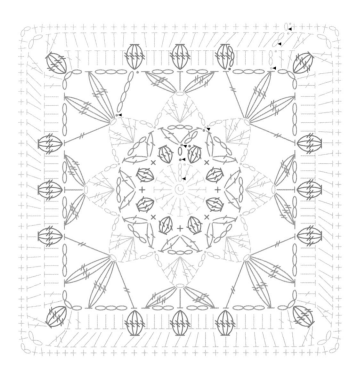

HESTIA

DESIGNER: HATTIE RISDALE

YARN

Sirdar Happy Cotton DK, light worsted (DK), in foll shades:
Colour 1: Puff (763)
Colour 2: Seaside (784)
Colour 3: Fizz (779)
Colour 4: Tea Time (751)

HOOK

US size G/6 (4mm) hook

GAUGE (TENSION)

A single motif measures approx 5⅛in (13cm) using a US size G/6 (4mm) hook.

SPECIAL ABBREVIATIONS

spike sc, sc worked in st two or more rows below
spike hdc, hdc worked in st two or more rows below
3tr-cl, cluster of 3 tr
5tr-cl, cluster of 5 tr

NOTE

In Rounds 6, 7 and 8 spaces worked into are not ch-sp.

PATTERN

Using G/6 hook and colour 1, make a magic ring.

Round 1: 2 ch (counts 1 hdc throughout), 15 hdc in ring, slst in 2nd ch of beg 2-ch to join. (16 hdc)

Fasten off colour 1.

Round 2: Join colour 2 with slst in top of any st, 1 ch (counts as 1 sc), 1 sc in same sp, *miss 1 st, (2 hdc, 2 ch, 2 hdc) in next st, miss 1 st, 2 sc in next st; rep from * twice more, miss 1 st, (2 hdc, 2 ch, 2 hdc) in next st, slst in beg 1-ch to join. (8 sc, 16 hdc, 4 x 2ch-sp corners)

Fasten off colour 2.

Round 3: Join colour 3 with slst in any 2ch-sp, 3 ch (counts as 1 dc), (2 dc, 2 ch, 3 dc) in same sp, *1 spike sc in hdc in Round 1 in which 2 sc were worked in Round 2, (3 dc, 2 ch, 3 dc) in 2ch-sp; rep from * twice more, 1 spike sc in hdc in Round 1 in which 2 sc were worked in Round 2, slst in 3rd ch of beg 3-ch to join. (24 dc, 4 spike sc, 4 x 2ch-sp corners)

Fasten off colour 3.

Round 4: Join colour 2 with slst in any 2ch-sp, 2 ch, (2 hdc, 2 ch, 3 hdc) in same sp, *slstBLO in next 3 dc, (slst, 4 ch, slst) in "v" of sc, slstBLO in next 3 dc, (3 hdc, 2 ch, 3 hdc) in 2ch-sp; rep from * twice more, slstBLO in next 3 dc, (slst, 4 ch, slst) in "v" of sc, slstBLO in next 3 dc, slst in 2nd ch of beg 2-ch to join. (24 hdc, 24 slstBLO, 4 x 4ch-sp, 8 slst, 4 x 2ch-sp corners)

Fasten off colour 2.

Round 5: Join colour 1 with slst in any 4ch-sp, (2 ch counts as first part of 3dc-cl, complete 3dc-cl, 5tr-cl, 3dc-cl, 4 ch) in same sp, (3dc-cl, 2 ch, 3dc-cl, 4 ch) in 2ch-sp, *(3dc-cl, 5tr-cl, 3dc-cl, 4 ch) in 4ch-sp, (3dc-cl, 2 ch, 3dc-cl, 4 ch) in 2ch-sp; rep from * twice more, slst in top of beg 3dc-cl to join. (16 x 3dc-cl, 4 x 5tr-cl, 8 x 4ch-sp, 4 x 2ch-sp corners)

Fasten off colour 1.

Round 6: Join colour 3 with slst in any 4ch-sp after a corner, 2 ch, 3 hdc in same sp, 3 hdc in space between 3dc-cl and 5tr-cl, 3 hdc in space between next 5tr-cl and 3dc-cl, 4 hdc in 4ch-sp, (2 dc, 2 ch, 2 dc) in 2ch-sp, *4 hdc in 4ch-sp, 3 hdc in space between 3dc-cl and 5tr-cl, 3 hdc in space between next 5tr-cl and 3dc-cl, 4 hdc in 4ch-sp, (2 dc, 2 ch, 2 dc) in 2ch-sp; rep from * twice more, slst in top of beg 2-ch to join. (56 hdc, 16 dc, 4 x 2ch-sp corners)

continued on next page >

Fasten off colour 3.

Round 7: Join colour 2 with slst in any space after 2 dc of corner, 2 ch, 1 hdc in same space, [skip 2 sts, 2 hdc in space] twice, [skip 3 sts, 2 hdc in space] twice, [skip 2 sts, 2 hdc in space] twice, skip 2 sts, (5tr-cl, 2 ch, 5tr-cl) in 2ch-sp, *[skip 2 sts, 2 hdc in next sp] 3 times, [skip 3 sts, 2 hdc in space] twice, [skip 2 sts, 2 hdc in space] twice, skip 2 sts, (5tr-cl, 2 ch, 5tr-cl) in 2ch-sp; rep from * twice more, slst in 2nd ch of beg 2-ch to join. (56 hdc, 8 x 5tr-cl, 4 x 2ch-sp corners)

Fasten off colour 2.

Round 8: Join colour 1 with slst in first space after any corner 5tr-cl, 2 ch (counts as 1 hdc), 1 hdc in same space, [skip 2 sts, 2 hdc in space] twice, skip 2 sts, 1 hdc in next space, skip next st, 2 spike hdc in space between two 3-hdc groups in Round 6, skip next st, 1 hdc in next space, [skip 2 sts, 2 hdc in space] 3 times, *(2 dc, 2 ch, 2 dc) in corner 2ch-sp, 2 hdc in space after 5tr-cl, [skip 2 sts, 2 hdc in space] twice, skip 2 sts, 1 hdc in next space, skip next st, 2 spike hdc in space between two 3-hdc groups in Round 6, skip next st, 1 hdc in next space, [skip 2 sts, 2 hdc in next space] 3 times; rep from * twice more, (2 dc, 2 ch, 2 dc) in 2ch-sp, slst in top of beg 2-ch to join. (64 hdc, 8 spike hdc, 16 dc, 4 x 2ch-sp corners)

Fasten off colour 1.

Round 9: Join colour 4 with slstBLO in any st, 1 ch (counts as 1 sc), 1 scBLO in each st around working (2 sc, 2 ch, 2 sc) in each corner, slst in beg 1-ch to join. (80 scBLO, 16 sc, 4 x 2ch-sp corners)

Fasten off and weave in ends.

COBBLESTONE
DESIGNER: ANNA NIKIPIROWICZ

YARN

Scheepjes Stone Washed, sport (4ply), in foll shades:
Colour 1: Smokey Quartz (802)
Colour 2: Crystal Quartz (814)
Colour 3: Moon Stone (801)

HOOK

US size E/4 (3.5mm) hook

GAUGE (TENSION)

A single motif measures approx 7in (18cm) using a US size E/4 (3.5mm) hook.

SPECIAL ABBREVIATIONS

4hdc-puff, puff st of 4 hdc
spike sc, single crochet worked in st two or more rows below

NOTE

Join yarn with standing sts unless otherwise indicated, and join round with invisible join in standing st.

PATTERN

Using E/4 hook and colour 1, make a magic ring.

Round 1: 1 ch (does not count as st throughout), [1 dc, 1 ch] 8 times in ring, enclosing yarn end as you work, pull on yarn end to close opening, make invisible join in first dc. (8 dc, 8 ch)

Fasten off colour 1.

Round 2: Join colour 2, 4hdc-puff in first 1ch-sp, 1 ch, skip next dc, *4hdc-puff in next 1ch-sp, 1 ch, skip next dc; rep from * to end, make invisible join in top of beg puff. (8 puff sts, 8 ch)

Fasten off colour 2.

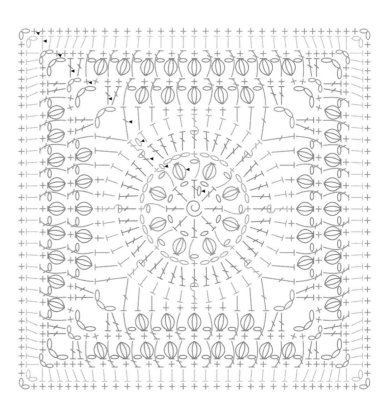

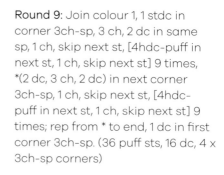

Round 3: Join colour 3 in first 1ch-sp, 1 ch, *1 spike sc in dc from Round 1, 3 ch, skip next puff; rep from * to end, make invisible join in top of beg spike st. (8 sc, 8 x 3ch-sp)

Fasten off colour 3.

Round 4: Join colour 1, 1 stdc in first spike sc, 4 dc in next 3ch-sp, *1 dc in next spike sc, 4 dc in next 3ch-sp; rep from * to end. (40 sts)

Fasten off colour 1.

Round 5: Join colour 3 in first st, 1 ch, 1 FPdc around post of stdc, 4 hdc, *1 FPdc around post of next dc, 4 hdc; rep from * to end, make invisible join in top of beg FPdc. (7 dc, 32 hdc)

Fasten off colour 3.

Round 6: Join colour 2, 1 stdc in first FPdc, 3 ch, 1 dc in same st, 2 hdc, 5 sc, 2 hdc, *(1 dc, 3 ch, 1 dc) in next FPdc, 2 hdc, 5 sc, 2 hdc; rep from * to end. (44 sts, 4 x 3ch-sp corners)

Fasten off colour 2.

Round 7: Join colour 1, 1 stdc in corner 3ch-sp, 3 ch, 2 dc in same sp, 1 ch, skip next st, [4hdc-puff in next st, 1 ch, skip next st] 5 times, *(2 dc, 3 ch, 2 dc) in next corner 3ch-sp, 1 ch, skip next st, [4hdc-puff in next st, 1 ch, skip next st] 5 times; rep from * to end, 1 dc in first corner 3ch-sp. (20 puff sts, 16 dc, 24 ch, 4 x 3ch-sp corners)

Fasten off colour 1.

Round 8: Join colour 2, 1 stsc in first corner 3ch-sp, 3 ch, 2 sc in same sp, 2 sc, 1 dc in skipped dc from prev round, making sure to work dc in front of 1-ch, [1 sc in top of next puff, 1 dc in skipped dc from prev round] 5 times, 2 sc, *(2 sc, 3 ch, 2 sc) in next corner 3ch-sp, 2 sc, 1 dc in skipped dc from prev round, [1 sc in top of next puff, 1 dc in skipped dc from prev round] 5 times, 2 sc; rep from * to end, 1 sc in first corner 3ch-sp. (52 sc, 24 dc, 4 x 3ch-sp corners)

Fasten off colour 2.

Round 9: Join colour 1, 1 stdc in corner 3ch-sp, 3 ch, 2 dc in same sp, 1 ch, skip next st, [4hdc-puff in next st, 1 ch, skip next st] 9 times, *(2 dc, 3 ch, 2 dc) in next corner 3ch-sp, 1 ch, skip next st, [4hdc-puff in next st, 1 ch, skip next st] 9 times; rep from * to end, 1 dc in first corner 3ch-sp. (36 puff sts, 16 dc, 4 x 3ch-sp corners)

Fasten off colour 1.

Round 10: Join colour 2, 1 stsc in first corner 3ch-sp, 3 ch, 2 sc in same sp, 2 sc, 1 dc in skipped dc from prev round, making sure to work dc in front of 1-ch, [1 sc in top of next puff, 1 dc in skipped dc from prev round] 9 times, 2 sc, *(2 sc, 2 ch, 2 sc) in next corner 3ch-sp, 2 sc, 1 dc in skipped dc from prev round, [1 sc in top of next puff, 1 dc in skipped dc from prev round] 9 times, 2 sc; rep from * to end, 1 sc in first corner 3ch-sp. (68 sc, 40 tr, 4 x 3ch-sp corners)

Fasten off colour 2.

Round 11: Join colour 3, 1 sthdc in corner 3ch-sp, 2 ch, 2 hdc in same sp, 1 hdc in each st to next corner sp, *(2 hdc, 2 ch, 2 hdc) in corner 2ch-sp, 1 hdc in each st to next corner sp; rep from * to end, 1 hdc in first corner sp. (124 hdc, 4 x 2ch-sp corners)

Fasten off colour 2.

Round 12: Join colour 2, 1 stsc in first corner 2ch-sp, 2 ch, 1 sc in same sp, 1 ch, 1 sc in each st to next corner 2ch-sp, *(1 sc, 2 ch, 1 sc) in corner 2ch-sp, 1 sc in each st to next corner 2ch-sp; rep from * to end. (132 sc, 4 x 2ch-sp corners)

Fasten off with invisible join, weave in all ends.

ESTRELLA

DESIGNER: JULIE YEAGER

YARN

Scheepjes Stone Washed, sport (4ply), in foll shades:

Colour 1: Pink Quartzite (821)

Colour 3: Peridot (827)

Scheepjes River Washed, sport (4ply), in foll shades:

Colour 2: Danube (948)

Colour 4: Rhine (952)

HOOK

US size G/6 (4mm)

GAUGE (TENSION)

A single motif measures approx 8in (20cm) using a US size G/6 (4mm) hook.

SPECIAL ABBREVIATIONS

2dc-cl, cluster of 2 dc

2dc-cl 3-group, ([2dc-cl, 2 ch] twice, 2dc-cl) in same sp

2dc-cl 5-group, ([2dc-cl, 2 ch] 4 times, 2dc-cl) in same sp

NOTES

When skipping sts, each ch counts as one stitch, and each cluster also counts as one stitch.

First few rounds quickly alternate from square to diamond to square so corners are transient and can be 1ch-sp, 2ch-sp, 3ch-sp or 4ch-sp.

To join with single crochet, yoh, insert in designated st, yoh and pull through (2 loops on hook), yoh and pull through both loops.

PATTERN

Using G/6 hook and colour 1, 5 ch, slst to join into a ring.

Round 1: 2 ch (counts as 1 hdc throughout), 1 dc in same sp to complete first 2dc-cl, 1 ch, 2dc-cl, [4 ch, 2dc-cl, 1 ch, 2dc-cl] 3 times, 4 ch, slst in top of 2dc-cl to join. (8 x 2dc-cl, 4 ch, 4 x 4ch-sp)

Fasten off colour 1.

Round 2: Join colour 2 with sc in any 4ch-sp, 4 sc in same sp, [1 FPsc around top of 2dc-cl, 1 ch, skip 1 ch, 1 FPsc around top of 2dc-cl, 5 sc in 4ch-sp] 4 times omitting last 5 sts, slst in first sc to join. (28 sc, 4 ch)

Fasten off colour 2.

Round 3: Join colour 3 with slst in 3rd sc of any 5-sc group, 2 ch, (1 dc, 1 ch, 1 dc, 1 hdc) in same st, [1 hdc, 1 sc, skip next st, (1 sc, 2 ch, 1 sc) in ch-sp, skip 1 st, 1 sc, 1 hdc, (1 hdc, 1 dc, 1 ch, 1 dc, 1 hdc) in next st] 4 times omitting last 5 sts, slst in top of beg 2-ch to join. (40 sts)

Fasten off colour 3.

Round 4: Join colour 4 with sc in any 1ch-sp, (2 ch, 1 sc) in same sp, [1 sc in dc, skip 3 sts, 2dc-cl, 1 ch, (2dc-cl, 3 ch, 2dc-cl) in 2ch-sp, 1 ch, 2dc-cl, skip 3 sts, 1 sc in dc, (1 sc, 2 ch, 1 sc) in 1ch-sp] 4 times omitting last 4 sts, slst in beg sc to join. (16 x 2dc-cl, 16 sc, 4 x 3ch-sp, 4 x 2ch-sp, 8 ch)

Fasten off colour 4.

Round 5: In this round sc to work into right after 2dc-cl 5-group is somewhat hidden. Join colour 1 with slst in any 2ch-sp, (2 ch, 1 dc in same st to complete first 2dc-cl, [2 ch, 2dc-cl] 4 times) in same sp for corner, [1 ch, 2dc-cl in next st, skip 2 sts, 1 sc in 1ch-sp, skip cluster, (1 sc, 2 ch, 1 sc) in 3-ch-sp, skip cluster, 1 sc in 1ch-sp, skip 2 sts, 2dc-cl in next st, 1 ch, 2dc-cl 5-group in next 2ch-sp] 4 times omitting last 2dc-cl 5-group, slst in top of 2dc-cl to join. (4 x 2dc-cl 5-groups, 8 x 2dc-cl, 16 sc, 4 x 2ch-sp, 8 ch)

Fasten off colour 1.

Round 6: Join colour 3 with sc in first 2ch-sp of any 2dc-cl 5-group, 1 sc in same sp, 2 sc in next 2ch-sp, *2 ch, [2 sc in next 2ch-sp] twice, skip 4 sts, 2dc-cl in next st, 1 ch, 2dc-cl 5-group in 2ch-sp, 1 ch, 2dc-cl in next st, skip 4 sts, [2 sc in next 2ch-sp] twice; rep from * 3 more times omitting last 4 sts, slst in beg sc to join. (28 x 2dc-cl, 32 sc, 20 x 2ch-sp, 8 ch)

Fasten off colour 3.

Round 7: Join colour 4 with sc in first 2ch-sp of any 2dc-cl 5-group, 1 sc in same sp, 2 sc in next 2ch-sp, *2 ch for corner, [2 sc in next 2ch-sp] twice, skip cluster, 2dc-cl in 1ch-sp, skip 3 sts, [2dc-cl in next st] twice, 2dc-cl 5-group in 2ch-sp, [2dc-cl in next st] twice, skip 3 sts, 2dc-cl in 1ch-sp, skip cluster, [2 sc in next 2ch-sp] twice; rep from * 3 more times omitting last 4 sts, slst in beg sc to join. (44 x 2dc-cl, 32 sc, 20 x 2ch-sp)

Fasten off colour 4.

Round 8: Join colour 1 with slst in any corner 2ch-sp, (2 ch, 1 dc in same st to complete first 2dc-cl, [2 ch, 2dc-cl] 4 times) in same

sp, [skip 5 sts, 2dc-cl 3-group in sp between clusters, 7 ch, skip 17 sts, 2dc-cl 3-group in sp between clusters, skip 5 sts, 2dc-cl 5-group in 2ch-sp] 4 times omitting last 2dc-cl 5-group, slst in top of beg 2dc-cl to join. (44 x 2dc-cl, 4 x 7ch-sp, 32 x 2ch-sp)

Fasten off colour 1. Push 7-ch "bridges" to back of work.

Round 9: Sc in this round are worked in 2ch-sp and around 7-ch bridge of Round 8. Join colour 3 with sc in first 2ch-sp of any 2dc-cl 5-group of Round 8, 1 sc in same sp, 2 sc in next 2ch-sp, *2 ch, [2 sc in next 2ch-sp] 4 times, 4 ch, 1 sc around 7-ch bridge, 4 ch, [2 sc in next 2ch-sp] 4 times; rep from * 3 more times omitting last 4 sts, slst in beg sc to join. (68 sc, 8 x 4ch-sp, 4 x 2ch-sp)

Round 10: 3 ch (counts as 1 dc), 3 dc, *(2 dc, 2 ch, 2 dc) in 2ch-sp), 4 dc, 2 hdc, 2 sc, [2 sc in 2ch-sp of Round 7, picking up 4ch-sp of Round 9] 4 times, 2 sc, 2 hdc, 4 dc; rep from * 3 more times omitting last 4 sts, slst in top of beg 3-ch to join. (48 dc, 16 hdc, 48 sc, 4 x 2ch-sp corners)

Fasten off and weave in ends.

CATALINA

DESIGNER: JULIE YEAGER

YARN

Scheepjes River Washed, sport (4ply), in foll shade:
Colour 1: Danube (948)
Scheepjes Stone Washed, sport (4ply), in foll shades:
Colour 2: Moon Stone (801)
Colour 3: Lemon Quartz (812)

HOOK

US size G/6 (4mm)

GAUGE (TENSION)

A single motif measures approx 8in (20cm) using a US size G/6 (4mm) hook.

SPECIAL ABBREVIATIONS

3tr-cl, cluster of 3 tr
3tr-cl group, ([3tr-cl, 3 ch] twice, 3tr-cl) in same sp
W-st, ([1 dc, 2 ch] twice, 1 dc) in same st or sp

NOTE

In Rounds 4 and 6 space between dc groups is not a ch-sp.

PATTERN

Using G/6 hook and colour 1, 4 ch, slst to join into a ring.

Round 1: 1 ch (does not count as st), 8 sc in ring, slst in first sc to join. (8 sc)

Fasten off colour 1.

Round 2: Join colour 2 with slst in any st, 6 ch (counts as 1 dc, 3 ch), [3tr-cl, 3 ch, 1 dc, 3 ch] 3 times, 3tr-cl, 3 ch, slst in 3rd ch of beg ch-6 to join. (4 dc, 4 x 3tr-cl, 8 x 3ch-sp)

Fasten off colour 2.

continued on next page >

Round 3: Join colour 3 with slst in any 3ch-sp, 3 ch (counts as 1 dc throughout), 4 dc in same sp, [5 dc in 3ch-sp] 7 times, slst in top of beg 3-ch to join. (40 dc)

Fasten off colour 3.

Round 4: Join colour 1 with slst in space between 5-dc groups above single dc in Round 2, 5 ch (counts as 1 dc, 2 ch), (1 dc, 2 ch, 1 dc) in same space, [3tr-cl group in next space, W-st in next space] 3 times, 3tr-cl group in next space, slst in 3rd ch of beg 5-ch to join. (4 W-sts, 4 x 3tr-cl groups)

Fasten off colour 1.

Round 5: Join colour 3 with slst in 3ch-sp between first and 2nd cluster of any 3tr-cl group, 3 ch, 5 dc in same sp, *1 ch, 6 dc in next 3ch-sp, [4 dc in 2ch-sp] twice, 6 dc in 3ch-sp; rep from * 3 more times omitting last 6 dc, slst in top of beg 3-ch to join. (80 dc, 4 x 1ch-sp corners)

Fasten off colour 3.

Round 6: Join colour 2 with slst in space between 4-dc group and first 6-dc group of corner, 5 ch (counts as 1 dc, 2 ch), (1 dc, 2 ch, 1 dc) in same space, [1 ch, 3tr-cl group in 1ch-sp, 1 ch, W-st in next space, 1 dc in next space, W-st in next sp] 4 times omitting last W-st, slst in 3rd ch of beg 5-ch to join. (8 W-sts, 4 x 3tr-cl groups, 4 dc, 8 ch)

Fasten off colour 2.

Round 7: Join colour 3 with slst in first 2ch-sp of W-st before corner, 2 ch (counts as 1 hdc), 2 hdc in same sp, *3 hdc in 2ch-sp, 2 dc in 1ch-sp, 4 dc in 3ch-sp, 1 FPtr around post of 3tr-cl, 4 dc in 3ch-sp, 2 dc in 1ch-sp, [3 hdc in 2ch-sp] twice, 1 dc between W-st and dc, 1 dc between dc and next W-st, 3 hdc in 2ch-sp; rep from * 3 more times omitting last 3 hdc, slst in top of beg 2-ch. (48 hdc, 56 dc, 4 FPtr)

Fasten off colour 3.

Round 8: Join colour 1 with slst in any st, 1 sc in each st and 3 sc in each FPtr, slst in beg sc to join. (116 sc)

Fasten off and weave in ends.

MANDALITA

DESIGNER: CAITIE MOORE

YARN

Nurturing Fibres Eco-Cotton, light
worsted (DK), in foll shades:
Colour 1: Sunglow
Colour 2: Denim
Colour 3: Lime
Colour 4: Vanilla
Colour 5: Aventurine

HOOK

US size G/6 (4mm) hook

GAUGE (TENSION)

A single motif measures approx 5½in
(14cm) using a US size G/6 (4mm) hook.

SPECIAL ABBREVIATIONS

2dc-bobble, bobble of 2 dc
4hdc-puff st, puff st of 4 hdc
4dc-PC, popcorn of 4-dc, 1 ch

NOTE

*Join yarn with standing sts unless
otherwise indicated, and join round with
invisible join in standing st.*

PATTERN

Using G/6 hook and colour 1, make a
magic ring.

Round 1: 8 hdc in ring, pull on tail to
close ring. (8 hdc)

Fasten off colour 1.

Round 2: Join colour 2 in any st,
*(2dc-bobble, 1 ch, 2dc-bobble, 1 ch)
in same st; rep from * to end. (16
bobbles)

Fasten off colour 2.

Round 3: Join colour 3 in any 1ch-sp,
(4hdc-puff st, 1 ch) in each 1ch-sp to
end. (16 puffs, 16 ch)

Fasten off colour 3.

Round 4: Join colour 4 in any 1ch-sp,
*(1 sc, 1 ch, 1 sc, 1 ch) in 1ch-sp, skip
puff and work in next 1ch-sp; rep
from * to end. (32 sc, 32 ch)

Fasten off colour 4.

Round 5: Join colour 1 in 1ch-sp
above puff st, *(2 sc, 2 ch) in 1ch-sp,
skip (1 sc, 1 ch, 1 sc) and work in the
next 1ch-sp; rep from * to end. (32 sc,
16 x 2ch-sp)

Fasten off colour 1.

Round 6: Join colour 5 in 2ch-sp,
*(1 sc in 2ch-sp, 4dc-PC around 2ch-
sp of Round 5 and 1ch-sp of Round
4, 1 sc in 2ch-sp), 1 ch, skip to next
2ch-sp; rep from * to end. (16 PC, 32
sc, 16 ch)

Fasten off colour 5.

Round 7: Join colour 4 in 1ch-sp,
*1 hdc, 1 hdc in sc, 1 hdc in 1-ch at
back of PC, 1 hdc in sc; rep from * to
end. (64 hdc)

Fasten off colour 4.

Round 8: Join colour 1 in hdc above
PC, *1 sc, 1 ch, skip 1 st; rep from * to
end. (32 sc, 32 ch)

Fasten off colour 1.

continued on next page >

Round 9: Join colour 4 in 1ch-sp, *3 hdc in 1ch-sp, skip 1 sc, work in next 1ch-sp; rep from * to end. (96 hdc)

Fasten off colour 4.

Round 10: Join colour 2 in 3rd loop of any st, *1 sc in 3rd loop of hdc, skip next hdc, 5 dc in next hdc, skip next hdc, 1 sc in 3rd loop of hdc, skip next hdc, 5 dc in next hdc, skip next hdc, [1 sc in 3rd loop of hdc] twice, 13 slst in 3rd loop, 1 sc in 3rd loop of next hdc; rep from * to end. (52 slst, 40 dc, 20 sc)

Fasten off colour 2.

Round 11: Join colour 3 in sc to right of first 5-dc group, *1 scBLO, 2 BPsc, 2 BPhdc, 1 BPdc, 2 dc in next sc, 1 ch, 2 dc in next dc, 1 BPdc around same dc, 2 BPhdc, 2 BPsc, 1 scBLO, 15 slstBLO; rep from * to end. (124 sts, 4 x 1ch-sp corners)

Fasten off colour 3.

Round 12: Join colour 2 in 1ch-sp, *(2 hdc, 1 ch, 2 hdc) in 1ch-sp, skip next st, [sc2togBLO, 1 scBLO] 9 times, sc2togBLO; rep from * to end. (92 sts, 4 x 1ch-sp corners)

Fasten off and weave in ends.

WAGON WHEEL

DESIGNER: CAITIE MOORE

YARN

Nurturing Fibres Eco-Cotton, light worsted (DK), in foll shades:
Colour 1: Sunglow
Colour 2: Persian
Colour 3: Baltic
Colour 4: Vanilla

HOOK

US G/6 (4mm) hook

OTHER TOOLS AND MATERIALS

8 stitch markers

GAUGE (TENSION)

A single motif measures approx 6¼in (16cm) using a US size G/6 (4mm) hook.

SPECIAL ABBREVIATION

5dc-bobble, bobble of 5 dc, 1 ch

NOTE

Join yarn with standing sts unless otherwise indicated, and join round with invisible join in standing st.

PATTERN

Using G/6 hook and colour 1, make a magic ring.

Round 1: 3 ch (counts as dc), 7 dc in ring. (8 dc)

Fasten off colour 1.

Round 2: Join colour 2 in any st, *(1 hdc, 1 FPhdc) in same st; rep from * to end. (16 sts)

Fasten off colour 2.

Round 3: Join colour 3 in any hdc, *(1 dc, place st marker, 1 FPdc) in same st, 1 dc; rep from * to end. (24 sts)

Fasten off colour 3.

Round 4: Join colour 4 in dc just to right of any FPdc, *(1 sc, 1 FPdc) in same st, 1 sc, 1 ch, skip next sc; rep from * to end. (24 sts, 8 ch)

Fasten off colour 4.

Round 5: Join colour 4 in any FPdc, *2 dc in same st, 1 sc, 3 dc in 1ch-sp, skip next st; rep from * to end. (48 sts)

Fasten off colour 4.

Round 6 (WS): With WS facing, join colour 3 in BLO of any skipped sc from Round 4 (back loop will be facing as you are working on WS), *1 dcBLO, 4 ch, 1 dcBLO in next skipped sc, 4 ch; rep from * to end. (8 dc, 8 x 4ch-sp)

Fasten off colour 3.

Round 7 (RS): With RS facing, join colour 3 in any dcBLO from Round 6, *1 sc in dcBLO from Round 6, 1 FPdc around marked dc from Round 3, 1 sc

back in same Round 6 dcBLO, 2 ch, skip 1 sc and 2 dc from Round 5, 2 hdc in next dc from Round 5 (3rd dc from 3-dc group), 2 ch; rep from * to end. (40 sts, 16 x 2ch-sp)

Fasten off colour 3.

Round 8: Join colour 4 in any sc from Round 5 (sc may be hidden behind FPdc from prev round, push FPdc to right to work in st), *3 dc in Round 5, skip 1 hdc in Round 7, 1 hdc in next st from Round 7, cont working in Round 5, 2 dc, skip over FPdc (push to right); rep from * to end. (48 sts)

Fasten off colour 4.

Round 9: Join colour 3 in any sc to right of FPdc from Round 7, *1 sc, 1 FPdc around FPdc from Round 7, 1 sc in next sc from Round 7, 5 ch; rep from * to end, slst to join. (24 sts, 8 x 5ch-sp)

Fasten off colour 3.

Round 10: Join colour 4 in any hdc from Round 8, work dc around, skipping over FPdc. (48 dc)

Fasten off colour 4.

Round 11: Join colour 3 in FPdc from Round 9, *1 FPdc in Round 9, cont in Round 10, 2 scBLO in next st, 5 scBLO; rep from * to end. (64 sts)

Fasten off colour 3.

Round 12: Join colour 3 in any st, 1 sc in each st to end. (64 sts)

Fasten off colour 3.

Round 13: Join colour 1 in sc to right of Round 12 FPdc from, *1 sc, 5dc-bobble; rep from * to end. (32 bobbles, 32 sc)

Fasten off colour 1.

Round 14: Join colour 2 in any sc, *2 sc in sc, 1 sc in 1ch-sp; rep from * to end. (96 sc)

Fasten off colour 2.

Round 15: Join colour 4 in any sc aligned with FPdc below, *(2 dc, 2 ch, 2 dc) in sc, 4 hdcBLO, 15 scBLO, 4 hdcBLO; rep from * to end. (108 sts, 4 x 2ch-sp corners)

Fasten off colour 4.

Round 16: Join colour 3 in 2ch-sp, *(2 dc, 2 ch, 2 dc) in 2ch-sp, 3 BPdc, 3 hdcBLO, sc2togBLO, 2 scBLO, 7 slstBLO, 2 scBLO, sc2togBLO, 3 hdcBLO, 3 BPdc; rep from * to end. (116 sts, 4 x 2ch-sp corners)

Fasten off, remove st markers and weave in ends.

TESSELLATION

DESIGNER: CAITIE MOORE

YARN

Nurturing Fibres Eco-Cotton, light worsted (DK), in foll shades:
Colour 1: Charcoal
Colour 2: Cobblestone
Colour 3: Mist

HOOK

US size G/6 (4mm) hook

GAUGE (TENSION)

A single motif measures approx 6in (15cm) using a US size G/6 (4mm) hook.

SPECIAL ABBREVIATIONS

2dc-bobble, bobble of 2 dc
3dc-bobble, bobble of 3 dc

NOTE

Join yarn with standing sts unless otherwise indicated, and join round with invisible join in standing st.

PATTERN

Using G/6 hook and colour 1, make a magic ring.

Round 1: 3 ch (counts as 1 hdc), 11 hdc in ring, pull on tail to close ring. (12 hdc)

Fasten off colour 1.

Round 2: Join colour 2 in any st, *2dc-bobble, 1 ch; rep from * to end. (12 bobbles, 12 ch)

Fasten off colour 2.

Round 3: Join colour 1 in any 1ch-sp, *2 hdc in same st, 1 ch; rep from * to end. (24 hdc, 12 ch)

Fasten off colour 1.

Round 4: Join colour 3 in 1ch-sp, *3 hdc in 1ch-sp, skip 1 hdc, 1 hdc in 3rd loop of hdc; rep from * to end. (48 sts)

Fasten off colour 3.

Round 5: Join colour 1 in 3rd loop of any hdc, 1 tr in 3rd loop of each hdc. (48 sts)

Fasten off colour 1.

Round 6: Join colour 3 through front and back loops of first hdc of any 3-hdc group in Round 4, dc3tog, 1 ch, 1 sc in tr attached to 2nd hdc of 3-hdc group in Round 4, 3 sc in Round 5, *dc3tog in next 3-hdc group in Round 4, 1 ch, 4 sc in Round 5; rep from * to end. (60 sts, 12 ch)

Fasten off colour 3.

Round 7: Join colour 2 in any sc, 2 hdc in each st around, skipping over dc3tog. (96 sts)

Fasten off colour 2.

Round 8: Join colour 3 in hdc to right of dc3tog, *1 sc, 3dc-bobble, 1 sc, skip 1 st; rep from * to end. (24 bobbles, 48 sc)

Fasten off colour 3.

Round 9: Join colour 1 in sc to immediate right of any bobble, keeping bobbles pushed to front, *1 hdc, 1 ch, skip bobble, 2 hdc in sc; rep from * to end. (72 hdc, 24 ch)

Fasten off colour 1.

Round 10: Join colour 2 in 1ch-sp above a bobble lying between two dc3tog, *(3 tr, 1 ch, 3 tr) in 1ch-sp, skip 1 st, 2 dc, 2 dc in 1ch-sp, skip 1 st, 2 hdc, 1 sc in 1ch-sp, skip 1 st, 2 sc, 1 sc in 1ch-sp, skip 1 st, 2 sc, 1 sc in 1ch-sp, skip 1 st, 2 hdc, 2 dc in 1ch-sp, skip 1 st, 2 dc; rep from * to end. (100 sts, 4 x 1ch-sp corners)

Fasten off and weave in ends.

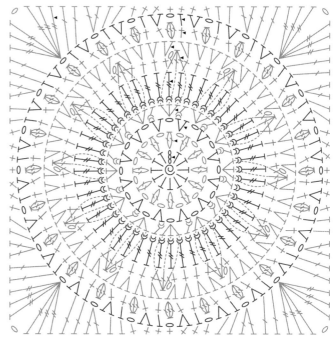

ECHO

DESIGNER: HATTIE RISDALE

YARN

Paintbox Yarns Cotton DK, light worsted (DK), in foll shades:

Colour 1: Champagne White (403)
Colour 2: Blush Pink (454)

HOOK

US size G/6 (4mm) hook

GAUGE (TENSION)

A single motif measures approx 6in (15cm) using a US size G/6 (4mm) hook.

SPECIAL ABBREVIATION

5tr-bobble, bobble of 5 tr

NOTE

To join colour 2 at beg of bobble rounds, insert hook in st in which bobble will be worked, pick up colour 2 and pull through to RS, join with slst, make 3 ch (counts as first part of bobble).

PATTERN

Work in colour 1 throughout, using colour 2 only for bobble. Make sure to work over bobble yarn tail when not using it, around whole of each bobble round.

Using G/6 hook and colour 1, make a magic ring.

Round 1: Working in ring, 1 ch (counts as 1 sc throughout), 2 sc, 2 ch, [3 sc, 2 ch] 3 times, slst in beg 1-ch to join. (12 sc, 4 x 2ch-sp corners)

Round 2: 3 ch (counts as 1 dc throughout), 1 dc in top loops of each st and (1 dc, 2 ch, 1 dc) in each corner 2ch-sp, slst in top of beg 3-ch to join. (20 dc, 4 x 2ch-sp corners)

Round 3 (bobble): 3 ch (counts as 1 dc), join colour 2 in next st, 5tr-bobble in same st, 2 dc, *(2 dc, 2 ch, 2 dc) in corner sp, 2 dc, 5tr-bobble in next st, 2 dc; rep from * twice more, (2 dc, 2 ch, 2 dc) in corner sp, 1 dc in next st, slst in top of beg 3-ch to join. (32 dc, 4 bobbles, 4 x 2ch-sp corners)

Fasten off colour 2.

Round 4: Cont in colour 1, 3 ch, 1 dc in each st and (2 dc, 2 ch, 2 dc) in each corner sp, slst in top of beg 3-ch to join. (52 dc, 4 x 2ch-sp corners)

Round 5 (bobble): 3 ch, 2 dc, join colour 2 in next st, 5tr-bobble in same st, 4 dc, *(2 dc, 2 ch, 2 dc) in corner sp, 4 dc, 5tr-bobble in next st, 3 dc, 5tr-bobble in next st, 4 dc; rep from * twice more, (2 dc, 2 ch, 2 dc) in corner sp, 4 dc, 5tr-bobble in next st, slst in top of beg 3-ch to join. (60 dc, 8 bobbles, 4 x 2ch-sp corners)

Fasten off colour 2.

Round 6: 3 ch, 1 dc in each st and (2 dc, 2 ch, 2 dc) in each corner sp, slst in beg 3-ch to join. (84 dc, 4 x 2ch-sp corners)

Round 7 (bobble): 3 ch, 4 dc, join colour 2 in next st, 5tr-bobble in same st, 6 dc, *(2 dc, 2 ch, 2 dc) in corner sp, 6 dc, 5tr-bobble in next st, 7 dc, 5tr-bobble, 6 dc; rep from * twice more, (2 dc, 2 ch, 2 dc) in corner sp, 6 dc, 5tr-bobble in next st, 2 dc, slst in top of beg 3-ch to join. (92 dc, 8 bobbles, 4 x 2ch-sp corners)

Fasten off colour 2.

Round 8: 1 ch, 1 sc in each st around and (2 sc, 2 ch, 2 sc) in each corner sp, slst in beg 1-ch to join. (116 sc, 4 x 2ch-sp corners)

Fasten off and weave in all ends.

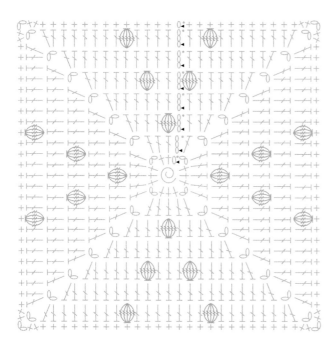

LOTUS BLOSSOM

DESIGNER: CAITIE MOORE

YARN

Nurturing Fibres Eco-Cotton, light worsted (DK), in foll shades:

Colour 1: Persian

Colour 2: Aventurine

Colour 3: Sunglow

Colour 4: Charcoal

Colour 5: Vanilla

HOOK

US size G/6 (4mm) hook

GAUGE (TENSION)

A single motif measures approx 6¼in (16cm) using a US size G/6 (4mm) hook.

SPECIAL ABBREVIATIONS

4dc-bobble, bobble of 4 dc

FP-bobble, 4dc-bobble worked round front post of st

2ch-picot, picot with 2 ch

3ch-picot, picot with 3 ch

NOTE

Join yarn with standing sts unless otherwise indicated, and join round with invisible join in standing st.

PATTERN

Using G/6 hook and colour 1, make a magic ring.

Round 1: 1 ch (does not count as st), 8 sc in ring. (8 sc)

Fasten off colour 1.

Round 2: Join colour 2 in any st, 2 sc in each st to end. (16 sc)

Fasten off colour 2.

Round 3: Join colour 3 in any st, *1 sc, 4dc-bobble; rep from * to end. (8 bobbles, 8 sc)

Fasten off colour 3.

Round 4: Join colour 4 in any sc, *3 sc in same st, 1 ch, skip bobble; rep from * to end. (24 sc, 8 ch)

Fasten off colour 4.

Round 5: Join colour 5 in any 1ch-sp, *(1 slst, 1 ch, 3 dc, 2ch-picot, 2 dc, 1 ch, 1 slst) in 1ch-sp, 1 ch, skip 3 sc; rep from * to end. (8 petals, 8 ch, 16 slst)

Fasten off colour 5.

Round 6: Join colour 2 in any 1ch-sp between petals from prev round, *1 sc, skip slst, skip 1 ch, 5 BPdc, skip 1 ch, skip slst; rep from * to end. (40 dc, 8 sc)

Fasten off colour 2.

Round 7: Join colour 2 in any sc, *1 slst, 1 sc, 1 hdc, (2 dc, 3ch-picot, 2 dc) in same st, 1 hdc, 1 sc; rep from * to end. (72 sts, 8 picot)

Fasten off colour 2.

Round 8 (WS): Join colour 2 around post of 3rd dc from any 5-BPdc group from Round 6, *1 FPsc, 3 ch, 1 FPsc around 3rd BPdc of next petal, 3 ch; rep from * to end. (8 sc, 8 x 3ch-sp)

Fasten off colour 2.

Round 9 (RS): Join colour 5 in any 3 ch-sp, *(4 sc, 3 ch, 1 sc in 2nd ch from hook, 1 hdc in 3rd ch from hook, 4 sc) in 3ch-sp; rep from * in each 3ch-sp. (104 sts)

Fasten off colour 5.

Round 10: Join colour 4 in 2nd sc to left of any Round 9 petal, *1 hdc, 1 dc, 2 dc in next st, 2 ch, 2 dc in next st, 1 dc, 1 hdc, 1 ch (work behind Round 9 petal), skip sc, skip petal, skip sc, 6 hdc, 1 ch, skip sc, skip petal, skip sc; rep from * to end. (64 sts, 4 x 2ch-sp corners)

Fasten off colour 4.

ROUNDS 1-7

ROUNDS 8-14

Round 11: Join colour 4 in any 2ch-sp, *(2 dc, 2 ch, 2 dc) in 2ch-sp, skip next st, 3 dc, 1 dc in 1ch-sp, skip next st, 5 dc, 1 dc in 1ch-sp, 3 dc; rep from * to end. (68 dc, 4 x 2ch-sp corners)

Fasten off colour 4.

Round 12: Join colour 1 in any 2ch-sp, (1 hdc, 2 dc, 1 ch, 2 dc, 1 hdc) in 2ch-sp, skip next st, 7 scBLO, 1 sc, FP-bobble in same st, 1 sc, 7 scBLO; rep from * to end. (88 sts, 4 bobbles, 4 x 1ch-sp corners)

Fasten off colour 1.

Round 13: Join colour 3 in any 1ch-sp, *(2 hdc, 1 ch, 2 hdc) in 1ch-sp, skip 1 st, 10 hdc, skip bobble, 10 hdc, skip 1 st; rep from * to end. (96 hdc, 4 x 1ch-sp corners)

Fasten off colour 3.

Round 14: Join colour 4 in any 1ch-sp, *(2 hdc, 1 ch, 2 hdc) in 1ch-sp, skip 1 st, [2 hdc in next st, skip 1 st] 11 times, 2 hdc in next st; rep from * to end. (112 hdc, 4 x 1ch-sp corners)

Fasten off and weave in ends.

WHEN FLOWERS GO BLUE

DESIGNER: ANA MORAIS SOARES

YARN

Rosários4 Belmonte, light worsted (DK), in foll shades:
Colour 1: Dark Blue (29)
Colour 2: White Pearl (21)
Colour 3: Light Blue (27)
Colour 4: Green (31)

HOOK

US size E/4 (3.5mm) hook

GAUGE (TENSION)

A single motif measures approx 7½in (19cm) using a US size E/4 (3.5mm) hook.

SPECIAL ABBREVIATION

5dc-bobble, bobble of 5 dc

NOTES

For neater work, change slst at end of rounds to invisible join. Bobbles worked in Round 12 are separated by lengths of ch. In Round 13 bobbles are brought to front and chain pushed to back and Round 13 sts are worked over chain.

PATTERN

Using E/4 hook and colour 1, make a magic ring.

Round 1: 3 ch (counts as 1 dc), 11 dc in ring, slst in top of beg 3-ch to join. (12 dc)

Fasten off colour 1.

Round 2: Join colour 2, *(1 dc, 5 ch, 1 dc) in any st (corner made), 2 FPdc; rep from * 3 more times, slst in first dc to join. (16 dc, 4 x 5ch-sp corners)

Fasten off colour 2.

Round 3: Join colour 3, *(5 dc, 2 ch, 5 dc) in 5ch-sp corner, 3 ch, skip next 4 sts; rep from * 3 more times, slst in first dc to join. (40 dc, 4 x 3ch-sp, 4 x 2ch-sp corners)

Fasten off colour 3.

Round 4: Join colour 4, *3 sc in 2ch-sp corner (corner made), 5 BPhdc, 1 FPtr around 2nd of pair of FPdc from Round 2 working in front of 3ch-sp from prev round, 2 ch, 1 FPtr around first of pair of FPdc from Round 2 working in front of 3ch-sp from prev round, 5 BPhdc; rep from * 3 more times, slst in first sc to join. (12 sc, 40 BPhdc, 8 FPtr, 4 x 2ch-sp, 4 x 3-sc corners)

Fasten off colour 4.

Round 5: Join colour 1, *3 hdc in middle sc of 3-sc corner (corner made), 6 hdc, 1 ch, skip next st (FPtr from prev round), 5dc-bobble in next 2ch-sp also catching 3ch-sp from Round 3, 1 ch, skip next st (FPtr from prev round), 6 hdc; rep from * 3 more times, slst in first hdc to join. (4 bobbles, 60 hdc, 8 ch, 4 x 3 hdc corners)

Fasten off colour 1.

Round 6: Join colour 2, *(2 hdc, 2 ch, 2 hdc) in middle hdc of 3-hdc corner (corner made), 7 BPhdc, 1 FPhdc around bobble, 7 BPhdc; rep from * 3 more

continued on next page >

- 61 -

times, slst in first hdc to join. (16 hdc, 56 BPhdc, 4 FPhdc, 4 x 2ch-sp corners)

Round 7: 2 ch (counts as 1 hdc), 1 hdc in next st, *(1 hdc, 2 ch, 1 hdc) in next 2ch-sp corner, 19 hdc; rep from * 3 more times omitting last 2 hdc, slst in top of beg 2-ch to join. (84 hdc, 4 x 2ch-sp corners)

Fasten off colour 2.

Round 8: Join colour 4, working entire round in 3rd loop of hdc from prev round (loop behind "v" of st), *(2 hdc, 2 ch, 2 hdc) in 2ch-sp corner, 21 hdc; rep from * 3 more times, slst in first hdc to join. (100 hdc, 4 x 2ch-sp corners)

Fasten off colour 4.

Round 9: Join colour 1, *(1 sc, 2 ch, 1 sc) in 2ch-sp corner, 25 scBLO; rep from * 3 more times, slst in first sc to join. (108 sc, 4 x 2ch-sp corners)

Fasten off colour 1.

Round 10: Join colour 3, *(1 sc, 2 ch, 1 sc) in 2ch-sp corner, 27 scBLO; rep from * 3 more times, slst in first sc to join. (116 sc, 4 x 2ch-sp corners)

Round 11: 1 ch (does not count as st), 1 sc in same st, *(1 sc, 2 ch, 1 sc) in next 2ch-sp corner, 29 sc; rep from * 3 more times omitting last sc, slst in first sc to join. (124 sc, 4 x 2ch-sp corners)

Fasten off colour 3.

Round 12: Join colour 1, *(1 sc, 2 ch, 1 sc) in 2ch-sp corner, 7 ch, skip next 7 sts, [5dc-bobble in next st, 7 ch, skip next 7 sts] 3 times; rep from * 3 more times, slst in first sc to join. (12 bobbles, 8 sc, 16 x 7ch-sp, 4 x 2ch-sp corners)

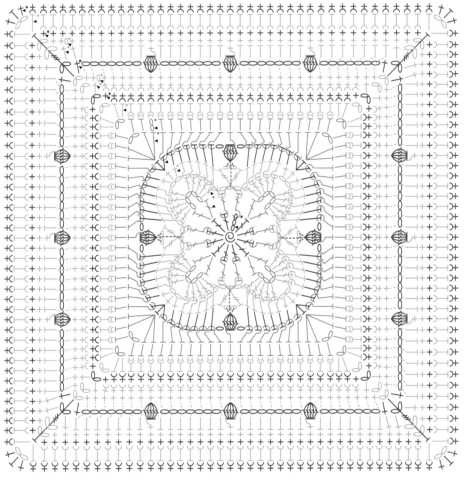

Fasten off colour 1.

Round 13: Join colour 3, working all hdc in skipped sts from Round 11 and in front of 7ch-sp to pull bobbles to front, *(1 sc, 2 ch, 1 sc) in 2ch-sp corner, skip first st (corner sc from prev round), 7 hdc, [1 FPsc around bobble, 7 hdc] 3 times, 1 sc in last st; rep from * 3 more times, slst in first sc to join. (112 hdc, 12 FPsc, 12 sc, 4 x 2ch-sp corners)

Round 14: 1 ch (does not count as st), 1 sc in same st, *(1 sc, 2 ch, 1 sc) in next 2ch-sp corner, 34 sc; rep from * 3 more times omitting last sc, slst in first sc to join. (144 sc, 4 x 2ch-sp corners)

Fasten off colour 3.

Round 15: Join colour 1, *(1 sc, 1 dtr in 2ch-sp from Round 11 working between two sc already there, 1 sc) in 2ch-sp corner, 36 sc; rep from * 3 more times, slst in first sc to join. (152 sc, 4 x dtr corners)

Fasten off colour 1.

Round 16: Join colour 4, *(1 hdc, 2 ch, 1 hdc) in dtr from prev round, 38 hdcBLO; rep from * 3 more times, slst in first hdc to join. (160 hdc, 4 x 2ch-sp corners)

Fasten off colour 4.

Round 17: Join colour 1, *(1 sc, 1 hdc, 1 sc) in 2ch-sp corner, 40 scBLO; rep from * 3 more times, slst in first sc to join. (168 sc, 4 x hdc corners)

Fasten off and weave in ends.

GROW YOUR GARDEN

DESIGNER: ANA MORAIS SOARES

YARN

Rosários4 Abraço, light worsted (DK), in foll shades:
Colour 1: White Pearl (01)
Colour 2: Pink (23)
Colour 3: Yellow (13)

HOOK

US size E/4 (3.5mm) hook

GAUGE (TENSION)

A single motif measures approx 7½in (19cm) using a US size E/4 (3.5mm) hook.

SPECIAL ABBREVIATIONS

V-st, (1 dc, 2 ch, 1 dc) in same st
2dc-cl, cluster of 2 dc
3dc-cl, cluster of 3 dc
4dc-bobble, bobble of 4 dc
2tr-cl, cluster of 2 tr

PATTERN

Using E/4 hook and colour 1, make a magic ring.

Round 1: 3 ch (counts as first dc of 3dc-cl), complete 3dc-cl, 3 ch, [3dc-cl, 3 ch] 5 times in ring, slst in top of 3-ch to join. (6 clusters, 6 x 3ch-sp)

Fasten off colour 1.

Round 2: Join colour 2, 3 ch (counts as first dc of 3dc-cl), complete 3dc-cl, 3 ch, [3dc-cl in 3ch-sp, 1 FPdc around next st, 3dc-cl in 3ch-sp, 3 ch] 5 times, 3dc-cl in 3ch-sp, 1 FPdc around next st, slst in top of 3-ch to join. (12 clusters, sts, 6 dc, 6 x 3ch-sp)

Fasten off colour 2.

Round 3: Join colour 3, [3 sc in 3ch-sp, 2 ch, skip 3dc-cl, 1 FPhdc around FPdc, 2 ch, skip 3dc-cl] 6 times, slst in first sc to join. (18 sc, 6 hdc, 12 x 2ch-sp)

Fasten off colour 3. Turn work.

Round 4 (WS): Join colour 1, [hdc in top of 3dc-cl from Round 1, 4 ch] 6 times, slst in first hdc to join. Turn work. (6 hdc, 6 x 4ch-sp)

Round 5 (RS): 1 ch (does not count as st), [5 hdc in 4ch-sp, 1 hdc in next st] 6 times, slst in first hdc to join. (36 hdc)

Round 6: 5 ch (counts as 1 dc, 2ch-sp), 1 dc in same st (first V-st made), skip next st, [V-st in next st, skip next st] 17 times, slst in 3rd ch of beg 5-ch to join. (18 V-sts)

Fasten off colour 1.

Round 7: Join colour 2, 4 sc in every 2ch-sp around, slst in first sc to join. (72 sc)

Fasten off colour 2.

Round 8: Join colour 3, 1 scBLO in last st from 4-sc group aligned with FPhdc from Round 3, [1 FPtr around FPhdc from Round 3, 12 scBLO (do not skip st behind FPtr)] 6 times omitting last sc, slst in first sc to join. (72 sc, 6 tr)

Fasten off colour 3.

Round 9: Join colour 1, [1 FPhdc around FPtr from prev round, skip st behind, 12 scBLO] 6 times, slst in first FPhdc to join. (72 sc, 6 hdc)

Fasten off colour 1.

Round 10: Join colour 2, 3 ch (counts as first dc of 4dc-bobble), complete 4dc-bobble, 12 scBLO, [4dc-bobble in FPhdc, 12 scBLO] 5 times, slst in first 4dc-bobble to join. (6 bobbles, 72 sc)

Fasten off colour 2.

continued on next page >

Round 11: Join colour 3, [scBLO in 4dc-bobble, 1 FPhdc around same 4dc-bobble, 12 scBLO] 6 times, slst in first scBLO to join. (78 sc, 6 hdc)

Fasten off colour 3.

Round 12: Join colour 1, *(2tr-cl, 2 ch, 2tr-cl, 2 ch, 2tr-cl) in 3rd st before FPhdc from prev round (corner), 2 ch, skip next 2 sts, 1 dc in FPhdc, 2 ch, skip next 2 sts, 1 hdc in next st, [2 ch, skip next 2 sts, 1 sc in next st] twice, 2 ch, skip next 2 sts, 1 hdc in next st, 2 ch, skip next 2 sts, 1 dc in next st, 2 ch, skip next 2 sts; rep from

* 3 more times, slst in first 2tr-cl to join. (8 dc, 8 hdc, 8 sc, 36 x 2ch-sp, 12 x 2tr-cl)

Round 13: 1 ch (does not count as st), 1 FPsc around 2tr-cl, 2 sc in next 2ch-sp, *(1 FPhdc, 2 ch, 1 FPhdc) around next st (corner), [2 sc in next 2ch-sp, 1 FPsc around next st] 8 times, 2 sc in next 2ch-sp; rep from * 3 more times omitting last FPsc and last 2 sc, slst in first FPsc to join. (112 sts, 4 x 2ch-sp corners)

Fasten off colour 1.

Round 14: Join colour 2, *(2 dc, 2 ch, 2 dc) in 2ch-sp corner, 28 dcBLO; rep from * 3 more times, slst in first dc to join. (128 dc, 4 x 2ch-sp corners)

Fasten off colour 2.

Round 15: Join colour 1, *(2 hdc, 2 ch, 2 hdc) in 2ch-sp corner, 32 BPhdc; rep from * 3 more times, slst in first hdc to join. (144 hdc, 4 x 2ch-sp corners)

Fasten off colour 1 and weave in ends.

Round 16: Join colour 3, *(2 dc, 2 ch, 2 dc) in 2ch-sp corner, 1 ch, skip next 2 sts, [1 dc in next st, 1 ch, skip next st] 17 times; rep from * 3 more times, slst in first dc to join. (84 dc, 72 x ch, 4 x 2ch-sp corners)

Fasten off colour 3.

Round 17: Join colour 1, *(1 sc, 2 ch, 1 sc) in 2ch-sp corner, 2 sc, 1 tr in 2nd skipped st from Round 15 working in front of ch-sp from prev round, skip ch-sp behind tr and next st, [2 sc in next ch-sp, skip next st] 16 times, tr in last skipped st from Round 15, skip ch-sp behind tr, 2 sc; rep from * 3 more times, slst in first sc to join. (8 tr, 152 sc, 4 x 2ch-sp corners)

Fasten off colour 1.

Round 18: Join colour 2, *(1 sc, 2 ch, 1 sc) in 2ch-sp corner, 3 scBLO, 4dc-bobble in tr, 8 scBLO, [4dc-bobble in next st,

7 scBLO] 3 times, 4 dc-bobble in next st, 3 scBLO; rep from * 3 more times, slst in first sc to join. (148 sc, 20 bobbles, 4 x 2ch-sp corners)

Fasten off colour 2.

Round 19: Join colour 1, *(1 sc, 2 ch, 1 sc) in 2ch-sp corner, 4 scBLO, 1 FPsc around 4dc-bobble, 8 scBLO, [1 FPsc around 4dc-bobble, 7 scBLO] 3 times, 1 FPsc around last 4dc-bobble, 4 scBLO; rep from * 3 more times, slst in first sc to join. (176 sc, 4 x 2ch-sp corners)

Round 20: *3 sc in 2ch-sp corner, 44 slstBLO; rep from * 3 more times, slst in beg st to join. (176 slsts, 4 x 3-sc corners)

Fasten off and weave in ends.

BOBBLE BURST

DESIGNED BY ANNA NIKIPIROWICZ

YARN

Scheepjes Stone Washed, sport (4ply), in foll shades:
Colour 1: Corundum Ruby (808)
Colour 2: Deep Amethyst (811)

HOOK

US size E/4 (3.5mm) hook

GAUGE (TENSION)

A single motif measures approx 7in (18cm) using a US size E/4 (3.5mm) hook.

SPECIAL ABBREVIATION

5tr-bobble, bobble of 5 tr

NOTE

Change to new colour on yoh of slst that joins round.

PATTERN

Using E/4 hook and colour 1, 5 ch, slst to join into a ring.

Round 1: 3 ch (counts as 1 dc throughout), 2 dc in ring, [2 ch, 3 dc in ring] 3 times, 2 ch, slst in top of beg 3-ch to join. (12 dc, 4 x 2ch-sp corners)

Round 2: 3 ch, 5tr-bobble, 1 dc, (2 dc, 2 ch, 2 dc) in 2ch-sp, *1 dc, 5tr-bobble, 1 dc, (2 dc, 2 ch, 2 dc) in 2ch-sp; rep from * twice more, slst in top of beg 3-ch to join. (24 dc, 4 bobbles, 4 x 2ch-sp corners)

Round 3: 3 ch, *1 dc in top of bobble, 1 dc, 5tr-bobble, 1 dc, (2 dc, 2 ch, 2 dc) in 2ch-sp, 1 dc, 5tr-bobble, 1 dc; rep from * 3 more times omitting last dc, slst in top of beg 3-ch to join. (36 dc, 8 bobbles, 4 x 2ch-sp corners)

continued on next page >

Round 4: 3 ch, *5tr-bobble, 1 dc, 1 dc in bobble, 1 dc, 5tr-bobble, 1 dc, (2 dc, 2 ch, 2 dc) in 2ch-sp, 1 dc, 5tr-bobble, 1 dc, 1 dc in bobble, 1 dc; rep from * 3 more times omitting last dc, slst in top of beg 3-ch to join. (48 dc, 12 bobbles, 4 x 2ch-sp corners)

Round 5: 3 ch, *1 dc in bobble, 1 dc, 5tr-bobble, 1 dc, 1 dc in bobble, 3 dc, (2 dc, 2 ch, 2 dc) in next 2ch-sp, 3 dc, 1 dc in bobble, 1 dc, 5tr-bobble, 1 dc; rep from * 3 more times omitting last dc, slst in top of beg 3-ch to join. (68 dc, 8 bobbles, 4 x 2ch-sp corners)

Round 6: 3 ch, *5tr-bobble, 1 dc, 1 dc in bobble, 7 dc, (2 dc, 2 ch, 2 dc) in next 2ch-sp, 7 dc, 1 dc in bobble, 1 dc; rep from * 3 more times omitting last dc, slst in top of beg 3-ch to join. (88 dc, 4 bobbles, 4 x 2ch-sp corners)

Fasten off colour 1.

Round 7: Join colour 2, 2 ch (counts as 1 hdc), 1 hdc in bobble, 11 hdc, (2 dc, 2 ch, 2 dc) in next 2ch-sp, 11 hdc; rep from *3 more times omitting last hdc, slst in top of beg 3-ch to join. (108 hdc, 4 x 2ch-sp corners)

Fasten off colour 2.

Round 8: Join colour 1 in any corner 2ch-sp, 4 ch (counts as first hdc, 2ch-sp) in same sp, 2 hdc in same sp, 1 BPdc around post of each st to next 2ch-sp, *(2 hdc, 2 ch, 2 hdc) in 2ch-sp, 1 BPdc around post of each st to next 2ch-sp; rep from * twice more, 1 hdc in same sp as beg 4-ch, slst in 2nd of beg 4-ch to join. (124 hdc, 4 x 2ch-sp corners)

Fasten off colour 1.

Round 9: Join colour 2 in any 2ch-sp, 3 ch (counts as first sc, 2ch-sp) in same sp, 2 sc in same sp, 1 BPhdc around post of each st to next 2ch-sp, *(2 sc, 2 ch, 2 sc) in 2ch-sp, 1 BPhdc around post of each st to next 2ch-sp; rep from * twice more, 1 sc in same sp as beg 4-ch, slst in first of beg 3-ch to join. (140 sts, 4 x 2ch-sp corners)

Fasten off and weave in ends.

BLUE BOBBLES

DESIGNER: RACHELE CARMONA

YARN

Scheepjes Colour Crafter, light worsted (DK), in foll shades:

Colour 1: Verviers (2017)
Colour 2: Middelburg (1003)
Colour 3: Texel (1019)

HOOK

US size G/6 (4mm) hook

GAUGE (TENSION)

A single motif measures approx 6in (15cm) using a US size G/6 (4mm) hook.

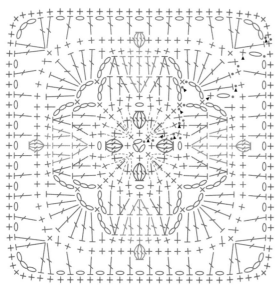

SPECIAL ABBREVIATION

4dc-bobble, bobble of 4 dc

NOTE

Change to next colour on last yoh of last st in old colour.

PATTERN

Using G/6 hook and colour 1, 3 ch, slst to join into a ring.

Round 1 (RS): Working in ring, 8 sc, using colour 2, slst in first sc to join, turn, do not fasten off colour 1. (8 sc)

Round 2: Using colour 2, [3 sc in next st, 4dc-bobble] 4 times, slst in first sc to join, turn. (4 bobbles, 12 sc)

Fasten off colour 2.

Round 3: Using colour 1, slst in same st as 3-sc, 5 sc in same st from Round 1 working over 3-sc, [1 ch, skip bobble, 5 sc in next st from Round 1 working over 3-sc] 3 times omitting final 5-sc, slst in first sc to join. (20 sc, 4 ch)

Round 4: Slst in next st, [3 sc in corner sc, 2 sc, 1 sc in ch-sp, 2 sc] 4 times, slst in first sc to join. (32 sc)

Make 4 bobbins each with about 8ft (2.5m) of colour 3.

Round 5: [1 sc in corner st, 3 ch, 1 dc, dc2tog, change to colour 3 on final yoh of dec, 3 dc in next st, change to colour 1 on 3rd dc, drop colour 3, using colour 1, dc2tog, 1 dc, 3 ch] 4 times, slst in first sc to join, turn. 4 bobbins of colour 3 now in use. (28 dc, 4 sc, 8 x 3ch-sp)

Round 6: Slst in 2nd ch of 3ch-sp, 1 sc in same ch-sp, *3 ch, dc2tog, change to colour 3 as before, 2 dc in next st, 1 dc, 2 dc in next st, change to colour 1, drop colour 3, using colour 1, dc2tog, [3 ch, 1 sc in next ch-sp] twice; rep from * 3

more times omitting final sc, slst in first sc to join, turn. (28 dc, 8 sc, 12 x 3ch-sp)

Round 7: (1 sc, 1 ch, 6 dc) in corner ch-sp (counts as 7 dc), [1 sc in next ch-sp, 1 sc in dc2tog, 1 sc, change to colour 3, 3 sc, change to colour 1 on 3rd sc, drop colour 3, 2 sc, 1 sc in next ch-sp, 7 dc in corner sp] 4 times omitting final 7 dc, slst in first ch to join, turn. (28 dc, 36 sc)

Round 8: Slst in next 2 sts, [3 sc in corner st, 7 sc, change to colour 3 in final sc, 4dc-bobble in next st, change to colour 1 on final step of bobble, 7 sc] 4 times, slst in first sc to join, turn. (4 bobbles, 68 sc)

Fasten off all colour 3 bobbins.

Round 9: (1 sc, 1 ch, 1 dc, 3 ch, 2 dc) in corner st (first sc and ch count as 1 dc), *[1 ch, skip 1 st, 1 dc] 8 times, 1 ch, skip 1 st, (2 dc, 3 ch, 2 dc) in corner st; rep from * 3 more times omitting final corner, slst in first ch to join. (48 dc, 36 ch, 4 x 3ch-sp corners)

Fasten off colour 1.

Round 10: Join colour 2 with a slst in any corner ch-sp, [5 sc in corner sp, 1 sc in 21 sts/sps to next corner sp] 4 times, slst in first sc to join. (104 sc)

Fasten off and weave in ends.

PEBBLE SPLASH

DESIGNER: CAITIE MOORE

YARN

Nurturing Fibres Eco-Cotton, light worsted (DK), in foll shades:
Colour 1: Charcoal
Colour 2: Vanilla
Colour 3: Watershed
Colour 4: Denim

HOOK

US size G/6 (4mm) hook

GAUGE (TENSION)

A single motif measures approx 5¾in (14.5cm) using a US size G/6 (4mm) hook.

SPECIAL ABBREVIATIONS

FP-bobble, bobble of 3 dc worked round front post of st
2ch-picot, picot with 2 ch
3ch-picot, picot with 3 ch

NOTE

Join yarn with standing sts unless otherwise indicated, and join round with invisible join in standing st.

PATTERN

Using G/6 hook and colour 1, make a magic ring.

Round 1: Working in ring, 4 ch (counts as dc, 1 ch), [1 dc, 1 ch] 7 times. (8 dc, 8 ch)

Fasten off colour 1.

Round 2: Join colour 2 around any dc, *1 FP-bobble, 1 sc in 1ch-sp; rep from * to end. (8 bobbles, 8 sc)

Fasten off colour 2.

Round 3: Join colour 1 in any sc, *(1 sc, 1 ch, 1 sc, 1 ch, 1 sc) in same st, 2 ch, skip FP-bobble, 1 sc, 2 ch, skip FP-bobble; rep from* to end. (16 sc, 8 x 2ch-sp, 8 ch)

Fasten off colour 1.

Round 4: Join colour 3 in first 2ch-sp to left of any 3-sc + 2-ch group, *2 sc in 2ch-sp, 1 ch, skip next sc, 2 sc in 2ch-sp, skip next sc, (1 slst, 2 hdc) in 1ch-sp, 2ch-picot, skip next sc, (2 hdc, 1 slst) in 1ch-sp, skip next st; rep from * to end. (16 sc, 16 hdc, 8 slsts, 4 ch, 4 picot)

Fasten off colour 3.

Round 5 (WS): Join colour 4 in any sc between petals of Round 3, cont to work in Round 3, *(1 FPhdc, 1 ch, 1 FPhdc, 1 ch, 1 FPhdc, 2 ch) around sc, skip 1 sc, (1 FPhdc, 1 ch, 1 FPhdc, 1 ch, 1 FPhdc, 2 ch) in 2nd sc of 3-sc group, skip next sc; rep from * to end. (24 hdc, 16 ch, 8 x 2ch-sp)

Fasten off colour 4.

ROUNDS 1-4

ROUNDS 5-6

Round 6 (RS): Join colour 4 in any 2ch-sp, *1 sc, skip next st, 3 dc in 1ch-sp, 3ch-picot, skip next st, 3 dc in 1ch-sp, skip next st; rep from * to end. (48 dc, 8 sc, 8 picot)

Fasten off colour 4.

Round 7 (WS): Join colour 2 around 2nd FPhdc of any petal of Round 5, *(1 FPdc, 1 ch, 1 FPdc, 1 ch, 1 FPdc, 2 ch) around FPdc in Round 5; rep from * to end. (24 dc, 16 ch, 8 x 2ch-sp)

Fasten off colour 2.

Round 8 (RS): Join colour 2 in any 2ch-sp, *1 sc in ch-sp, skip next st, (3 dc, 2 tr, 3ch-picot) in 1ch-sp, skip next st, (2 tr, 3 dc) in next 1ch-sp, skip next st; rep from * to end. (88 sts, 8 picot)

Fasten off colour 2.

Round 9: Join colour 1 in first dc of any petal, *5 scBLO, 1 ch, skip picot, 5 scBLO, skip sc; rep from * to end. (80 sts, 8 ch)

Fasten off colour 1.

Round 10: Find 1ch-sp aligned between 2 petals from Round 4 (not aligned with petal), count to right by 5 sts, join colour 3 in 6th st, *1 slstBLO, 3 hdcBLO, 2 dcBLO, 3 dc in 1ch-sp, 2 dcBLO, 3 hdcBLO, 1 slstBLO, 6 ch, skip (4 sts, 1 ch, 4 sts); rep from * to end. (60 sts, 4 x 6ch-sp)

Fasten off colour 3.

Round 11: Join colour 4 in 2nd dc of any 3-dc group from Round 10, *(2 hdc, 1 ch, 2 hdc) in same st, 6 hdc, skip slst, 2 sc in 6ch-sp, 3 hdc around 6ch-sp from Round 10 and 1ch-sp from Round 9, 2 sc in 6ch-sp, skip slst, 6 hdc; rep from * to end. (92 sts, 4 x 1ch-sp corners)

Fasten off colour 4.

Round 12: Join colour 3 in any 1ch-sp, *(2 dc, 1 ch, 2 dc) in 1ch-sp, 10 dc, 3 hdc in 3rd loop of hdc, 10 dc; rep from * to end. (108 sts, 4 x 1ch-sp corners)

Fasten off and weave in ends.

ROUNDS 7-10

ROUNDS 11-12

DELFT BLUES

DESIGNER: CAITIE MOORE

YARN

Nurturing Fibres Eco-Cotton, light worsted (DK), in foll shades:
Colour 1: Vanilla
Colour 2: Denim
Colour 3: Watershed

HOOK

4mm (US G/6) hook

GAUGE (TENSION)

A single motif measures approx 6¼in (16cm) using a US size G/6 (4mm) hook.

SPECIAL ABBREVIATIONS

2dc-bobble, bobble of 2 dc
3ch-picot, picot with 3 ch
4ch-picot, picot with 4 ch

NOTE

Join yarn with standing sts unless otherwise indicated, and join round with invisible join in standing st.

PATTERN

Using G/6 hook and colour 1, make a magic ring.

Round 1: 6 hdc in ring, pull on tail to close ring. (6 hdc)

Fasten off colour 1.

Round 2: Join colour 2 to any st, (2dc-bobble, 1 ch, 2dc-bobble, 1 ch) in each st to end. (12 bobbles, 12 ch)

Fasten off colour 2.

Round 3: Join colour 1, 3 dc in each 1ch-sp. (36 dc)

Fasten off colour 1.

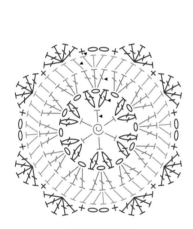

ROUNDS 1-5

ROUND 6

ROUND 7

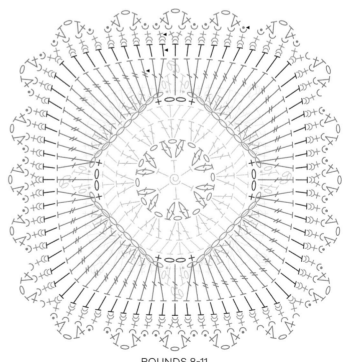

ROUNDS 8-11

Round 4: Join colour 3 in any st, *8 hdc, 3 hdc in same st; rep from * to end. (44 hdc)

Fasten off colour 3.

Round 5: Join colour 2 in any st, *1 sc, skip 1 st, 5 dc in next st, skip 1 st, 1 sc, skip 1 st, 5 dc in next st, skip 1 st, 1 sc, 2 ch, skip 2 sts; rep from * to end. (40 dc, 12 sc, 4 x 2ch-sp)

Fasten off colour 2.

Round 6: Keeping ch back, join colour 3 in first of 2 skipped sts, *(1 slst, 1 ch, 1 dc, 3ch-picot) in same st, (1 dc, 1 ch, 1 slst) in next st, 10 ch behind 5-dc groups, skip to next 2 skipped sts; rep from * to end. (4 petals, 4 x 10ch-sp)

Fasten off colour 3.

Round 7: Join colour 3 in sc to right of first 5-dc group in Round 5, *1 sc, (3 BPsc, 2 BPhdc) in 5-dc group, (2 FPdc, 4ch-picot, 1 FPdc) around sc, (2 BPhdc, 3 BPsc) in next 5-dc group, 1 sc in next sc, 3 sc in Round 5 2ch-sp (behind petal from prev round); rep from * to end. (72 sts, 4 picot)

Fasten off colour 3.

Round 8: Join colour 1 in 10ch-sp from Round 6, *13 tr in 10-ch, 2 dc in sc, 1 dc in ch-sp, 2 dc in sc; rep from * to end. (52 tr, 20 dc)

Fasten off colour 1.

Round 9: Join colour 2 in any st, 1 hdc in each st. (72 hdc)

Fasten off colour 2.

Round 10: Join colour 3 in 3rd loop of any st, *8 sc in 3rd loop, 2 sc in 3rd loop of next st; rep from * to end. (80 sc)

Fasten off colour 3.

Round 11: Join colour 1 in front loop, *1 slstFLO, (1 scFLO, 1 hdcFLO, 1 ch) in same st, (1 hdcFLO, 1 scFLO) in next st, 1 slstFLO; rep from * to end. (120 sts, 20 ch)

Fasten off colour 1.

Round 12: Join colour 3 in back loop of sc from Round 10 above 4ch-picot from Round 7, *(2 dc, 1 ch, 2 dc) in same st, 2 dc, 15 hdc, 2 dc; rep from * to end. (60 hdc, 32 dc, 4 x 1ch-sp corners)

Fasten off colour 3.

Round 13: Join colour 1 in 1ch-sp, *(2 hdc, 1 ch, 2 hdc) in 1ch-sp, 4 FPhdc, 7 sc, sc2tog, 6 sc, (1 sc, 1 FPhdc) in same st, 3 FPhdc; rep from * to end. (108 sts, 4 x 1ch-sp corners)

Fasten off and weave in ends.

ROUNDS 12-13

MINDFUL MANDALA

DESIGNER: CAITIE MOORE

YARN

Nurturing Fibres Eco-Cotton, light
worsted (DK), in foll shades:
Colour 1: Old Gold
Colour 2: Aventurine
Colour 3: Pecan
Colour 4: Denim
Colour 5: Mint
Colour 6: Watershed

HOOK

US size G/6 (4mm) hook

GAUGE (TENSION)

A single motif measures approx 8in
(20cm) using a US size G/6 (4mm) hook.

SPECIAL ABBREVIATIONS

2dc-bobble, bobble of 2 dc
4dc-bobble, bobble of 4 dc
4dc-PC, popcorn of 4 dc, 1 ch

NOTE

*Join yarn with standing sts unless
otherwise indicated, and join round with
invisible join in standing st.*

PATTERN

Using G/6 hook and colour 1, make a
magic ring.

Round 1: 8 sc, in ring, pull tail to close
ring. (8 sc)

Fasten off colour 1.

Round 2: Join colour 2 in FLO of
any st, *(1 hdcFLO, 2 ch, 1 hdcFLO)
in same st; rep from * in each st
around. (16 hdc, 16 ch)

Fasten off colour 2.

Round 3: Join colour 3 in BLO of
Round 1, *3 trBLO in same st; rep
from * in each st around. (24 tr)

Fasten off colour 3.

Round 4: Join colour 4 in any st, *2
sc, 2 sc in same st; rep from * to end.
(32 sc)

Fasten off colour 4.

Round 5: Join colour 1 in any st,
*2dc-bobble, 5 ch, skip 3 sts; rep
from * to end. (8 bobbles, 8 x 5ch-sp)

Fasten off colour 1.

Round 6: Join colour 5 to Round
4 in sc to left of bobble from prev
round, keeping 5-ch in back as you
work around, *2 dcBLO in same st,
1 dcBLO, 2 dcBLO in same st, 2 ch,
skip bobble; rep from * to end. (40
dc, 8 x 2ch-sp)

Fasten off colour 5.

Round 7: Join colour 1 to 5-ch from
Round 5, *1 sc, 4dc-PC in 2dc-
bobble, 1 sc in 5ch-sp (ch may be
in back, pull forward and work at
front), 5 ch, skip 5 dc from Round 6,
insert hook under 2-ch from Round
6 to work next st around 5-ch from
Round 5; rep from * to end. (8 PC, 16
sc, 8 x 5ch-sp)

Fasten off colour 1.

Round 8: Join colour 5 in sc from
Round 7 to right of PC, *1 hdc, 3 dc
in 1 ch of PC, 1 hdc in next sc, with
Round 7 5-ch in back, cont working
in Round 6, sc2tog, 1 sc, sc2tog; rep
from * to end. (64 sts)

Fasten off colour 5.

Round 9: Join colour 4 in any st,
1 hdc in each st around. (64 hdc)

Fasten off colour 4.

Round 10: Join colour 6 in any
st, 1 hdc in 3rd loop of each hdc
around. (64 hdc)

Fasten off colour 5.

Round 11: Join colour 2 in any st,
*1 sc, skip next st, (3 dc, 2ch-picot, 3
dc) in same st, skip next st, 1 sc; rep
from * around. (96 tr, 16 sc, 16 picot)

Fasten off colour 2.

Round 12: Join colour 3 in 3rd loop of
any hdc from Round 10, *7 tr in third
loops, 2 tr in third loop in same st;
rep from * to end. (72 tr)

ROUNDS 1-11

Fasten off colour 3.

Round 13: Join colour 1 in any st, *2 hdc in same st, 1 ch, skip next st; rep from * to end. (72 hdc, 36 ch)

Fasten off colour 1.

Round 14: Join colour 3 in any 1 ch-sp, *2 hdc in same st, 1 ch, skip 2 hdc and work in next 1 ch-sp; rep from * to end. (72 hdc, 36 ch)

Fasten off colour 3.

Round 15: Join colour 6 in hdc to right of 1-ch, *1 sc, 4dc-bobble in 1 ch-sp, skip next st; rep from * to end. (36 bobbles, 36 sc)

Fasten off colour 5.

Round 16: Join colour 4 in sc, *(2 tr, 1 ch , 2 tr) in same st (corner), 1 ch, skip bobble, 3 dc in sc, 1 ch, skip bobble, 3 hdc, 1 ch, skip bobble, 3 sc, 1 ch, skip bobble, 3 sc, 1 ch, skip bobble, 3 sc, 1 ch, skip bobble, 3 sc, 1 ch, skip bobble, 3 hdc, 1 ch, skip bobble, 3 dc, 1 ch, skip bobble; rep from * to end. (112 sts, 40 ch)

Fasten off and weave in ends.

ROUNDS 12-16

LOVE IN A MIST

DESIGNER: CAITIE MOORE

YARN

Nurturing Fibres Eco-Cotton, light worsted (DK), in foll shades:

Colour 1: Sunglow
Colour 2: Persian
Colour 3: Baltic
Colour 4: Vanilla
Colour 5: Aventurine

HOOK

US size G/6 (4mm) hook

GAUGE (TENSION)

A single motif measures approx 6in (15cm) using a US size G/6 (4mm) hook.

SPECIAL ABBREVIATIONS

croc st, 5 dc bottom to top up post of first dc, 2ch-picot, 5 dc top to bottom down post of next dc
2ch-picot, picot with 2 ch
3dc-bobble, bobble of 3 dc, 1 ch

NOTE

Join yarn with standing sts unless otherwise indicated, and join round with invisible join in standing st.

PATTERN

Using G/6 hook and colour 1, make a magic ring.

Round 1: 8 hdc in ring. (8 hdc)

Fasten off colour 1.

Round 2: Join colour 2 in any st, *(1 sc, 1 ch, 1 dc, 1 ch, 1 sc) in same st; rep from * to end. (16 sc, 8 dc, 16 ch)

Fasten off colour 2.

Round 3: Join colour 3 in 3rd loop of hdc from Round 1, 3 dc in each st around. (24 dc)

Fasten off colour 3.

Round 4: Join colour 4 in any st, *2 hdc, 2 hdc in same st; rep from * around. (32 hdc)

Fasten off colour 4.

Round 5: Join colour 5 in any st, *2 dc, 3 ch, skip 2 sts; rep from * to end. (16 dc, 8 x 3ch-sp)

Fasten off colour 5.

Round 6: Join colour 5 to Round 4 in hdc to right of dc from Round 5, *1 sc, croc st around 2-dc from Round 5, 1 sc in Round 4; rep from * to end. (96 sts, 8 picot)

Fasten off colour 5.

Round 7: Join colour 1 in 3ch-sp from Round 5, *8 dc in 3ch-sp, skip 2 dc; rep from * to end. (64 dc)

Fasten off colour 1.

Round 8: Join colour 4 in any st, *7 hdc, 2 hdc in same st; rep from * to end. (72 hdc)

Fasten off colour 4.

Round 9: Join colour 4 in any st, 72 FPdc.

ROUNDS 1-6

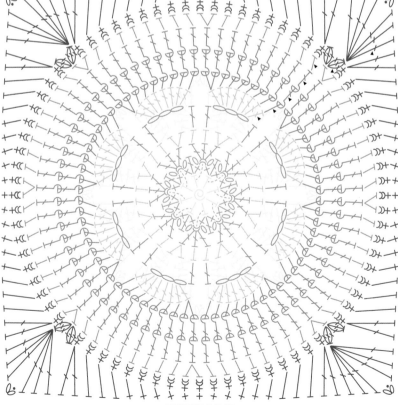

ROUNDS 7-13

Fasten off colour 4.

Round 10: Join colour 4 in any st, 72 FPdc.

Fasten off colour 4.

Round 11: Join colour 5 in any st, *8 hdc, 2 hdc in same st; rep from * to end. (80 hdc)

Fasten off colour 5.

Round 12: Join colour 2 in st aligned with Round 6 petal, *[3dc-bobble] twice in same st, 1 sc in 3rd loop of next 19 hdc; rep from * to end. (76 sc, 8 bobbles)

Fasten off colour 2.

Round 13: Join colour 3 in 1 ch of first 3dc-bobble, *(3 dc, 2ch-picot, 3 dc) in same st, skip bobble, 2 dc in same st, 3 hdc, 11 sc, 3 hdc, 2 dc in same st; rep from * to end. (108 sts, 4 picot corners)

Fasten off and weave in ends.

CRESCENT QUARTER

DESIGNER: RACHELE CARMONA

YARN

Scheepjes Merino Soft, light worsted (DK), in foll shades:
Colour 1: Chagall (655)
Colour 2: Velázquez (650)
Colour 3: Rothko (623)
Colour 4: Copley (634)

HOOK

US size G/6 (4mm) hook

GAUGE (TENSION)

A single motif measures approx 7in (18cm) using a US size G/6 (4mm) hook.

SPECIAL ABBREVIATION

4dc-PC, popcorn of 4 dc

PATTERN

Using G/6 hook and colour 1, 3 ch, slst to join into a ring.

Row 1 (RS): Working in ring, 1 sc, 1 ch (these count as first dc here and throughout), 4 dc, turn. (5 dc)

Row 2: (1 sc, 1 ch, 1 dc) in first st, skip 1 st, (1 dc, 1 ch, 1 dc) in next st, skip 1 st, 2 dc in last st, turn. (6 dc, 1 ch)

Fasten off colour 1.

Row 3: Join colour 2 with slst in first st, 1 sc in same st, 2 ch, 1 tr in first skipped dc from Row 1, 1 ch, (1 dc, 1 ch, 1 dc) in ch-sp, 1 ch, 1 tr in next skipped dc from Row 1, 1 ch, 1 dc in last st, turn. (2 tr, 4 dc, 5 ch)

Row 4: 1 sc, 2 ch, 3 dc in tr, 1 ch, 3 dc in middle ch-sp, 1 ch, 3 dc in tr, 1 ch, 1 dc in last st, turn. (11 dc, 4 ch)

Fasten off colour 2.

Row 5: Join colour 3 with slst in first st, 1 sc, 2 ch, 1 dtr in first ch-sp from Row 3, *1 ch, skip 1 dc, (1 dc, 1 ch, 1 dc) in next dc, 1 ch, 1 dtr in next ch-sp from Row 3; rep from * twice more, 1 ch, 1 dc in last st, turn. (4 dtr, 8 dc, 11 ch-sp)

Row 6: 1 sc, 2 ch, [1 dc in dtr, 1 ch, skip 1 ch-sp, 3 dc in next ch-sp] 3 times, 1 ch, 1 dc in dtr, 1 ch, 1 dc in final st, turn. (15 dc, 8 ch-sp)

Fasten off colour 3.

Row 7: Join colour 4 with slst in first st, 1 sc in same st, 2 ch, *skip one ch-sp from Row 5, 1 dtr in next ch-sp from Row 5, 1 ch, 1 dtr in prev skipped ch-sp from Row 5, 1 ch, skip next dc in Row 6, (1 dc, 1 ch, 1 dc) in next dc, 1 ch; rep from * twice more, 1 dtr in final ch-sp of Row 5, 1 ch, 1 dtr in previous ch-sp from Row 5, 1 ch, 1 dc in last st of Row 6t, turn. (8 dtr, 8 dc, 15 ch)

Row 8: 1 sc, 2 ch, [skip 1 ch-sp, 3 dc in next ch-sp, 1 ch] 7 times, 1 dc in last st, turn. (23 dc, 8 ch)

Row 9: 1 sc in first st, [1 sc in ch-sp, 1 sc in dc, 1 FPdc in next st, 1 sc in next dc] 7 times, 1 sc in ch-sp, 1 sc in last st, turn. (7 FPdc, 24 sc)

continued on next page >

Row 10: (1 sc, 1 ch, 2 dc) in first st, skip 2 dc on Row 9, 1 BPdtr in next st on Row 8, skip 2 sts on Row 9, [3 dc in next sc, skip next st, 1 BPdtr in next st on Row 8, skip next 2 sts] 6 times, skip 1 more st, 3 dc in last st, turn. (24 dc, 7 BPdtr)

Fasten off colour 4.

Row 11: Join colour 1 with slst in first st, 1 sc, 1 ch, 2 dc in next st, [skip 1 dc, 1 ch, 4dc-PC in front post of BPdtr, 1 ch, skip 1 dc, 3 dc in next st] 7 times omitting final dc, 1 dc in last st, turn. (7 x 4dc-PC, 24 dc, 14 ch)

Row 12: 1 sc, 2 ch, 2 dc in next st, *1 ch, skip 2 dc, (2 dc, 1 ch, 2 dc) in next st; rep from * 5 more times, 1 ch, skip 2 dc, (2 dc, 1 ch, 1 dc) in last st, do not turn. (30 dc, 15 ch)

Fasten off colour 1.

Row 13 (WS): Join colour 2 with slst in first ch-sp, 1 sc, 2 ch, (1 dc, 1 ch, 1 dc, 1 ch) in next 13 ch-sps, 1 dc in last ch-sp, turn. (28 dc, 27 ch)

Row 14: (1 sc, 1 ch, 1 dc) in first st, [1 ch, skip one ch-sp, 3 dc in next ch-sp, 1 ch, skip one ch-sp, 2 dc in next ch-sp] 7 times working final 2 dc in last st, turn. (37 dc, 14 ch)

Row 15: 1 sc in all sts/sps across, turn. (51 sc)

Row 16: Slst in 10 sts, 3 sc, 3 hdc, (1 dc, 2 tr) in next st, [1 ch, skip 1 sc, 1 tr] 8 times, 1 ch, (2 tr, 1 dc) in next st, 3 hdc, 3 sc, turn, leaving rem sts unworked. (12 tr, 2 dc, 6 hdc, 6 sc, 9 ch)

Row 17: Slst in 9 sts, 1 sc in next 17 sts/sps, turn, leaving rem sts unworked. (17 sc)

Fasten off colour 2.

Row 18: Join colour 4 with slst in second sc, 1 sc in same st, 1 ch, dc2tog (these count as first dc3tog), 1 ch, skip 2 sts, 3 dc in next st, skip 3 sts, 3 dc in next st, 1 ch, skip 2 sts, dc3tog, turn. (2 x dc3tog, 6 dc, 3 ch)

Row 19: 1 sc in first ch-sp, 1 sc in next 8 sts/ sps, turn. (9 sc)

Row 20: Skip first st, 1 sc in next st, 1 ch, dc2tog (these count as first dc3tog), 1 dc, dc3tog, turn. (2 x dc3tog, 1 dc)

Row 21: Sc3tog.

Fasten off colour 4

BORDER

Round 1: Join colour 2 with slst in corner, [3 sc in corner st, 25 sc evenly across to next corner] 4 times, slst in first sc to join. (112 sc)

Round 2: [3 sc in corner st, 1 sc in each st to next corner] 4 times, slst in first sc to join. (120 sc)

Fasten off yarn and weave in all ends.

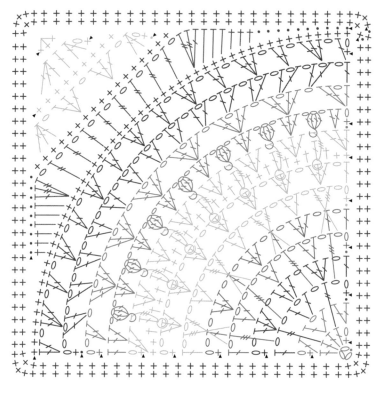

INDIAN TERRACOTTA

DESIGNER: EMMA POTTER

YARN

Stylecraft Special DK, light worsted (DK), in foll shades:
Colour 1: Copper (1029)
Colour 2: White (1001)

HOOK

US size G/6 (4mm) hook

GAUGE (TENSION)

A single motif measures approx 4¾in (12cm) using a US size G/6 (4mm) hook.

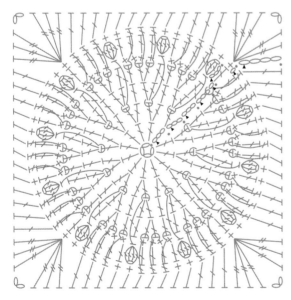

SPECIAL ABBREVIATION

4dc-PC, popcorn of 4 dc

GAUGE (TENSION)

A single motif measures approx 4¾in (12cm) using a US size G/6 (4mm) hook.

PATTERN

Using G/6 hook and colour 1, 4 ch, slst to join into a ring.

Round 1: 3 ch (counts as first dc throughout), 11 dc in ring, slst in top of beg 3-ch to join. (12 dc)

Round 2: 3 ch, 1 dc in same place as 3-ch, 2 dc in each dc around, slst in top of beg 3-ch to join. (24 dc)

Fasten off colour 1.

Round 3: Join colour 2 in same place, 3 ch, 2 dc in next dc, [1 dc, 2 dc in next st] around, slst in top of beg 3-ch to join. (36 dc)

Fasten off colour 2.

Round 4: Join colour 1 in same place, 3 ch, 1 dc, 2 dc in next dc, [2 dc, 2 dc in next dc] around, slst in top of beg 3-ch to join. (48 dc)

Fasten off colour 1.

Round 5: Join colour 2 in same place, 1 ch (counts as 1 sc throughout), 1 FPdc around colour 2 dc two rounds below, 1 sc, 2 sc in next st, [1 sc, 1 FPdc around dc two rounds below, 1 sc, 2 sc in next st] around, slst in beg FPdc to join. (12 dc, 48 sc)

Round 6: 3 ch, 3 dc in same place, remove loop from hook, insert hook in top of beg 3-ch and draw loop through to create first 4dc-PC, [4 dc,

4dc-PC in FPdc] around, slst in beg PC to join. (12 PC, 48 dc)

Fasten off colour 2.

Round 7: Join colour 1 in same place, 1 ch (does not count as st), 1 sc in same place, 1 sc in next st, 1 FPdc around next 3 dc in colour 1 two rounds below, [2 sc, 3 FPdc] around, slst in beg sc to join. (60 sts)

Round 8: 4 ch (counts as tr), (2 tr, 2 ch, 3 tr) in same place, skip 1 sc, 3 dc, 7 hdc, 3 dc, [(3 tr, 2 ch, 3 tr) in next st, skip 1 sc, 3 dc, 7 hdc, 3 dc] around, slst in top of beg-ch to join. (76 sts, 4 x 2ch-sp corners)

Fasten off and weave in ends.

POPCORN FANTASY

DESIGNER: JOHANNA LINDAHL

YARN

Scheepjes Colour Crafter, light worsted (DK), in foll shades:

Colour 1: Gouda (1081)
Colour 2: Lelystad (1026)
Colour 3: Leek (1132)
Colour 4: Goes (1820)
Colour 5: Alphen (1722)
Colour 6: Alkmaar (1708)

HOOKS

US size G/6 (4mm) hook
US size 7 (4.5mm) hook

GAUGE (TENSION)

A single motif measures 7in (18cm) using US size G/6 (4mm) and US size 7 (4.5mm) hooks.

SPECIAL ABBREVIATION

4dc-PC, popcorn of 4 dc, 1 ch

PATTERN

Using G/6 hook and colour 1, make a magic ring.

Round 1: Working into ring, 5 ch (counts as 1 dc, 2ch-sp), [1 dc, 4dc-PC, 1 dc, 2 ch] 3 times, 1 dc, 4dc-PC, slst in 3rd ch of beg 5-ch to join. (8 dc, 4 PC, 4 x 2ch-sp corners)

Fasten off colour 1.

Round 2: Join colour 2 in any corner 2ch-sp, 2 ch (does not count as st throughout), (4dc-PC, 1 dc, 2 ch, 1 dc, 4dc-PC) in corner 2ch-sp, *(1 FPdc, 1 ch, 1 FPdc) in next PC, (4dc-PC, 1 dc, 2 ch, 1 dc, 4dc-PC) in next 2ch-sp; rep from * twice more, (1 FPdc, 1 ch, 1 FPdc) in next PC, slst in first PC to join. (16 dc, 8 PC, 4 ch-sp, 4 x 2ch-sp corners)

Fasten off colour 2.

Round 3: Join colour 3 in any corner 2ch-sp, 2 ch, (4dc-PC, 1 dc, 2 ch, 1 dc, 4dc-PC) in corner 2ch-sp, *(1 FPdc, 1 ch, 1 FPdc) in next PC, 4dc-PC in next 1ch-sp, (1 FPdc, 1 ch, 1 FPdc) in next PC, (4dc-PC, 1 dc, 2 ch, 1 dc, 4dc-PC) in next 2ch-sp; rep from * twice more, (1 FPdc, 1 ch, 1 FPdc) in next PC, 4dc-PC in next 1ch-sp, (1 FPdc, 1 ch, 1 FPdc) in next PC, slst in first PC to join. (24 dc, 12 PC, 8 ch-sp, 4 x 2ch-sp corners)

Fasten off colour 3.

Round 4: Join colour 2 in any corner 2ch-sp, 2 ch, (4dc-PC, 1 dc, 2 ch, 1 dc, 4dc-PC) in corner 2ch-sp, *[(1 FPdc, 1 ch, 1 FPdc) in next PC, 4dc-PC in next 1ch-sp] twice, (1 FPdc, 1 ch, 1 FPdc) in next PC, (4dc-PC, 1 dc, 2 ch, 1 dc, 4dc-PC) in next 2ch-sp; rep from * twice more, [(1 FPdc, 1 ch, 1 FPdc) in next PC, 4dc-PC in next 1ch-sp] twice, (1 FPdc, 1 ch, 1 FPdc) in next PC, slst in first PC to join. (32 dc, 16 PC, 12 ch-sp, 4 x 2ch-sp corners)

Fasten off colour 2.

Round 5: Join colour 1 in any corner 2ch-sp, 2 ch, (4dc-PC, 1 dc, 2 ch, 1 dc, 4dc-PC) in corner 2ch-sp, *[(1 FPdc, 1 ch, 1 FPdc) in next PC, 4dc-PC in next 1ch-sp] 3 times, (1 FPdc, 1 ch, 1 FPdc) in next PC, (4dc-PC, 1 dc, 2 ch, 1 dc, 4dc-PC) in next 2ch-sp; rep from * twice more, [(1 FPdc, 1 ch, 1 FPdc) in next PC, 4dc-PC in next 1ch-sp] 3 times, (1 FPdc, 1 ch, 1 FPdc) in next PC, slst in first PC to join. (40 dc, 20 PC, 16 ch-sp, 4 x 2ch-sp corners)

Fasten off colour 1.

Round 6: Join colour 3 in any corner 2ch-sp, 2 ch, (4dc-PC, 1 dc, 2 ch, 1 dc, 4dc-PC) in corner 2ch-sp, *[(1 FPdc, 1 ch, 1 FPdc) in next PC, 4dc-PC in next 1ch-sp] 4 times, (1 FPdc, 1 ch, 1 FPdc) in next PC, (4dc-PC, 1 dc, 2 ch, 1 dc, 4dc-PC) in next 2ch-sp; rep from * twice more, [(1 FPdc, 1 ch, 1 FPdc) in next PC, 4dc-PC in next 1ch-sp] 4 times, (1 FPdc, 1 ch, 1 FPdc) in next PC, slst in first PC to join. (48 dc, 24 PC, 20 ch-sp, 4 x 2ch-sp corners)

Fasten off colour 3.

Change to US 7 hook.

Round 7: Join colour 4 in any corner 2ch-sp, 3 ch (counts as 1 sc, 2ch-sp throughout), 1 sc in corner 2ch-sp, *[1 ch, 1 FPsc in next PC, 1 ch, 1 sc in next 1ch-sp] 5 times, 1 ch, 1 FPsc in next PC, 1 ch (1 sc, 2 ch, 1 sc) in next 2ch-sp; rep from * twice more, [1 ch, 1 FPsc in next PC, 1 ch, 1 sc in next 1ch-sp] 5 times, 1 ch, 1 FPsc in next PC, 1 ch, slst in first ch of beg 3-ch to join. (52 sc, 48 ch-sp, 4 x 2ch-sp corners)

Fasten off colour 4.

Round 8: Join colour 3 in any corner 2ch-sp, 3 ch, 1 sc in corner 2ch-sp, *[1 ch, 1 sc in next 1ch-sp] 12 times, 1 ch, (1 sc, 2 ch, 1 sc) in next 2ch-sp; rep from * twice more, [1 ch, 1 sc in next 1ch-sp] 12 times, 1 ch, slst in first ch of beg 3-ch to join. (56 sc, 52 ch-sp, 4 x 2ch-sp corners)

Fasten off colour 3.

Round 9: Join colour 5 in any corner 2ch-sp, 3 ch, 1 sc in corner 2ch-sp, *[1 ch, 1 sc in next 1ch-sp] 13 times, 1 ch, (1 sc, 2 ch, 1 sc) in next 2ch-sp; rep from * twice more, [1 ch, 1 sc in next 1ch-sp] 13 times, 1 ch, slst in first ch of beg 3-ch to join. (60 sc, 56 ch-sp, 4 x 2ch-sp corners)

Fasten off colour 5.

Round 10: Join colour 3 in any corner 2ch-sp, 3 ch, 1 sc in corner 2ch-sp, *[1 ch, 1 sc in next 1ch-sp] 14 times, 1 ch, (1 sc, 2 ch, 1 sc) in next 2ch-sp; rep from * twice more, [1 ch, 1 sc in next 1ch-sp] 14 times, 1 ch, slst in first ch of beg 3-ch to join. (64 sc, 60 ch-sp, 4 x 2ch-ch corners)

Fasten off colour 3.

Round 11: Join colour 6 in any corner 2ch-sp, 3 ch, 1 sc in corner 2ch-sp, *[1 ch, 1 sc in next 1ch-sp] 15 times, 1 ch, (1 sc, 2 ch, 1 sc) in next 2ch-sp; rep from * twice more, [1 ch, 1 sc in next 1ch-sp] 15 times, 1 ch, slst in first ch of beg 3-ch to join. (68 sc, 64 ch-sp, 4 x 2ch-sp corners)

Round 12: Slst in next corner 2ch-sp, 3 ch, 1 sc in corner 2ch-sp, *[1 ch, 1 sc in next 1ch-sp] 16 times, 1 ch, (1 sc, 2 ch, 1 sc) in next 2ch-sp; rep from * twice more, [1 ch, 1 sc in next 1ch-sp] 16 times, 1 ch, slst in first ch of beg 3-ch to join. (72 sc, 68 ch-sp, 4 x 2ch-sp corners)

Fasten off and weave in ends

FRASERA

DESIGNER: CAITIE MOORE

YARN

Nurturing Fibres Eco-Cotton, light worsted (DK), in foll shades:

Colour 1: Watershed
Colour 2: Vanilla
Colour 3: Sunglow
Colour 4: Persian
Colour 5: Charcoal
Colour 6: Cobblestone

HOOK

US size G/6 (4mm) hook

GAUGE (TENSION)

A single motif measures approx 6in (15cm) using a US size G/6 (4mm) hook.

SPECIAL ABBREVIATIONS

5dc-PC, popcorn of 5 dc, 1 ch
4dc-PC, popcorn of 4 dc, 1 ch
2ch-picot, picot with 2 ch

NOTES

Join yarn with standing sts unless otherwise indicated, and join round with invisible join in standing st.
When working in popcorn, always work in 1ch-sp at back.

PATTERN

Using G/6 hook and colour 1, make a magic ring.

Round 1: 6 sc, pull on tail to close ring. (6 sc)

Fasten off colour 1.

Round 2: Join colour 1 in front loop of any st, *(1 slstFLO, 1 ch, 1 hdcFLO, 1 ch, 1 slstFLO) in same st; rep from * around. (18 sts, 12 ch)

Fasten off colour 1.

Round 3: Join colour 1 in back loop from Round 1, 2 sc in each st. (12 sc)

Fasten off colour 1.

Round 4: Join colour 1 in front loops from Round 3, *(1 slstFLO, 1 ch, 1 hdcFLO, 1 ch, 1 slstFLO) in same st; rep from * around. (36 sts, 24 ch)

Fasten off colour 1.

Round 5: Join colour 1 in back loops from Round 3, *1 sc, 2 sc in same st; rep from * to end. (18 sc)

Fasten off colour 1.

Round 6: Join colour 1 in any st, *2 hdc, 2 hdc in same st; rep from * to end. (24 hdc)

Fasten off colour 1.

Round 7: Join colour 2 in any st through back loop and 3rd loop and work entire round this way, *1 hdc, 2 hdc in same st; rep from * to end. (36 hdc)

Fasten off colour 2.

Round 8: Join colour 3 in any st through back loop and 3rd loop and work entire round this way, *1 sc, 5dc-PC, 1 sc, 5dc-PC, 1 sc, 5 ch, skip 4 sts; rep from * to end. (12 sc, 8 PC, 4 x 5ch-sp)

Fasten off colour 3.

Round 9: Join colour 2 in front loop from Round 7 (in front of sc in back loop) immediately to right of first PC, *1 sc, 1 ch, 1 hdc in PC, 3 hdc in sc between two PCs, 1 hdc in PC, 1 ch, 1 scFLO in next sc in Round 7, cont working in Round 7, 4 hdc; rep from * to end. (44 sts, 8 ch)

Fasten off colour 2.

Round 10: Join colour 3 in 1 ch-sp to right of first PC, *1 slst, 1 ch, skip next hdc, 1 sc in first hdc of 3-hdc group, 5dc-PC, 1 sc, 1 ch, skip next hdc, 1 slst in 1ch-sp, 5 ch; rep from * to end. (4 PC, 8 sc, 8 slsts, 8 ch, 4 x 5ch-sp)

Fasten off colour 3.

Round 11: Join colour 2 to Round 9 in 1ch-sp to right of PC from prev round,

*2 sc in Round 9 1ch-sp (working over slst from Round 9), 3 dc in first hdc of group from Round 9 (working over sc from prev round), (2 dc, 1 ch, 2 dc) in PC, 3 dc in 3rd hdc of group from Round 9 (working over sc from prev round), 2 sc in Round 9 1ch-sp (working over slst from Round 9), 7 sc in 6ch-sp; rep from * to end. (84 sts, 4 ch)

Fasten off colour 2.

Round 12: Join colour 4 in first of 7-sc (worked in 6ch-sp in prev round), *1 sc, 1 FPdc around first hdc from Round 9 below, 1 FPdc around next hdc, skip 2 sts in Round 11, 1 sc, without skipping any sts in Round 9, 2 FPdc, skip 2 sts in Round 11, 1 sc, 8 ch behind petal; rep from * to end. (28 sts, 4 x 8ch-sp)

Fasten off colour 4.

Round 13: Join colour 2 to Round 9 in sc to right of pair of PC, *1 dc, now work in Round 11 around petal, 1 sc in sc, 6 hdc, (2 dc, 2ch-picot, 2 dc) in 1ch-sp, 6 hdc, 1 sc, 1 dc in round 9, skip Round 12 sc and cont in Round 11, 2 hdc, skip next st, 2 hdc, skip next st; rep from * to end. (96 sts, 4 picot)

Fasten off colour 2.

Round 14: Join colour 4 to Round 12 and work only in Round 12, *1 slst in first sc after 8-ch behind Round 13, 2 FPdc around FPdcs, skip 1 sc, 2 FPdc around FPdcs, 1 slst in sc, 8 ch behind petal; rep from * to end. Do not fasten off. (24 sts, 4 x 8ch-sp)

Round 15: Cont with colour 4, *1 slst in slst after 8-ch from prev round, 4dc-PC in each FPdc, 1 slst, 8 ch behind petal; rep from * to end. (16 PC, 8 slsts, 4 x 8ch-sp)

Fasten off colour 4.

Round 16: Join colour 5 to 8ch-sp, *10 hdc in 8ch-sp, 3 dc in first PC, 2 tr in next PC, 2 ch, 2 tr in next PC (corner), 3 dc in last PC; rep from * to end. (40 hdc, 24 dc, 16 tr, 4 x 2ch-sp corners)

Fasten off colour 5.

Round 17: Join colour 6 in 2ch-sp, *(3 dc, 1 ch, 3 dc) in 2ch-sp, 8 dc, dc2tog twice, 8 dc; rep from * to end. (96 dc, 4 x 1ch-sp corners)

Fasten off and weave in ends.

COUNTRY POSY

DESIGNER: CAITIE MOORE

YARN

Nurturing Fibres Eco-Cotton, light worsted (DK), in foll shades:

Colour 1: Sunglow

Colour 2: Aventurine

Colour 3: Vanilla

Colour 4: Persian

Colour 5: Lime

Colour 6: Watershed

HOOK

US size G/6 (4mm) hook

GAUGE (TENSION)

A single motif measures approx 6in (15cm) using a US size G/6 (4mm) hook.

SPECIAL ABBREVIATIONS

3dc-PC, popcorn of 3 dc, 1 ch

modPC1, 3 dc in first st, 2ch-picot, 3 dc in next st, pull up loop, remove hook, insert hook from front to back through first dc, catch working loop and pull through, 1 ch

modPC2, 2 dc, 2ch-picot, 2 dc, in same st, pull up loop, remove hook, insert hook from front to back through first dc of st, catch loop and pull through, 1 ch

2ch-picot, picot with 2 ch

3ch-picot, picot with 3 ch

NOTES

Join yarn with standing sts unless otherwise indicated, and join round with invisible join in standing st.
In Round 10 space between PCs is a gap not a ch sp.

PATTERN

Using G/6 hook and colour 1, make a magic ring.

Round 1: 8 sc in ring, pull on tail to close ring. (8 sc)

Fasten off colour 1.

Round 2: Join colour 2 in any st, *(1 scFLO, 1 hdcFLO, 1 scFLO in same st; rep from * to end. (24 sts)

Fasten off colour 2.

Round 3: Join colour 3 in BLO from Round 1, 2 hdcBLO in each st. (16 hdc)

Fasten off colour 3.

Round 4: Join colour 3 in any st, *(1 dc, 1 ch, 1 dc) in same st, 4 ch, skip 3 sts; rep from * to end. (8 dc, 4 ch, 4 x 4ch-sp)

Fasten off colour 3.

Round 5: Join colour 1 to Round 3 in first hdc after dc, *with 4ch-sp in back, work three 3dc-PC, 2 ch (skip over dcs from Round 4), skip 1 hdc; rep from * to end. (12 PC, 4 x 2ch-sp)

Fasten off colour 1.

Round 6: Join colour 4 in 4ch-sp from Round 4, *10 dc in 4ch-sp, skip dc, 2 dc in 1ch-sp, skip dc; rep from * to end. (48 dc)

Fasten off colour 4.

ROUNDS 1-5

ROUNDS 6-9

Round 7: Join colour 3 in first dc of 10-dc group, *10 scBLO, keep 2-ch from Round 5 to back, 1 FPdc around dc from Round 4, 2 scBLO, 1 FPdc around next dc from Round 4; rep from * to end. (56 sts)

Fasten off colour 3.

Round 8: Join colour 5 in the first FPdc (of a pair) from prev round, *1 sc, modPC1, 1 sc in next FPdc, 8 ch; rep from * to end. (4 modPC1, 8 sc, 4 x 8ch-sp)

Fasten off colour 5.

Round 9: Join colour 3 to Round 7 FPdc to right of any modPC1, *1 FPdc around FPdc from Round 7, now work in Round 8 around modPC1, (1 sc, 3dc-PC) in sc from Round 8, 3 3dc-PC in 1ch-sp at top of modPC1, (3dc-PC, 1 sc) in sc, 1 FPdc around next FPdc from Round 7, 10 sc in Round 7; rep from * to end, keeping ch from prev round in back. (20 PC, 48 sc, 8 dc)

Fasten off colour 3.

Round 10: Join colour 6 to sc to left of rightmost FPdc, between FPdc and PC, *2 hdc in same st, skip PC, [2 hdc in space between PC, skip PC] twice, (1 hdc, 2-ch picot, 1 hdc) in space between PC, [skip PC, 2 hdc in space between PC] twice, 2 hdc in sc, skip FPdc, sc2tog, skip 6 sts from Round 9 and work in FLO from Round 6, 6 dcFLO, work back in Round 9, sc2tog, skip FPdc; rep from * to end. (88 sts, 4 picot)

Fasten off colour 6.

Round 11: Join colour 3 to first hdc at base of a petal (bottom right), *1 hdc in 3rd loop of next 6 hdc, 2 hdc in 3rd loop of same st, skip picot, 3ch-picot, 2 hdc in 3rd loop of same st, 1 hdc in 3rd loop of next 6 hdc, 3 scBLO, sc2togBLO, 3 scBLO; rep from * to end. (92 sts)

Fasten off colour 3.

Round 12: Join colour 2 in any sc2tog, *(1 sc, modPC2, 1 sc) in same st, 12 ch (keeping ch in back); rep from * to end. (4 modPC2, 8 sc, 4 x 12ch-sp)

Fasten off colour 2.

Round 13: Join colour 3 in rightmost hdc at base of a petal in Round 11, *7 dcBLO, 2 dcBLO in same st, 3ch-picot, 2 dcBLO in same st, 10 dcBLO, 1 ch behind PC, 3 dcBLO; rep from * to end. (96 dc, 4 ch, 4 picot)

Fasten off colour 3.

Round 14: Join colour 4 in 1 ch-sp, *2 hdc in 1ch-sp, skip 1 st, 11 scBLO, 3 ch, skip picot, 11 scBLO, skip 1 st; rep from * to end. (96 sts, 4 x 3ch-sp corners)

Fasten off and weave in ends.

ROUNDS 10–11

ROUNDS 12–14

ANNIE

DESIGNER: ROSINA PLANE

YARN

Stylecraft Naturals Bamboo+Cotton DK, light worsted (DK), in foll shades:
Colour 1: Night (7160)
Colour 2: Pale Pink (7132)
Colour 3: Blush (7133)
Colour 4: Azalea (7135)

HOOK

US size E/4 (3.5mm) hook

GAUGE (TENSION)

A single motif measures approx 8¼in (21cm) using a US size E/4 (3.5mm) hook.

SPECIAL ABBREVIATION

FLMdc, double crochet worked in front loop two rounds below

NOTES

Motif is worked in overlay mosaic crochet in Rounds 2 to 18, with RS facing.
To change colour, or join new colour, pull up a loop in new colour after joining slst, leaving prev colour on WS.
Unless directed otherwise, work corner sc in individual ch, NOT in ch sps.
Final scBLO on all rounds is worked in slst at end of prev round.
Rounds 19 and 20 begin with standing sts, and finish with invisible join. Do not pull too tight as will work in this st.

PATTERN

Using E/4 hook and colour 4, make a magic ring.

Round 1 (RS): 5 ch (counts as 1 dc, 2 ch), [3 dc, 2 ch] 3 times in ring, 2 dc in ring, slst in 3rd of beg 5-ch to join. (12 dc, 4 x 2ch-sp corners)

Fasten off colour 4, join colour 1.

Round 2: 1 ch (does not count as st throughout), *1 sc in first corner ch, 2 ch, 1 sc in 2nd corner ch, 3 scBLO; rep from * 3 more times, slst in beg sc to join. (20 dc, 4 x 2ch-sp corners)

Round 3: Join colour 3, 1 ch, *1 sc in first corner ch, 2 ch, 1 sc in 2nd corner ch, 5 scBLO; rep from * 3 more times, slst in beg sc to join. (28 dc, 4 x 2ch-sp corners)

Round 4: Pull up colour 1 loop, 1 ch, *1 sc in first corner ch, 2 ch, 1 sc in 2nd corner ch, 1 scBLO, 1 FLMdc, 3 scBLO, 1 FLMdc, 1 scBLO; rep from * 3 more times, slst in beg sc to join. (28 sc, 8 dc, 4 x 2ch-sp corners)

Round 5: Pull up colour 3 loop, 1 ch, *1 sc in first corner ch, 2 ch, 1 sc in 2nd corner ch, 3 scBLO, 3 FLMdc, 3 scBLO; rep from * 3 more times, slst in beg sc to join. (32 sc, 12 dc, 4 x 2ch-sp corners)

Round 6: Pull up colour 1 loop, 1 ch, *1 sc in first corner ch, 2 ch, 1 sc in 2nd corner ch, 1 scBLO, 1 FLMdc, 7 scBLO, 1 FLMdc, 1 scBLO; rep from * 3 more times, slst in beg sc to join. (44 sc, 8 dc, 4 x 2ch-sp corners)

Round 7: Pull up colour 3 loop, 1 ch, *1 sc in first corner ch, 2 ch, 1 sc in 2nd corner ch, 1 scBLO, 1 FLMdc, 1 scBLO, 7 FLMdc, 1 scBLO, 1 FLMdc, 1 scBLO; rep from * 3 more times, slst in beg sc to join. (24 sc, 36 dc, 4 x 2ch-sp corners)

Round 8: Pull up colour 1 loop, 1 ch, *1 sc in first corner ch, 2 ch, 1 sc in 2nd corner ch, 3 scBLO, 1 FLMdc, 7 scBLO, 1 FLMdc, 3 scBLO; rep from * 3 more times, slst in beg sc to join. (60 sc, 8 dc, 4 x 2ch-sp corners)

Round 9: Pull up colour 3 loop, 1 ch, *1 sc in first corner ch, 2 ch, 1 sc in 2nd corner ch, 1 scBLO, 1 FLMdc, 5 scBLO, 3 FLMdc, 5 scBLO, 1 FLMdc, 1 scBLO; rep from * 3 more times, slst in beg sc to join. (56 sc, 20 dc, 4 x 2ch-sp corners)

Fasten off colour 3.

Round 10: Pull up colour 1 loop, 1 ch, *1 sc in first corner ch, 2 ch, 1 sc in 2nd corner ch, [3 scBLO, 1 FLMdc] 4 times, 3 scBLO; rep from * 3 more times, slst in beg sc to join. (68 sc, 16 dc, 4 x 2ch-sp corners)

Round 11: Join colour 2, 1 ch, *1 sc in first corner ch, 2 ch, 1 sc in 2nd corner ch, 21 scBLO; rep from * 3 more times, slst in beg sc to join. (92 sc, 4 x 2ch-sp corners)

Round 12: Pull up colour 1 loop, 1 ch, *1 sc in first corner ch, 2 ch, 1 sc in 2nd corner ch, 1 scBLO, [1 FLMdc, 3 scBLO] 5 times, 1 FLMdc, 1 scBLO; rep from * 3 more times, slst in beg sc to join. (76 sc, 24 dc, 4 x 2ch-sp corners)

Round 13: Pull up colour 2 loop, 1 ch, *1 sc in first corner ch, 2 ch, 1 sc in 2nd corner ch, 3 scBLO, 3 FLMdc, 5 scBLO, 1 FLMdc, 1 scBLO, 1 FLMdc, 5 scBLO, 3 FLMdc, 3 scBLO; rep from * 3 more times, slst in beg sc to join. (76 sc, 32 dc, 4 x 2ch-sp corners)

Round 14: Pull up colour 1 loop, 1 ch, *1 sc in first corner ch, 2 ch, 1 sc in 2nd corner ch, 1 scBLO, [1 FLMdc, 7 scBLO] 3 times, 1 FLMdc, 1 scBLO; rep from * 3 more times, slst in beg sc to join. (100 sc, 16 dc, 4 x 2ch-sp corners)

Round 15: Pull up colour 2 loop, 1 ch, *1 sc in first corner ch, 2 ch, 1 sc in 2nd corner ch, 1 scBLO, 1 FLMdc, 1 scBLO, 7 FLMdc, [1 scBLO, 1 FLMdc] 4 times, 1 scBLO, 7 FLMdc, 1 scBLO, 1 FLMdc, 1 scBLO; rep from * 3 more times, slst in beg sc to join. (44 sc, 80 dc, 4 x 2ch-sp corners)

Round 16: Pull up colour 1 loop, 1 ch, *1 sc in first corner ch, 2 ch, 1 sc in 2nd corner ch, 3 scBLO, [1 FLMdc, 7 scBLO] 3 times, 1 FLMdc, 3 scBLO; rep from * 3 more times, slst in beg sc to join. (116 sc, 16 dc, 4 x 2ch-sp corners)

Round 17: Pull up colour 2 loop, 1 ch, *1 sc in first corner ch, 2 ch, 1 sc in 2nd corner ch, 1 scBLO, 1 FLMdc, 5 scBLO, 3 FLMdc, 5 scBLO, 1 FLMdc, 1 scBLO, 1 FLMdc, 5 scBLO, 3 FLMdc, 5 scBLO, 1 FLMdc, 1 scBLO; rep from * 3 more times, slst in beg sc to join. (100 sc, 40 dc, 4 x 2ch-sp corners)

Fasten off colour 2.

Round 18: Pull up colour 1 loop, 1 ch, *1 sc in first corner ch, 2 ch, 1 sc in 2nd corner ch, [3 scBLO, 1 FLMdc] 8 times, 3 scBLO; rep from * 3 more times, slst in beg sc to join. (116 sc, 32 dc, 4 x 2ch-sp corners)

Fasten off colour 1.

Round 19: Join colour 2 with a stsc in first ch in any corner, *2 ch, 1 sc in 2nd corner ch, scBLO across to next corner, 1 sc in first corner ch; rep from * 3 more times omitting last sc on final rep. (156 sc, 4 x 2ch-sp corners)

Fasten off colour 2, sew to stsc with invisible join.

Round 20: Join colour 4 with a sthdc in any corner 2ch-sp, *2 ch, 1 hdc in same sp, BPhdc across to next corner, 1 hdc in 2ch-sp; rep from * 3 more times omitting last hdc on final rep. (164 hdc, 4 x 2ch-sp corners)

Fasten off colour 4, sew to sthdc with invisible join, weave in all ends.

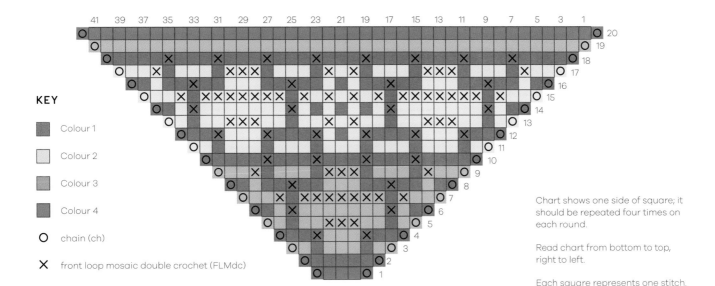

KEY

- ■ Colour 1
- □ Colour 2
- ■ Colour 3
- ■ Colour 4
- O chain (ch)
- X front loop mosaic double crochet (FLMdc)

Chart shows one side of square; it should be repeated four times on each round.

Read chart from bottom to top, right to left.

Each square represents one stitch.

HAND-PAINTED

DESIGNER: ANA MORAIS SOARES

YARN

Rosários4 Meia, sport (4ply), in foll shade:
Colour 1: Dark Blue (12)
Rosários4 Meia Print, sport (4ply), in foll shade:
Colour 2: Purples and Yellow (119)

HOOK

US size C/2 or D/3 (3mm) hook

GAUGE (TENSION)

A single motif measures approx 7in (18cm) using a US size C/2 or D/3 (3mm) hook.

SPECIAL ABBREVIATION

FLMdc, double crochet worked in front loop two rounds below

NOTES

Motif is worked in overlay mosaic crochet in Rounds 3 to 21, with RS facing using colour 1 and contrast colour 2. Do NOT fasten off at end of each round (after making 3-ch string). First st after 3-ch string and first st of next 2ch-sp corner are worked over same 3-ch string.

PATTERN

Using US size C/2 or D/3 hook and colour 1, make a magic ring.

Round 1: 1 ch (does not count as st), [1 sc, 2 ch] 4 times, slst in first sc to join, do not cut yarn. (4 sc, 4 x 2ch-sp corners)

Round 2: 1 ch, (does not count as st), *(1 sc, 2 ch, 1 sc) in next 2ch-sp corner, 1 sc in next st; rep from * 3 more times, slst in first sc to join, 3 ch, remove hook. (12 sc, 4 x 2ch-sp corners, 1 x 3-ch string)

Round 3: Join colour 2, (1 sc, 2 ch, 1 sc) in 2ch-sp corner opposite 3-ch string, *3 scBLO, (1 sc, 2 ch, 1 sc) in next 2ch-sp corner*, 2 scBLO, working over 3-ch string from prev round, 1 scBLO in next st, 1 sc in next 2ch-sp corner (string is in position for next round), 2 ch, (not working over string) 1 sc in same 2ch-sp corner; rep from * to * once, 3 scBLO, slst in first sc to join, 3 ch, remove hook. (20 sc, 4 x 2ch-sp corners, 1 x 3-ch string)

Round 4: Insert hook in colour 1 loop (from Round 2), *(1 sc, 2 ch, 1 sc) in 2ch-sp corner, 5 scBLO; rep from * 3 more times, (work over 3-ch string with last sc before 3rd corner and first sc in same corner), slst in first sc to join, 3 ch, remove hook. (28 sc, 4 x 2ch-sp corners, 1 x 3-ch string)

Round 5: Insert hook in colour 2 loop (from Round 3), *(1 sc, 2 ch, 1 sc) in 2ch-sp corner, 7 scBLO; rep from * 3 more times, (work over 3-ch string with last sc before 3rd corner and first sc in same corner), slst in first sc to join, 3 ch, remove hook. (36 sc, 4 x 2ch-sp corners, 1 x 3-ch string)

Round 6: Insert hook in colour 1 loop (from Round 4), *(1 sc, 2 ch, 1 sc) in 2ch-sp corner, 4 scBLO, 1 FLMdc, 4 scBLO; rep from * 3 more times, (work over 3-ch string with last sc before 3rd corner and first sc in same corner), slst in first sc to join, 3 ch, remove hook. (40 sc, 4 dc, 4 x 2ch-sp corners, 1 x 3-ch string)

Round 7: Insert hook in colour 2 loop (from Round 5), *(1 sc, 2 ch, 1 sc) in 2ch-sp corner, 2 scBLO, FLMdc, 5 scBLO, 1 FLMdc, 2 scBLO; rep from * 3 more times, (work over 3-ch string with last sc before 3rd corner and first sc in same corner), slst in first sc to join, 3 ch, remove hook. (44 sc, 8 dc, 4 x 2ch-sp corners, 1 x 3-ch string)

Round 8: Insert hook in colour 1 loop (from Round 6), *(1 sc, 2 ch, 1 sc) in 2ch-sp corner, 2 scBLO, 1 FLMdc, 1 scBLO, 1 FLMdc, 3 scBLO, 1 FLMdc, 1 scBLO, 1 FLMdc, 2 scBLO; rep from * 3 more times, (work over 3-ch string with last sc before 3rd corner and first sc in same corner), slst in first sc to join, 3 ch, remove hook. (44 sc, 16 dc, 4 x 2ch-sp corners, 1 x 3-ch string)

Round 9: Insert hook in colour 2 loop (from Round 7), *(1 sc, 2 ch, 1 sc) in 2ch-sp corner, 2 scBLO, 1 FLMdc, 3 scBLO, 1 FLMdc, 1 scBLO, 1 FLMdc, 3 scBLO, 1 FLMdc, 2 scBLO; rep from * 3 more times, (work over 3-ch string with last sc before 3rd corner and first sc in same corner), slst in first sc to join, 3 ch, remove hook. (52 sc, 16 dc, 4 x 2ch-sp corners, 1 x 3-ch string)

Round 10: Insert hook in colour 1 loop (from Round 8), *(1 sc, 2 ch,1 sc) in 2ch-sp corner, 2 scBLO, [1 FLMdc, 1 scBLO] twice, 1 FLMdc, 3 scBLO, [1 FLMdc, 1 scBLO] 3 times, 1 scBLO; rep from * 3 more times, (work over 3-ch string with last sc before 3rd corner and first sc in same corner), slst in first sc to join, 3 ch, remove hook. (52 sc, 24 dc, 4 x 2ch-sp corners, 1 x 3-ch string)

Round 11: Insert hook in colour 2 loop (from Round 9), *(1 sc, 2 ch, 1 sc) in 2ch-sp corner, 2 scBLO, [1 FLMdc, 1 scBLO] twice, 1 FLMdc, 5 scBLO, [1 FLMdc, 1 scBLO] 3 times, 1 scBLO; rep from * 3 more times, (work over 3-ch string with last sc before 3rd corner and first sc in same corner), slst in first sc to join, 3 ch, remove hook. (60 sc, 24 dc, 4 x 2ch-sp corners, 1 x 3-ch string)

Round 12: Insert hook in colour 1 loop (from Round 10), *(1 sc, 2 ch, 1 sc) in 2ch-sp corner, 2 scBLO, [1 FLMdc, 1 scBLO] twice, 1 FLMdc, 7 scBLO, [1 FLMdc, 1 scBLO] 3 times, 1 scBLO; rep from * 3 more times, (work over 3-ch string with last sc before 3rd corner and first sc in same corner), slst in first sc to join, 3 ch, remove hook. (68 sc, 24 dc, 4 x 2ch-sp corners, 1 x 3-ch string)

Round 13: Insert hook in colour 2 loop (from Round 11), *(1 sc, 2 ch, 1 sc) in 2ch-sp corner, 2 scBLO, [1 FLMdc, 1 scBLO] twice, 1 FLMdc, 9 scBLO, [1 FLMdc, 1 scBLO] 3 times, 1 scBLO; rep from * 3 more times, (work over 3-ch string with last sc before 3rd corner and first sc in same corner), slst in first sc to join, 3 ch, remove hook. (76 sc, 24 dc, 4 x 2ch-sp corners, 1 x 3-ch string)

Round 14: Insert hook in colour 1 loop (from Round 12), *(1 sc, 2 ch, 1 sc) in 2ch-sp corner, 25 scBLO; rep from * 3 more times, (work over 3-ch string with last sc before 3rd corner and first sc in same corner), slst in first sc to join, 3 ch, remove hook. (108 sc, 4 x 2ch-sp corners, 1 x 3-ch string)

Round 15: Insert hook in colour 2 loop (from Round 13), *(1 sc, 2 ch, 1 sc) in 2ch-sp corner, 27 scBLO; rep from * 3 more times, (work over 3-ch string with last sc before 3rd corner and first sc in ame corner), slst in first sc to join, 3 ch, remove hook. (116 sts, 4 x 2ch-sp corners, 1 x 3-ch string)

Round 16: Insert hook in colour 1 loop (from Round 14), *(1 sc, 2 ch, 1 sc) in 2ch-sp corner, 6 scBLO, [1 FLMdc, 7 scBLO] twice, 1 FLMdc, 6 scBLO; rep from * 3 more times, (work over 3-ch string with last sc before 3rd corner and first sc in same corner), slst in first sc to join, 3 ch, remove hook. (112 sc, 12 dc, 4 x 2ch-sp corners, 1 x 3-ch string)

Round 17: Insert hook in colour 2 loop (from Round 15), *(1 sc, 2 ch, 1 sc) in 2ch-sp corner, 4 scBLO, [1 FLMdc, 5 scBLO, 1 FLMdc, 1 scBLO] twice, 1 FLMdc, 5 scBLO, 1 FLMdc, 4 scBLO; rep from * 3 more times, (work over 3-ch string with last sc before 3rd corner and first sc in same corner), slst in first sc to join, 3 ch, remove hook. (108 sc, 24 dc, 4 x 2ch-sp corners, 1 x 3-ch string)

continued on next page >

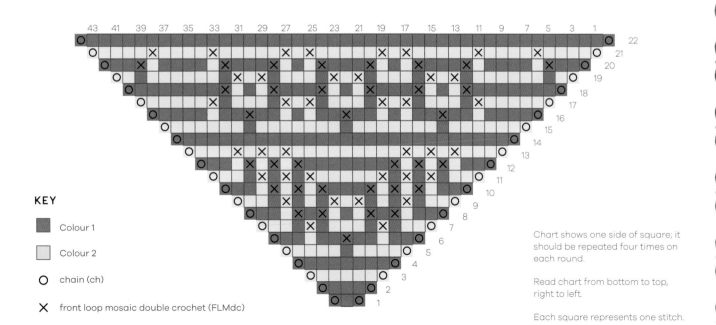

KEY

■ Colour 1

□ Colour 2

O chain (ch)

X front loop mosaic double crochet (FLMdc)

Chart shows one side of square; it should be repeated four times on each round.

Read chart from bottom to top, right to left.

Each square represents one stitch.

Round 18: Insert hook in colour 1 loop (from Round 16), *(1 sc, 2 ch, 1 sc) in 2ch-sp corner, 6 scBLO, [1 FLMdc, 3 scBLO] 5 times, 1 FLMdc, 6 scBLO; rep from * 3 more times, (work over 3-ch string with last sc before 3rd corner and first sc in same corner), slst in first sc to join, 3 ch, remove hook. (116 sc, 24 dc, 4 x 2ch-sp corners, 1 x 3-ch string)

Round 19: Insert hook in colour 2 loop (from Round 17), *(1 sc, 2 ch, 1 sc) in 2ch-sp corner, 8 scBLO, [1 FLMdc, 1 scBLO, 1 FLMdc, 5 scBLO] twice, 1 FLMdc, 1 scBLO, 1 FLMdc, 8 scBLO; rep from * 3 more times, (work over 3-ch string with last sc before 3rd corner and first sc in same corner), slst in first sc to join, 3 ch, remove hook. (124 sc, 24 dc, 4 x 2ch-sp corners, 1 x 3-ch string)

Round 20: Insert hook in colour 1 loop (from Round 18), *(1 sc, 2 ch, 1 sc) in 2ch-sp corner, 1 scBLO, 1 FLMdc, 6 scBLO, [1 FLMdc, 3 scBLO] 5 times, 1 FLMdc, 6 scBLO, 1 FLMdc, 1 scBLO; rep from * 3 more times, (work over 3-ch string with last sc before 3rd corner and first sc in same corner), slst in first sc to join, 3 ch, remove hook. (124 sc, 32 dc, 4 x 2ch-sp corners, 1 x 3-ch string)

Round 21: Insert hook in colour 2 loop (from Round 19), *(1 sc, 2 ch, 1 sc) in 2ch-sp corner, 3 scBLO, 1 FLMdc, 4 scBLO, [1 FLMdc, 5 scBLO, 1 FLMdc, 1 scBLO] 3 times, 3 scBLO, 1 FLMdc, 3 scBLO; rep from * 3 more times, (work over 3-ch string with last sc before 3rd corner and first sc in same corner), slst in first sc to join. (132 sc, 32 dc, 4 x 2ch-sp corners)

Fasten off.

EDGING

Insert hook in colour 1 loop (from Round 20), *(1 sc, 2 ch, 1 sc) in 2ch-sp corner, 41 scBLO; rep from * 3 more times, slst in beg st to join. (172 sc. 4 x 2ch-sp corners)

Fasten off and weave in ends.

SNOWFLAKE SWEETS

DESIGNER: ANA MORAIS SOARES

YARN

Rosários4 Regata, light worsted (DK), in foll shades:
Colour 1: Pink (43)
Colour 2: Aqua (113)

HOOK

US size E/4 (3.5mm) hook

GAUGE (TENSION)

A single motif measures approx 7½in (19cm) using a US size E/4 (3.5mm) hook.

SPECIAL ABBREVIATION

FLMdc, double crochet worked in front loop two rounds below

NOTES

Motif is worked in overlay mosaic crochet in Rounds 2 to 21, with RS facing using colour 1 and contrast colour 2.
Do NOT fasten off at end of each round (after making 3-ch string). First st after 3-ch string and first st of next 2ch-sp corner are worked over same 3-ch string.

PATTERN

Using E/4 hook and colour 1, make a magic ring.

Round 1 (RS): 1 ch (does not count as st), [1 sc, 2 ch] 4 times in ring, slst in first sc to join, 3 ch, remove hook. (4 sts, 1 x 3-ch string)

Round 2: Join colour 2, (1 sc, 2 ch, 1 sc) in 2ch-sp corner opposite 3-ch string, *1 scBLO, (1 sc, 2 ch, 1 sc) in next 2ch-sp corner*, working over 3-ch string from prev round, 1

scBLO in next st, 1 sc in next 2ch-sp corner (string is in position for next round), 2 ch, (not working over string), 1 sc in same 2ch-sp corner; rep from * to * once more, 1 scBLO, slst in first sc to join, 3 ch, remove hook. (12 sc, 4 x 2ch-sp corners, 1 x 3-ch string)

Round 3: Insert hook in colour 1 loop (from Round 1), [(1 sc, 2 ch, 1 sc) in 2ch-sp corner, 1 scBLO, 1 FLMdc, 1 scBLO] 4 times (work over 3-ch string with last scBLO before 3rd corner and first sc in same corner), slst in first sc to join, 3 ch, remove hook. (16 sc, 4 dc, 4 x 2ch-sp corners, 1 x 3-ch string)

Round 4: Insert hook in colour 2 loop (from Round 2), [(1 sc, 2 ch, 1 sc) in 2ch-sp corner, 5 scBLO] 4 times (work over 3-ch string with last scBLO before 3rd corner and first sc in same corner), slst in first sc to join, 3 ch, remove hook. (28 sc, 4 x 2ch-sp corners, 1 x 3-ch string)

Round 5: Insert hook in colour 1 loop (from Round 3), *(1 sc, 2 ch, 1 sc) in 2ch-sp corner, [1 scBLO, 1 FLMdc, skip st behind] 3 times, 1 scBLO; rep from * 3 more times (work over 3-ch string with last scBLO before 3rd corner and first sc in same corner), slst in first sc to join, 3 ch, remove

hook. (24 sc, 12 dc, 4 x 2ch-sp corners, 1 x 3-ch string)

Round 6: Insert hook in colour 2 loop (from Round 4), *(1 sc, 2 ch, 1 sc) in 2ch-sp corner, 3 scBLO, 1 FLMdc, 1 scBLO, 1 FLMdc, 3 scBLO; rep from * 3 more times (work over 3-ch string with last scBLO before 3rd corner and first sc in same corner), slst in first sc to join, 3 ch, remove hook. (36 sc, 8 dc, 4 x 2ch-sp corners, 1 x 3-ch string)

Round 7: Insert hook in colour 1 loop (from Round 5), *(1 sc, 2 ch, 1 sc) in 2ch-sp corner, 1 scBLO, [1 FLMdc, 3 scBLO] twice, 1 FLMdc, 1 scBLO; rep from * 3 more times (work over 3-ch string with last scBLO before 3rd corner and first sc in same corner), slst in first sc to join, 3 ch, remove hook. (40 sc, 12 dc, 4 x 2ch-sp corners, 1 x 3-ch string)

Round 8: Insert hook in colour 2 loop (from Round 6), *(1 sc, 2 ch, 1 sc) in 2ch-sp corner, 3 scBLO, 3 FLMdc, 1 scBLO, 3 FLMdc, 3 scBLO; rep from * 3 more times (work over 3-ch string with last scBLO before 3rd corner and first sc in same corner), slst in first sc to join, 3 ch, remove hook. (36 sc, 24 dc, 4 x 2ch-sp corners, 1 x 3-ch string)

Round 9: Insert hook in colour 1 loop (from Round 7), *(1 sc, 2 ch, 1 sc) in 2ch-sp corner, 1 scBLO, [1 FLMdc, 5 scBLO] twice, 1 FLMdc, 1 scBLO; rep from * 3 more times (work over 3-ch string with last scBLO before 3rd corner and first sc in same corner), slst in first sc to join, 3 ch, remove hook. (56 sc, 12 dc, 4 x 2ch-sp corners, 1 x 3-ch string)

Round 10: Insert hook in colour 2 loop (from Round 8), *(1 sc, 2 ch, 1 sc) in 2ch-sp corner, 3 scBLO, [4 FLMdc, 3 scBLO] twice; rep from * 3 more times (work over 3-ch string with last scBLO before 3rd corner and first sc in same corner), slst in first sc to join, 3 ch, remove hook. (44 sc, 32 dc, 4 x 2ch-sp corners, 1 x 3-ch string)

Round 11: Insert hook in colour 1 loop (from Round 9), *(1 sc, 2 ch, 1 sc) in 2ch-sp corner, 1 scBLO, [1 FLMdc, 7 scBLO] twice, 1 FLMdc, 1 scBLO; rep from * 3 more times (work over 3-ch string with last scBLO before 3rd corner and first sc in same corner), slst in first sc to join, 3 ch, remove hook. (72 sc, 12 dc, 4 x 2ch-sp corners, 1 x 3-ch string)

continued on next page >

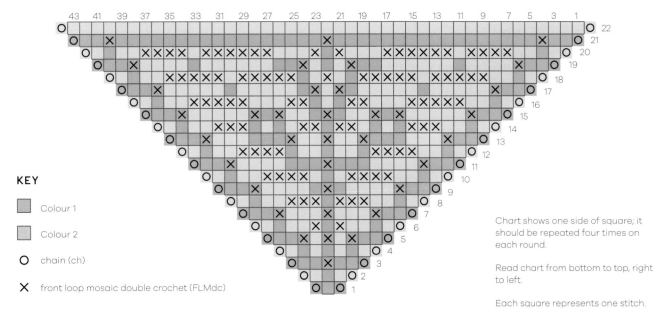

KEY

■ Colour 1

■ Colour 2

O   chain (ch)

X   front loop mosaic double crochet (FLMdc)

Chart shows one side of square; it should be repeated four times on each round.

Read chart from bottom to top, right to left.

Each square represents one stitch.

Round 12: Insert hook in colour 1 loop (from Round 10), *(1 sc, 2 ch, 1 sc) in 2ch-sp corner, 3 scBLO, 4 FLMdc, 7 scBLO, 4 FLMdc, 3 scBLO; rep from * 3 more times (work over 3-ch string with last scBLO before 3rd corner and first sc in same corner), slst in first sc to join, 3 ch, remove hook. (60 sc, 32 dc, 4 x 2ch-sp corners, 1 x 3-ch string)

Round 13: Insert hook in colour 1 loop (from Round 11), *(1 sc, 2 ch, 1 sc) in 2ch-sp corner, 1 scBLO, 1 FLMdc, 6 scBLO, [1 FLMdc, 2 scBLO] twice, 1 FLMdc, 6 scBLO, 1 FLMdc, 1 scBLO; rep from * 3 more times (work over 3-ch string with last sc before 3rd corner and first sc in same corner), slst in first sc to join, 3 ch, remove hook. (80 sc, 20 dc, 4 x 2ch-sp corners, 1 x 3-ch string)

Round 14: Insert hook in colour 2 loop (from Round 12), *(1 sc, 2 ch, 1 sc) in 2ch-sp corner, 3 scBLO, 3 FLMdc, 4 scBLO, 2 FLMdc, 1 scBLO, 2 FLMdc, 4 scBLO, 3 FLMdc, 3 scBLO; rep from * 3 more times (work over 3-ch string with last scBLO before 3rd corner and first sc in same corner), slst in first sc to join, 3 ch, remove hook. (68 sc, 40 dc, 4 x 2ch-sp corners, 1 x 3-ch string)

Round 15: Insert hook in colour 1 loop (from Round 13), *(1 sc, 2 ch, 1 sc) in 2ch-sp corner, 1 scBLO, 1 FLMdc, 5 scBLO, 1 FLMdc, 1 scBLO, [1 FLMdc, 3 scBLO] twice, 1 FLMdc, 1 scBLO, 1 FLMdc, 5 scBLO, 1 FLMdc, 1 scBLO; rep from * 3 more times (work over 3-ch string with last scBLO before 3rd corner and first sc in same corner), slst in first sc to join, 3 ch, remove hook. (88 sc, 28 dc, 4 x 2ch-sp corners, 1 x 3-ch string)

Round 16: Insert hook in colour 2 loop (from Round 14), *(1 sc, 2 ch, 1 sc) in 2ch-sp corner, 3 scBLO, 5 FLMdc, [3 scBLO, 2 FLMdc] twice, 3 scBLO, 5 FLMdc, 3 scBLO; rep from * 3 more times (work over 3-ch string with last scBLO before 3rd

corner and first sc in same corner), slst in first sc to join, 3 ch, remove hook. (68 sc, 56 dc, 4 x 2ch-sp corners, 1 x 3-ch string)

Round 17: Insert hook in colour 1 loop (from Round 15), *(1 sc, 2 ch, 1 sc) in 2ch-sp corner, 1 scBLO, 1 FLMdc, 12 scBLO, 1 FLMdc, 1 scBLO, 1 FLMdc, 12 scBLO, 1 FLMdc, 1 scBLO; rep from * 3 more times (work over 3-ch string with last scBLO before 3rd corner and first sc in same corner), slst in first sc to join, 3 ch, remove hook. (116 sc, 16 dc, 4 x 2ch-sp corners, 1 x 3-ch string)

Round 18: Insert hook in colour 2 loop (from Round 16), *(1 sc, 2 ch, 1 sc) in 2ch-sp corner, 3 scBLO, 5 FLMdc, 1 scBLO, 5 FLMdc, 2 scBLO, 1 FLMdc, 2 scBLO, 5 FLMdc, 1 scBLO, 5 FLMdc, 3 scBLO; rep from * 3 more times (work over 3-ch string with last scBLO before 3rd corner and first sc in same corner), slst in first sc to join, 3 ch, remove hook. (56 sc, 84 dc, 4 x 2ch-sp corners, 1 x 3-ch string)

Round 19: Insert hook in colour 1 loop (from Round 17), *(1 sc, 2 ch, 1 sc) in 2ch-sp corner, 1 scBLO, 1 FLMdc, 13 scBLO, 1 FLMdc, 3 scBLO, 1 FLMdc, 13 scBLO, 1 FLMdc, 1 scBLO; rep from * 3 more times (work over 3-ch string with last scBLO before 3rd corner and first sc in same corner), slst in first sc to join, 3 ch, remove hook. (132 sc, 16 dc, 4 x 2ch-sp corners, 1 x 3-ch string)

Round 20: Insert hook in colour 2 loop (from Round 18), *(1 sc, 2 ch, 1 sc) in 2ch-sp corner, 3 scBLO, 4 FLMdc, 1 scBLO, 6 FLMdc, 3 scBLO, 1 FLMdc, 1 scBLO, 1 FLMdc, 3 scBLO, 6 FLMdc, 1 scBLO, 4 FLMdc, 3 scBLO; rep from * 3 more times (work over 3-ch string with last scBLO before 3rd corner and first sc in same corner), slst in first sc to join, 3 ch, remove hook. (68 sc, 88 dc, 4 x 2ch-sp corners, 1 x 3-ch string)

Round 21: Insert hook in colour 1 loop (from Round 19), *(1 sc, 2 ch, 1 sc) in 2ch-sp corner, 1 scBLO, 1 FLMdc, 17 scBLO, 1 FLMdc, 17 scBLO, 1 FLMdc, 1 scBLO; rep from * 3 more times (work over 3-ch string with last scBLO before 3rd corner and first sc in same corner), slst in first sc to join. (152 sc, 12 dc)

Fasten off.

Edging: Insert hook in colour 2 loop (from Round 18), *(1 sc, 2 ch, 1 sc) in 2ch-sp corner, 41 scBLO; rep from * 3 more times, slst in beg st to join. (172 sc)

Fasten off and weave in ends.

PLAYING WITH CUBES

DESIGNER: ANA MORAIS SOARES

YARN

Rosários4 Regata, light worsted (DK), in foll shades:
Colour 1: Copper (47)
Colour 2: Blush (23)

HOOK

US size E/4 (3.5mm) hook

GAUGE (TENSION)

A single motif measures approx 7in (18cm) using a US size E/4 (3.5mm) hook.

SPECIAL ABBREVIATION

FLMdc, double crochet worked in front loop two rounds below

NOTES

Motif is worked in overlay mosaic crochet in Rounds 2 to 20, with RS facing using colour 1 and contrast colour 2. Do NOT fasten off at end of each round (after making 3-ch string). First st after 3-ch string and first st of next 2ch-sp corner are worked over same 3-ch string.

PATTERN

Using E/4 hook and colour 1, make a magic ring.

Round 1: 1 ch (does not count as st), [1 sc, 2 ch] 4 times in ring, slst in first sc to join, 3 ch, remove hook. (4 sc, 4 x 2ch-sp corners, 1 x 3-ch string)

Round 2: Join colour 2, [1 sc, 2 ch, 1 sc] in 2ch-sp corner opposite 3-ch string, *1 scBLO, (1 sc, 2 ch, 1 sc) in next 2ch-sp corner*, working over 3-ch string from prev round, 1 scBLO in next st, 1 sc in next 2ch-sp corner (string is in position for next round), 2 ch, (not working over string), 1 sc in same 2ch-sp corner; rep from * to * once more, 1 scBLO, slst in first sc to join, 3 ch, remove hook. (12 sc, 4 x 2ch-sp corners, 1 x 3-ch string)

Round 3: Insert hook in colour 1 loop (from Round 1), [(1 sc, 2 ch, 1 sc) in 2ch-sp corner, 1 scBLO, 1 FLMdc, 1 scBLO] 4 times (work over 3-ch string with last scBLO before 3rd corner and first sc in same corner), slst in first sc t to join, 3 ch, remove hook. (16 sc, 4 dc, 4 x 2ch-sp corners, 1 x 3-ch string)

Round 4: Insert hook in colour 2 loop (from Round 2), *(1 sc, 2 ch, 1 sc) in 2ch-sp corner, [1 scBLO, 1 FLMdc, skip st behind] twice, 1 scBLO; rep from * 3 more times (work over 3-ch string with last scBLO before 3rd corner and first sc in same corner), slst in first sc to join, 3 ch, remove hook. (20 sc, 8 dc, 4 x 2ch-sp corners, 1 x 3-ch string)

Round 5: Insert hook in colour 1 loop (from Round 3), *(1 sc, 2 ch, 1 sc) in 2ch-sp corner, 7 scBLO; rep from * 3 more times (work over 3-ch string with last scBLO before 3rd corner and first sc in same corner), slst in first sc to join, 3 ch, remove hook. (36 sc, 4 x 2ch-sp corners, 1 x 3-ch string)

Round 6: Insert hook in colour 2 loop (from Round 4), *(1 sc, 2 ch, 1 sc) in 2ch-sp corner, 9 scBLO; rep from * 3 more times, (work over 3-ch string with last scBLO before 3rd corner and first sc in same corner), slst in first sc to join, 3 ch, remove hook. (44 sc, 4 x 2ch-sp corners, 1 x 3-ch string)

Round 7: Insert hook in colour 1 loop (from Round 5), *(1 sc, 2 ch, 1 sc) in 2ch-sp corner, 4 scBLO, 1 FLMdc, 1 scBLO, 1 FLMdc, 4 scBLO; rep from * 3 more times (work over 3-ch string with last scBLO before 3rd corner and first sc in same corner), slst in first sc to join, 3 ch, remove hook. (44 sc, 8 dc, 4 x 2ch-sp corners, 1 x 3-ch string)

continued on next page >

Round 8: Insert hook in colour 2 loop (from Round 6), *(1 sc, 2 ch, 1 sc) in 2ch-sp corner, 3 scBLO, 1 FLMdc, 5 scBLO, 1 FLMdc, 3 scBLO; rep from * 3 more times (work over 3-ch string with last scBLO before 3rd corner and first sc in same corner), slst in first sc to join, 3 ch, remove hook. (52 sc, 8 dc, 4 x 2ch-sp corners, 1 x 3-ch string)

Round 9: Insert hook in colour 1 loop (from Round 7), *(1 sc, 2 ch, 1 sc) in 2ch-sp corner, 1 scBLO, 1 FLMdc, 1 scBLO, [1 FLMdc, 3 scBLO] twice, [1 FLMdc, 1 scBLO] twice; rep from * 3 more times (work over 3-ch string with last scBLO before 3rd corner and first sc in same corner), slst in first sc to join, 3 ch, remove hook. (48 sc, 20 dc, 4 x 2ch-sp corners, 1 x 3-ch string)

Round 10: Insert hook in colour 2 loop (from Round 8), *(1 sc, 2 ch, 1 sc) in 2ch-sp corner, 5 scBLO, [1 FLMdc, 5 scBLO] twice; rep from * 3 more times (work over 3-ch string with last scBLO before 3rd corner and first sc in same corner), slst in first sc to join, 3 ch, remove hook. (68 sc, 8 dc, 4 x 2ch-sp corners, 1 x 3-ch string)

Round 11: Insert hook in colour 1 loop (from Round 9), *(1 sc, 2 ch, 1 sc) in 2ch-sp corner, 1 scBLO, 1 FLMdc, 6 scBLO, 1 FLMdc, 1 scBLO, 1 FLMdc, 6 scBLO, 1 FLMdc, 1 scBLO; rep from

* 3 more times (work over 3-ch string with last scBLO before 3rd corner and first sc in same corner), slst in first sc to join, 3 ch, remove hook. (68 sc, 16 dc, 4 x 2ch-sp corners, 1 x 3-ch string)

Round 12: Insert hook in colour 2 loop (from Round 10), *(1 sc, 2 ch, 1 sc) in 2ch-sp corner, 21 scBLO; rep from * 3 more times (work over 3-ch string with last scBLO before 3rd corner and first sc in same corner), slst in first sc to join, 3 ch, remove hook. (92 sc, 4 x 2ch-sp corners, 1 x 3-ch string)

Round 13: Insert hook in colour 1 loop (from Round 11), *(1 sc, 2 ch, 1 sc) in 2ch-sp corner, 23 scBLO; rep from * 3 more times (work over 3-ch string with last scBLO before 3rd corner and first sc in same corner), slst in first st to join, 3 ch, remove hook. (100 sc, 4 x 2ch-sp corners, 1 x 3-ch string)

Round 14: Insert hook in colour 2 loop (from Round 12), *(1 sc, 2 ch, 1 sc) in 2ch-sp corner, [5 scBLO, 1 FLMdc, skip st behind] twice, 1 scBLO, [1 FLMdc, 5 scBLO] twice; rep from * 3 more times (work over 3-ch string with last scBLO before 3rd corner and first sc in same corner), slst in first sc to join, 3 ch, remove hook. (92 sc, 16 dc, 4 x 2ch-sp corners, 1 x 3-ch string)

Round 15: Insert hook in colour 1 loop (from Round 13), *(1 sc, 2 ch, 1 sc) in 2ch-sp corner, 3 scBLO, 1 FLMdc, 1 scBLO, 1 FLMdc, [7 scBLO, 1 FLMdc, skip st behind] twice, 1 scBLO, 1 FLMdc, 3 scBLO; rep from * 3 more times (work over 3-ch string with last scBLO before 3rd corner and first sc in same corner), slst in first sc to join, 3 ch, remove hook. (96 sc, 20 dc, 4 x 2ch-sp corners, 1 x 3-ch string)

Round 16: Insert hook in colour 2 loop (from Round 14), *(1 sc, 2 ch, 1 sc) in 2ch-sp corner, 7 scBLO, 1 FLMdc, 3 scBLO, 1 FLMdc, 5 scBLO, 1 FLMdc, 3 scBLO, 1 FLMdc, 7 scBLO; rep from * 3 more times (work over 3-ch string with last scBLO before 3rd corner and first sc in same corner), slst in first sc to join, 3 ch, remove hook. (108 sc, 16 dc, 4 x 2ch-sp corners, 1 x 3-ch string)

Round 17: Insert hook in colour 1 loop (from Round 15), *(1 sc, 2 ch, 1 sc) in 2ch-sp corner, 2 scBLO, [1 FLMdc, 1 scBLO] twice, 7 scBLO, [1 FLMdc, 1 scBLO] 3 times, 7 scBLO, [1 FLMdc, 1 scBLO] twice, 1 scBLO; rep from * 3 more times (work over 3-ch string with last scBLO before 3rd corner and first sc in same corner), slst in first sc to join, 3 ch, remove hook. (104 sc, 28 dc, 4 x 2ch-sp corners, 1 x 3-ch string)

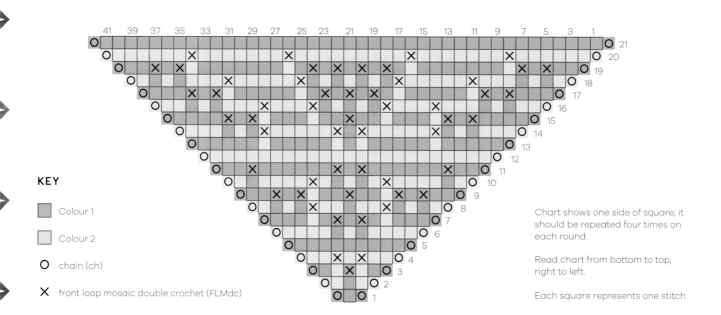

KEY

█ Colour 1

░ Colour 2

O chain (ch)

X front loop mosaic double crochet (FLMdc)

Chart shows one side of square; it should be repeated four times on each round.

Read chart from bottom to top, right to left.

Each square represents one stitch.

Round 18: Insert hook in colour 2 loop (from Round 16), *(1 sc, 2 ch, 1 sc) in 2ch-sp corner, 6 scBLO, 1 FLMdc, 5 scBLO, 1 FLMdc, 7 scBLO, 1 FLMdc, 5 scBLO, 1 FLMdc, 6 scBLO; rep from * 3 more times (work over 3-ch string with last scBLO before 3rd corner and first sc in same corner), slst in beg st to join, 3 ch, remove hook. (124 sc, 16 dc, 4 x 2ch-sp corners, 1 x 3-ch string)

Round 19: Insert hook in colour 1 loop (from Round 16), *(1 sc, 2 ch, 1 sc) in 2ch-sp corner, 1 scBLO, [1 FLMdc, 1 scBLO] twice, 9 scBLO, [1 FLMdc, 1 scBLO] 4 times, 9 scBLO, [1 FLMdc, 1 scBLO] twice; rep from * 3 more times (work over 3-ch string with last scBLO before 3rd corner and first sc in same corner), slst in first sc to join, 3 ch, remove hook. (116 sc, 32 dc, 4 x 2ch-sp corners, 1 x 3-ch string)

Round 20: Insert hook in colour 2 loop (from Round 18), *(1 sc, 2 ch, 1 sc) in 2ch-sp corner, 5 scBLO, 1 FLMdc, 7 scBLO, 1 FLMdc, 9 scBLO, 1 FLMdc, 7 scBLO, 1 FLMdc, 5 scBLO; rep from * 3 more times (work over 3-ch string with last scBLO before 3rd corner and first sc in same corner), slst in first sc to join. (140 sc, 16 dc, 4 x 2ch-sp corners)

Fasten off.

Edging: Insert hook in colour 1 loop (from Round 19), *(1 sc, 2 ch, 1 sc) in 2ch-sp corner, 39 scBLO; rep from * 3 more times, slst in first sc to join. (164 sc, 4 x 2ch-sp corners)

Fasten off and weave in ends.

SAMUEL

DESIGNER: ROSINA PLANE

YARN

Stylecraft Naturals Bamboo+Cotton DK, light worsted (DK), in foll shades:
Colour 1: Night (7160)
Colour 2: Pale Pink (7132)
Colour 3: Blush (7133)
Colour 4: Azalea (7135)

HOOK

US size E/4 (3.5mm) hook

GAUGE (TENSION)

A single motif measures approx 8¼in (21cm) using a US size E/4 (3.5mm) hook.

SPECIAL ABBREVIATION

mdc, double crochet worked in skipped st three rows below

NOTES

Motif is worked in inset mosaic crochet in Rounds 2 to 23. To keep pattern straight turn work when stated.
Colours are changed every two rounds; to change colour, or join new colour, pull up loop in corner 2ch-sp, leaving prev colour on WS.
You do not increase on every round – every 4th round only has 1 ch in each corner; following WS round skips corner ch-sp.
Place a marker in joining slst at end of all RS rounds.
Rounds 24 and 25 begin with standing sts and end with invisible join. Do not pull too tight as you will work in this st.
In st counts each 2ch-sp counts as one st and each 3ch-sp counts as two sts.

PATTERN

Using E/4 hook and colour 2, make a magic ring.

Round 1 (RS): 5 ch (counts as 1 dc, 2 ch), [3 dc, 2 ch] 3 times in ring, 2 dc, slst in 3rd of beg 5-ch to join. (12 dc)

Fasten off colour 2.

Round 2 (RS): Join colour 1 in 2ch-sp, 2 ch, (counts as 1 turning ch + 1 ch throughout), *1 sc in same sp, 3 sc, 1 sc in 2ch-sp, 1 ch; rep from * 3 more times omitting last ch on final rep, slst loosely in beg 2ch-sp to join, turn. (20 sc, 4 x 1ch-sp corners)

Round 3 (WS): 1 ch (does not count as st throughout), skip joining slst, *5 sc, 2 ch, skip corner ch-sp; rep from * 3 more times, slst in beg sc, inserting hook from RS to WS, to join, turn. (20 sc, 4 x 2ch-sp corners)

Round 4 (RS): Join colour 4 in 2ch-sp, 3 ch (counts as 1 turning ch + 2 ch throughout), *1 sc in same ch-sp, 2 sc, 2 ch, skip 1 st, 2 sc, 1 sc in 2ch-sp, 2 ch; rep from * 3 more times omitting last 2 ch on final rep, slst loosely in beg 3ch-sp to join. Turn. (28 sc)

Round 5 (WS): 1 ch, 1 sc in joining slst, *3 sc, 2 ch, skip ch-sp, 3 sc, [1 sc, 2 ch, 1 sc] in corner ch-sp; rep from * 3 more times omitting last sc on final rep, slst in beg sc, inserting hook from RS to WS, to join, turn. (36 sc)

Fasten off colour 4.

continued on next page >

Round 6 (RS): Pull up colour 1 loop in 2ch-sp, 2 ch, *1 sc in same ch-sp, 4 sc, 1 mdc, 4 sc, 1 sc in 2ch-sp, 1 ch; rep from * 3 more times omitting last ch on final rep, slst in beg 2ch-sp to join, turn. (44 sts, 4 x 1ch-sp corners)

Round 7 (WS): 1 ch, skip joining slst, *11 sc, 2 ch, skip corner 1ch-sp; rep from * 3 more times, slst in beg sc, inserting hook from RS to WS, to join, turn. (44 sc, 4 x 2ch-sp corners)

Round 8 (RS): Join colour 3 in 2ch-sp, 3 ch, *1 sc in same ch-sp, 1 sc, 3 ch, skip 2 sts, 5 sc, 3 ch, skip 2 sts, 1 sc, 1 sc in 2ch-sp, 2 ch; rep from * 3 more times omitting last 2 ch on final rep, slst loosely in beg 3ch-sp to join, turn. (52 sc)

Round 9 (WS): 1 ch, 1 sc in joining slst, *2 sc, 3 ch, skip ch-sp, 5 sc, 3 ch, skip ch-sp, 2 sc, [1 sc, 2 ch, 1 sc] in corner ch-sp; rep from * 3 more times omitting last sc on final rep, slst in beg sc, inserting hook from RS to WS, to join, turn. (44 sc)

Round 10 (RS): Pull up colour 1 loop in 2ch-sp, 2 ch, *1 sc in same ch-sp, 3 sc, 2 mdc, 3 ch, skip 2 sts, 1 sc, 3 ch, skip 2 sts, 2 mdc, 3 sc, 1 sc in 2ch-sp, 1 ch; rep from * 3 more times omitting last ch on final rep, slst in beg 2ch-sp to join, turn. (60 sts, 4 x 1ch-sp corners)

Round 11 (WS): 1 ch, skip joining slst, *6 sc, 3 ch, skip ch-sp, 1 sc, 3 ch, skip ch-sp, 6 sc, 2 ch, skip corner 1ch-sp; rep from * 3 more times, slst in beg sc, inserting hook from RS to WS, to join, turn. (60 sc, 4 x 2ch-sp corners)

Round 12 (RS): Pull up colour 3 loop in 2ch-sp, 3 ch, *1 sc in same ch-sp, 3 ch, skip 2 sts, 4 sc, 2 mdc, 1 sc, 2 mdc, 4 sc, 3 ch, skip 2 sts, 1 sc in 2ch-sp, 2 ch; rep from * 3 more times omitting last 2 ch on final rep, slst loosely in beg 3ch-sp to join, turn. (76 sts)

Round 13 (WS): 1 ch, 1 sc in joining slst, *1 sc, 3 ch, skip ch-sp, 13 sc, 3 ch, skip ch-sp, 1 sc, [1 sc, 2 ch, 1 sc] in corner ch-sp; rep from * 3 more times omitting last sc on final rep, slst in beg sc, inserting hook from RS to WS, to join, turn. (84 sc)

Round 14 (RS): Pull up colour 1 loop in 2ch-sp, 2 ch, *1 sc in same ch-sp, 3 ch, skip 2 sts, 2 mdc, 3 ch, skip 2 sts, 1 sc, 3 ch, skip 2 sts, 3 sc, 3 ch, skip 2 sts, 1 sc, 3 ch, skip 2 sts, 2 mdc, 3 ch, skip 2 sts, 1 sc in 2ch-sp, 1 ch; rep from * 3 more times omitting last ch on final rep, slst in beg 2ch-sp to join, turn. (92 sts, 4 x 1ch-sp corners)

Round 15 (WS): 1 ch, skip joining slst, *1 sc, 3 ch, skip ch-sp, 2 sc, 3 ch, skip ch-sp, 1 sc, 3 ch, skip ch-sp, 3 sc, 3 ch, skip ch-sp, 1 sc, 3 ch, skip ch-sp, 2 sc, 3 ch, skip ch-sp, 1 sc, 2 ch, skip corner 1ch-sp; rep from * 3 more times, slst in beg sc, inserting hook from RS to WS, to join, turn. (92 sc, 4 x 2ch-sp corners)

Round 16 (RS): Pull up colour 3 loop in 2ch-sp, 3 ch, *1 sc in same ch-sp, 1 sc, 2 mdc, 3 ch, skip 2 sts, 2 mdc, 1 sc, 2 mdc, 3 sc, 2 mdc, 1 sc, 2 mdc, 3 ch, skip 2 sts, 2 mdc, 1 sc, 1 sc in 2ch-sp, 2 ch; rep from * 3 more times omitting last 2 ch on final rep, slst loosely in beg 3ch-sp to join, turn. (100 sts)

Round 17 (WS): 1 ch, 1 sc in joining slst, *4 sc, 3 ch, skip ch-sp, 13 sc, 3 ch, skip ch-sp, 4 sc, [1 sc, 2 ch, 1 sc] in corner ch-sp; rep from * 3 more times omitting last sc on final rep, slst in beg sc, inserting hook from RS to WS, to join. Turn. (108 sc)

Round 18 (RS): Pull up colour 1 loop in 2ch-sp, 2 ch, *1 sc in same ch-sp, 5 sc, 2 mdc, 4 sc, 3 ch, skip 2 sts, 1 sc, 3 ch, skip 2 sts, 4 sc, 2 mdc, 5 sc, 1 sc in 2ch-sp, 1 ch; rep from * 3 more times omitting last ch on final rep, slst in beg 2ch-sp to join. Turn. (116 sts, 4 x 1ch-sp corners)

Round 19 (WS): 1 ch, skip joining slst, *12 sc, 3 ch, skip ch-sp, 1 sc, 3 ch, skip ch-sp, 12 sc, 2 ch, skip corner 1ch-sp; rep from * 3 more times, slst in beg sc, inserting hook from RS to WS, to join. Turn. (116 sc, 4 x 2ch-sp corners)

Round 20 (RS): Pull up colour 3 loop in 2ch-sp, 3 ch, *1 sc in same ch-sp, [2 sc, 3 ch, skip 2 sts] 3 times, 2 mdc, 1 sc, 2 mdc, [3 ch, skip 2 sts, 2 sc] 3 times, 1 sc in 2ch-sp, 2 ch; rep from * 3 more times omitting last 2 ch on final rep, slst loosely in beg 3ch-sp to join. Turn. (124 sts)

Round 21 (WS): 1 ch, 1 sc in joining slst, *3 sc, [3 ch, skip ch-sp, 2 sc] twice, 3ch, skip ch-sp, 5 sc, [3 ch, skip ch-sp, 2 sc] 3 times, 1 sc, [1 sc, 2 ch, 1 sc] in corner ch-sp; rep from * 3 more times omitting last sc on final rep, slst in beg sc, inserting hook from RS to WS, to join. Turn. (132 sc)

Fasten off colour 3.

Round 22 (RS): Pull up colour 1 loop in 2ch-sp, 3 ch, *1 sc in same ch-sp, 4 sc, [2 mdc, 2 sc] twice, 2 mdc, 5 sc, [2 mdc, 2 sc] 3 times, 2 ch, 1 sc in 2ch-sp, 2 ch; rep from * 3 more times omitting last 2 ch on final rep, slst in beg 2ch-sp to join. Turn. (140 sts)

Round 23 (WS): 1 ch, 1 sc in joining sl st, *35 sc, [1 sc, 2 ch, 1 sc] in corner ch-sp; rep from * 3 more times omitting last sc on final rep, sl st in beg sc to join inserting hook from RS to WS, fasten off colour 1. Turn. (148 sc)

Round 24 (RS): Join colour 2 with a stsc in any corner 2ch-sp, *2 ch, 1 sc in same sp, sc across to next corner, 1 sc in 2ch-sp; rep from * 3 more times omitting last sc on final rep. (156 sc)

Fasten off colour 2 with invisible join.

Round 25 (RS): Join colour 4 with a sthdc in any corner 2ch-sp, *2 ch, 1 hdc in same sp, BPhdc across to next corner, 1 hdc in 2ch-sp; rep from * 3 more times omitting last hdc on final rep. (164 hdc)

Fasten off colour 4 with invisible join, weave in all ends.

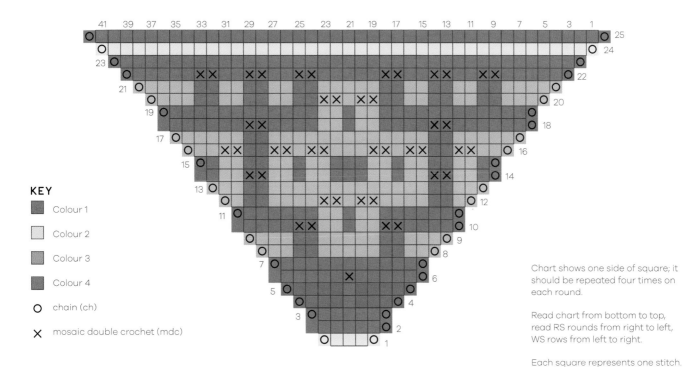

KEY

- Colour 1
- Colour 2
- Colour 3
- Colour 4
- O chain (ch)
- X mosaic double crochet (mdc)

Chart shows one side of square; it should be repeated four times on each round.

Read chart from bottom to top, read RS rounds from right to left, WS rows from left to right.

Each square represents one stitch.

CONCENTRIC ZIGZAGS

DESIGNER: CAROL IBBETSON

YARN

Lion Brand 24/7 Cotton, worsted (aran), in foll shades:
Colour 1: White (100)
Colour 2: Denim (108)

HOOK

US size E/4 (3.5mm) hook

GAUGE (TENSION)

A single motif measures approx 8in (20cm) using a US size E/4 (3.5mm) hook.

SPECIAL ABBREVIATION

mdc, double crochet worked in skipped st three rounds below

NOTES

Motif is worked in inset mosaic crochet in Rounds 5 to 19.
Two rounds are worked in each colour and work is turned after EACH round.
Carry unused yarn across WS of work.
In st counts each 3ch-sp counts as 2 sts.

PATTERN

Using E/4 hook and colour 1, make a magic ring.

Round 1 (RS): 4 sc in ring, slst in first sc to join, turn. (4 sc)

Chart starts here.

Round 2 (WS): 1 ch (does not count as st throughout), 1 sc, *(1 sc, 2 ch, 1 sc) in next st; rep from * twice more, 1 sc, 2 ch, slst in first st from back to front to join, turn. (8 sts)

Round 3: Change to colour 2, slst in corner 2ch-sp, (2 ch, 1 sc) in same 2ch-sp, *2 sc, (1 sc, 2 ch, 1 sc) in 2ch-sp; rep from * twice more, 2 sc,

1 sc in corner 2ch-sp, slst in first 2ch-sp to join, turn. (16 sts)

Round 4: 1 ch, 1 sc in corner 2ch-sp, *4 sc, (1 sc, 2 ch, 1 sc) in 2ch-sp; rep from * twice more, 4 sc, (1 sc, 2 ch) in corner 2ch-sp, slst in first st from back to front to join, turn. (24 sts)

Round 5: Change to colour 1, slst in corner 2ch-sp, (2 ch, 1 sc) in same 2ch-sp, *2 sc, 3 ch, skip 2 sts, 2 sc, (1 sc, 2 ch, 1 sc) in 2ch-sp; rep from * twice more, 2 sc, 3 ch, skip 2 sts, 2 sc, 1 sc in corner 2ch-sp, slst in first 2ch-sp to join, turn. (32 sts)

Round 6: 1 ch, 1 sc in corner 2ch-sp, *3 sc, 3 ch, skip 3ch-sp, 3 sc, (1 sc, 2 ch, 1 sc) in 2ch-sp; rep from * twice more, 3 sc, 3 ch, skip 3ch-sp, 3 sc, (1 sc, 2 ch) in corner 2ch-sp, slst in first st from back to front to join, turn. (40 sts)

Round 7: Change to colour 2, slst in corner 2ch-sp, (2 ch, 1 sc) in same 2ch-sp, *2 sc, 3 ch, skip 2 sts, 2 mdc, 3 ch, skip 2 sts, 2 sc, (1 sc, 2 ch, 1 sc) in 2ch-sp; rep from * twice more, 2 sc, 3 ch, skip 2 sts, 2 mdc, 3 ch, skip 3ch-

sp, 2 sc, 1 sc in corner 2ch-sp, slst in first 2ch-sp to join, turn. (48 sts)

Round 8: 1 ch, 1 sc in corner 2ch-sp, *1 sc, [2 sc, 3 ch, skip 3ch-sp] twice, 3 sc, (1 sc, 2 ch, 1 sc) in 2ch-sp; rep from * twice more, 1 sc, [2 sc, 3 ch, skip 3ch-sp] twice, 3 sc, (1 sc, 2 ch) in corner 2ch-sp, slst in first st from back to front to join, turn. (56 sts)

Round 9: Change to colour 1, slst in corner 2ch-sp, (2 ch, 1 sc) in same 2ch-sp, *2 sc, 3 ch, skip 2 sts, 2 mdc, 2 sc, 2 mdc, 3 ch, skip 2 sts, 2 sc, (1 sc, 2 ch, 1 sc) in 2ch-sp; rep from * twice more, 2 sc, 3 ch, skip 2 sts, 2 mdc, 2 sc, 2 mdc, 3 ch, skip 2 sts, 2 sc, 1 sc in corner 2ch-sp, slst in first 2ch-sp to join, turn. (64 sts)

Round 10: 1 ch, sc in corner 2ch-sp, *3 sc, 3 ch, skip 3ch-sp, 6 sc, 3 ch, skip 3ch-sp, 3 sc, (1 sc, 2 ch, 1 sc) in 2ch-sp; rep from * twice more, 3 sc, 3 ch, skip 3ch-sp, 6 sc, 3 ch, skip 3ch-sp, 3 sc, (1 sc, 2ch) in corner 2ch-sp, slst in first st from back to front to join, turn. (72 sts)

Round 11: Change to colour 2, slst in corner 2ch-sp, (2 ch, 1 sc) in same 2ch-sp, *2 sc, 3 ch, skip 2 sts, 2 mdc, 6 sc, 2 mdc, 3 ch, skip 2 sts, 2 sc, (1 sc, 2 ch, 1 sc) in 2ch-sp; rep from * twice more, 2 sc, 3 ch, skip 2 sts, 2 mdc, 6 sc, 2 mdc, 3 ch, skip 3ch-sp, 2 sc, 1 sc in corner 2ch-sp, slst in first 2ch-sp to join, turn. (80 sts)

Round 12: 1 ch, 1 sc in corner 2ch-sp, *3 sc, 3 ch, skip 3ch-sp, 10 sc, 3 ch, skip 3ch-sp, 3 sc, (1 sc, 2 ch, 1 sc) in 2ch-sp; rep from * twice more, 3 sc, 3 ch, skip 3ch-sp, 10 sc, 3 ch, skip 3ch-sp, 3 sc, (1 sc, 2 ch) in corner 2ch-sp, slst in first st from back to front to join, turn. (88 sts)

Round 13: Change to colour 1, slst in corner 2ch-sp, (2 ch, 1 sc) in same 2ch-sp, *2 sc, 3 ch, skip 2 sts, 2 mdc, 4 sc, 3 ch, skip 2 sts, 4 sc, 2 mdc, 3 ch, skip 2 sts, 2 sc, [1 sc, 2 ch, 1 sc] in 2ch-sp; rep from * twice more, 2 sc, 3 ch, skip 2 sts, 2 mdc, 4 sc, 3 ch, skip 2 sts, 4 sc, 2 mdc, 3 ch, skip 3ch-sp, 2 sc, 1 sc in corner 2ch-sp, slst in first 2ch-sp to join, turn. (96 sts)

Round 14: 1 ch, 1 sc in corner 2ch-sp, *3 sc, 3 ch, skip 3ch-sp, 6 sc, 3 ch, skip 3ch-sp, 6 sc, 3 ch, skip 3ch-sp, 3 sc, (1 sc, 2 ch, 1 sc) in 2ch-sp; rep from * twice more, 3 sc, 3 ch, skip 3ch-sp, 6 sc, 3 ch, skip 3ch-sp, 6 sc, 3 ch, skip 3ch-sp, 3 sc, (1 sc, 2 ch) in corner 2ch-sp, slst in first st from back to front to join, turn. (104 sts)

Round 15: Change to colour 2, slst in corner 2ch-sp, (2 ch, 1 sc) in same 2ch-sp, *2 sc, 3 ch, skip 2 sts, 2 mdc, 4 sc, 3 ch, skip 2 sts, 2 mdc, 3 ch, skip 2 sts, 4 sc, 2 mdc, 3 ch, skip 2 sts, 2 sc, (1 sc, 2 ch, 1 sc) in 2ch-sp; rep from * twice more, 2 sc, 3 ch, skip 2 sts, 2 mdc, 4 sc, 3 ch, skip 2 sts, 2 mdc, 3 ch, skip 2 sts, 4 sc, 2 mdc, 3 ch, skip 2 sts, 2 sc, 1 sc in corner 2ch-sp, slst in first 2ch-sp to join, turn. (112 sts)

Round 16: 1 ch, 1 sc in corner 2ch-sp, *3 sc, 3 ch, skip 3ch-sp, 6 sc, 3 ch, skip 3ch-sp, 2 sc, 3 ch, skip 3ch-sp, 6 sc, 3 ch, skip 3ch-sp, 3 sc, (1 sc, 2 ch, 1 sc) in 2ch-sp; rep from * twice more, 3 sc, 3 ch, skip 3ch-sp, 6 sc, 3 ch, skip 3ch-sp, 2 sc, 3 ch, skip 3ch-sp, 6 sc, 3 ch, skip 3ch-sp, 3 sc, (1 sc, 2ch) in corner 2ch-sp, slst in first st from back to front to join, turn. (120 sts)

Round 17: Change to colour 1, slst in corner 2ch-sp, (2 ch, 1 sc) in same 2ch-sp, *2 sc, 3 ch, skip 2 sts, 2 mdc, 4 sc, 3 ch, skip 2 sts, 2 mdc, 2 sc, 2 mdc, 3 ch, skip 2 sts, 4 sc, 2 mdc, 3 ch, skip 2 sts, 2 sc, (1 sc, 2 ch, 1 sc) in 2ch-sp; rep from * twice more, 2 sc, 3 ch, skip 2 sts, 2 mdc, 4 sc, 3 ch, skip 2 sts, 2 mdc, 2 sc, 2 mdc, 3 ch, skip 2 sts, 4 sc, 2 mdc, 3 ch, skip 2 sts, 2 sc, 1 sc in corner 2ch-sp, slst in first 2ch-sp to join, turn. (128 sts)

Round 18: 1 ch, 1 sc in corner 2ch-sp, *3 sc, [3 ch, skip 3ch-sp, 6 sc] 3 times, 3 ch, skip 3ch-sp, 3 sc, (1 sc, 2 ch, 1 sc) in 2ch-sp; rep from * twice more, 3 sc, [3 ch, skip 3ch-sp, 6 sc] 3 times, 3 ch, skip 3ch-sp, 3 sc, (1 sc, 2ch) in corner 2ch-sp, slst in first st from back to front to join, turn. (136 sts)

Round 19: Change to colour 2, slst in corner 2ch-sp, (2 ch, 1 sc) in same 2ch-sp, *4 sc, [2 mdc, 6 sc] 3 times, 2 mdc, 4 sc, [1 sc, 2 ch, 1 sc] in 2ch-sp; rep from * twice more, 4 sc, [2 mdc, 6 sc] 3 times, 2 mdc, 4 sc, 1 sc in corner 2ch-sp, slst in first 2ch-sp to join, turn. (144 sts)

Round 20: 1 ch, 1 sc in corner 2ch-sp, *1 sc in each st to 2ch-sp, (1 sc, 2 ch, 1 sc) in 2ch-sp; rep from * twice more, 1 sc in each st to 2ch-sp, (1 sc, 2ch) in corner 2ch-sp, slst in first st from back to front to join, turn. (152 sts)

Fasten off and weave in ends.

Chart shows one side of square; it should be repeated four times on each round. Turn after every round

Each square represents one stitch.

Odd numbered (RS) rounds are worked in an anti-clockwise direction. Even numbered (WS) rounds are worked in a clockwise direction.

Start with magic ring of 4 sc using colour 1, then **chart starts at Round 2** using colour 1 working in clockwise direction.

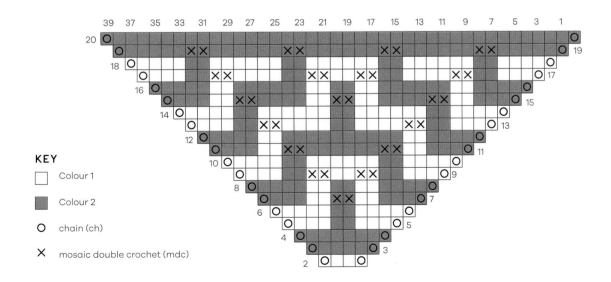

KEY

☐ Colour 1

▨ Colour 2

O chain (ch)

✕ mosaic double crochet (mdc)

ZIGZAG SWIRLS

DESIGNER: CAROL IBBETSON

YARN

Lion Brand 24/7 Cotton, worsted (aran), in foll shades:

Colour 1: Ecru (098)

Colour 2: Succulent (116)

HOOK

US size E/4 (3.5mm) hook

GAUGE (TENSION)

A single motif measures approx 8in (20cm) using a US size E/4 (3.5mm) hook.

SPECIAL ABBREVIATION

mdc, double crochet worked in skipped st three rounds below

NOTES

Motif is worked in inset mosaic crochet in rounds.
Two rounds are worked in each colour, work is turned after EACH round.
Carry unused yarn across WS of work.
In st counts each 3ch-sp counts as two sts.

PATTERN

Using E/4 hook and colour 1, make a magic ring.

Round 1 (RS): 4 sc in ring, slst in first sc to join, turn. (4 sc)

Chart starts here.

Round 2 (WS): 1 ch [does not count as st throughout], 1 sc, *(1 sc, 2 ch, 1 sc) in next st; rep from * twice more, 1 sc, 2 ch, slst in first st from back to front to join, turn. (8 sts)

Round 3: Change to colour 2, slst in corner 2ch-sp, (2 ch, 1 sc) in same 2ch-sp; *2 sc, (1 sc, 2 ch, 1 sc) in 2ch-sp; rep from * twice more, 2 sc, 1 sc in corner 2ch-sp, slst in first 2ch-sp to join, turn. (16 sts)

Round 4: 1 ch, 1 sc in corner 2ch-sp, *4 sc, (1 sc, 2 ch, 1 sc) in 2ch-sp; rep from * twice more, 4 sc, (1 sc, 2 ch) in corner 2ch-sp, slst in first st from back to front to join, turn. (24 sts)

Round 5: Change to colour 1, slst in corner 2ch-sp, (2 ch, 1 sc) in same 2ch-sp, *2 sc, 3 ch, skip 2 sts, 2 sc, (1 sc, 2 ch, 1 sc) in 2ch-sp; rep from * twice more, 2 sc, 3 ch, skip 2 sts, 2 sc, 1 sc in corner 2ch-sp, slst in first 2ch-sp to join, turn. (32 sts)

Round 6: 1 ch, 1 sc in corner 2ch-sp, *3 sc, 3 ch, skip 3ch-sp, 3 sc, (1 sc, 2 ch, 1 sc) in 2ch-sp; rep from * twice more, 3 sc, 3 ch, skip 3ch-sp, 3 sc, (1 sc, 2 ch) in corner 2ch-sp, slst in first st from back to front to join, turn. (40 sts)

Round 7: Change to colour 2, slst in corner 2ch-sp, (2 ch, 1 sc) in same 2ch-sp, *2 sc, 3 ch, skip 2 sts, 2 mdc, 4 sc, (1 sc, 2 ch, 1 sc) in 2ch-sp; rep from * twice more, 2 sc, 3 ch, skip 2 sts, 2 mdc, 4 sc, 1 sc in corner 2ch-sp, slst in first 2ch-sp to join, turn. (48 sts)

Round 8: 1 ch, 1 sc in corner 2ch-sp, *7 sc, 3 ch, skip 3ch-sp, 3 sc, (1 sc, 2 ch, 1 sc) in 2ch-sp; rep from * twice more, 7 sc, 3 ch, skip 3ch-sp, 3 sc, (1 sc, 2 ch) in corner 2ch-sp, slst in first st from back to front to join, turn. (56 sts)

Round 9: Change to colour 1, slst in corner 2ch-sp, (2 ch, 1 sc) in same 2ch-sp, *2 sc, 3 ch, skip 2 sts, 2 mdc, 4 sc, 3 ch, skip 2 sts, 2 sc, (1 sc, 2 ch, 1 sc) in 2ch-sp; rep from * twice more, 2 sc, 3 ch, skip 2 sts, 2 mdc, 4 sc, 3 ch, skip 2 sts, 1 sc in corner 2ch-sp, slst in first 2ch-sp to join, turn. (64 sts)

Round 10: 1 ch, 1 sc in corner 2ch-sp, *3 sc, 3 ch, skip 3ch-sp, 6 sc, 3 ch, skip 3ch-sp, 3 sc, (1 sc, 2 ch, 1 sc) in 2ch-sp; rep from * twice more, 3 sc, 3 ch, skip 3ch-sp, 6 sc, 3 ch, skip 3ch-sp, 3 sc, (1 sc, 2 ch) in corner 2ch-sp, slst in first st from back to front to join, turn. (72 sts)

Round 11: Change to colour 2, slst in corner 2ch-sp, (2 ch, 1 sc) in same 2ch-sp, *2 sc, [3 ch, skip 2 sts, 2 mdc,

4 sc] twice, (1 sc, 2 ch, 1 sc) in 2ch-sp; rep from * twice more, 2 sc, [3 ch, skip 2 sts, 2 mdc, 4 sc] twice, 1 sc in corner 2ch-sp, slst in first 2ch-sp to join, turn. (80 sts)

Round 12: 1 ch, 1 sc in corner 2ch-sp, *7 sc, 3 ch, skip 3ch-sp, 6 sc, 3 ch, skip 3ch-sp, 3 sc, (1 sc, 2 ch, 1 sc) in 2ch-sp; rep from * twice more, 7 sc, 3 ch, skip 3ch-sp, 6 sc, 3 ch, skip 3ch-sp, 3 sc, (1 sc, 2 ch) in corner 2ch-sp, slst in first st from back to front to join, turn. (88 sts)

Round 13: Change to colour 1, slst in corner 2ch-sp, (2 ch, 1 sc) in same 2ch-sp, *2 sc, [3 ch, skip 2 sts, 2 mdc, 4 sc] twice, 3 ch, skip 2 sts, 2 sc, (1 sc, 2 ch, 1 sc) in 2ch-sp; rep from * twice more, 2 sc, [3 ch, skip 2 sts, 2 mdc, 4 sc] twice, 3 ch, skip 2 sts, 2 sc, 1 sc in corner 2ch-sp, slst in first 2ch-sp to join, turn. (96 sts)

Round 14: 1 ch, 1 sc in corner 2ch-sp, *3 sc, [3 ch, skip 3ch-sp, 6 sc] twice, 3 ch, skip 3ch-sp, 3 sc, (1 sc, 2 ch, 1 sc) in 2ch-sp; rep from * twice more, 3 sc, [3 ch, skip 3ch-sp, 6 sc] twice, 3 ch, skip 3ch-sp, 3 sc, (1 sc, 2 ch) in corner 2ch-sp, slst in first st from back to front to join, turn. (104 sts)

Round 15: Change to colour 2, slst in corner 2ch-sp, (2 ch, 1 sc) in same 2ch-sp, *2 sc, [3 ch, skip 2 sts, 2 mdc, 4 sc] 3 times, (1 sc, 2 ch, 1 sc) in 2ch-sp; rep from * twice more, 2 sc, [3 ch, skip 2 sts, 2 mdc, 4 sc] 3 times, 1 sc in corner 2ch-sp, slst in first 2ch-sp to join, turn. (112 sts)

Round 16: 1 ch, 1 sc in corner 2ch-sp, *7 sc, [3 ch, skip 3ch-sp, 6 sc] twice, 3 ch, skip 3ch-sp, 3 sc, (1 sc, 2 ch, 1 sc) in 2ch-sp; rep from * twice more, 7 sc, [3 ch, skip 3ch-sp, 6 sc] twice, 3 ch, skip 3ch-sp, 3 sc, (1 sc, 2 ch) in corner 2ch-sp, slst in first st from back to front to join, turn. (120 sts)

Round 17: Change to colour 1, slst in corner 2ch-sp, (2 ch, 1 sc) in same 2ch-sp, *2 sc, [3 ch, skip 2 sts, 2 mdc, 4 sc] 3 times, 3 ch, skip 2 sts, 2 sc, (1 sc, 2 ch, 1 sc) in 2ch-sp; rep from * twice more, 2 sc, [3 ch, skip 2 sts, 2 mdc, 4 sc] 3 times, 3 ch, skip 2 sts, 2 sc, 1 sc in corner 2ch-sp, slst in first 2ch-sp to join, turn. (128 sts)

Round 18: 1 ch, 1 sc in corner 2ch-sp, *3 sc, [3 ch, skip 3ch-sp, 6 sc] 3 times, 3 ch, skip 3ch-sp, 3 sc, (1 sc, 2 ch, 1 sc) in 2ch-sp; rep from * twice more, 3 sc, [3 ch, skip 3ch-sp, 6 sc] 3 times, 3 ch, skip 3ch-sp, 3 sc, (1 sc, 2 ch) in corner 2ch-sp, slst in first st from back to front to join, turn. (136 sts)

Round 19: Change to colour 2, slst in corner 2ch-sp, (2 ch, 1 sc) in same 2ch-sp, *4 sc, [2 mdc, 6 sc] 3 times, 2 mdc, 4 sc, (1 sc, 2 ch, 1 sc) in 2ch-sp; rep from * twice more, 4 sc, [2 mdc, 6 sc] 3 times, 2 mdc, 4 sc, 1 sc in corner 2ch-sp, slst in first 2ch-sp to join, turn. (144 sts)

Round 20: 1 ch, 1 sc in corner 2ch-sp, *1 sc in each st to 2ch-sp, (1 sc, 2 ch, 1 sc) in 2ch-sp; rep from * twice more, 1 sc in each st to 2ch-sp, (1 sc, 2 ch) in corner 2ch-sp, slst in first st from back to front to join, turn. (152 sts)

Fasten off and weave in ends.

Chart shows one side of square; it should be repeated four times on each round. Turn after every round.

Each square represents one stitch.

Odd numbered (RS) rounds are worked in an anti-clockwise direction. Even numbered (WS) rounds are worked in a clockwise direction.

Start with magic ring of 4 sc using colour 1, then chart starts at Round 2 using colour 1 working in clockwise direction.

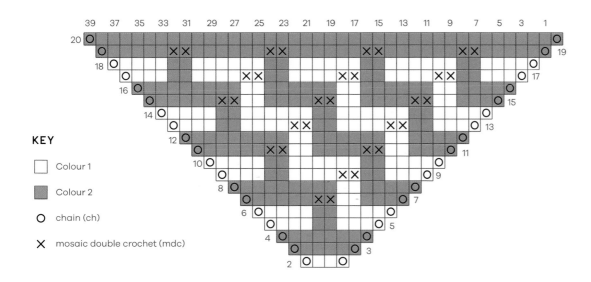

KEY

☐ Colour 1

▨ Colour 2

○ chain (ch)

✕ mosaic double crochet (mdc)

SHINING STAR

DESIGNER: CAROL IBBETSON

YARN

Lion Brand 24/7 Cotton, worsted (aran), in foll shades:
Colour 1: Rose (142)
Colour 2: Ecru (098)

HOOK

US size E/4 (3.5mm) hook

GAUGE (TENSION)

A single motif measures approx 8in (20cm) using a US size E/4 (3.5mm) hook.

SPECIAL ABBREVIATION

mdc, double crochet worked in skipped st three rounds below

NOTES

Motif is worked in inset mosaic crochet in rounds.
Two rounds are worked in each colour (after Round 1) and work is turned after EACH round.
Carry unused yarn across WS of work.
In st counts each 2ch-sp counts as one st.

PATTERN

Using E/4 hook and colour 1, make a magic ring.

Round 1 (WS): 8 sc in ring, slst in first sc to join, turn. (8 sc)

Chart starts here.

Round 2: Change to colour 2, 1 ch (does not count as st throughout), *(1 sc, 2 ch, 1 sc) in next st, 2 ch, skip 1 st; rep from * 3 more times, slst in first st to join, turn. (12 sts)

Round 3: 1 ch, *2 ch, skip 2ch-sp, 1 sc, (1 sc, 2 ch, 1 sc) in 2ch-sp, 1 sc; rep from * 3 more times, slst in first 2ch-sp to join, turn. (20 sts)

Round 4: Change to colour 1, 1 ch, *2 ch, skip 1 st, 1 sc, (1 sc, 2 ch, 1 sc) in 2ch-sp, 1 sc, 2 ch, skip 1 st, 1 mdc; rep from * 3 more times, slst in first 2ch-sp to join, turn. (28 sts)

Round 5: 1 ch, *1 sc, 2 ch, skip 2ch-sp, 2 sc, (1 sc, 2 ch, 1 sc) in 2ch-sp, 2 sc, 2 ch, skip 2ch-sp; rep from * 3 more times, slst in first st to join, turn. (36 sts)

Round 6: Change to colour 2, 1 ch, *1 mdc, 2 ch, skip 1 st, 2 sc, (1 sc, 2 ch, 1 sc) in 2ch-sp, 2 sc, 2 ch, skip 1 st, 1 mdc, 1 sc; rep from * 3 more times, slst in first st to join, turn. (44 sts)

Round 7: 1 ch, *2 sc, 2 ch, skip 2ch-sp, 3 sc, (1 sc, 2 ch, 1 sc) in 2ch-sp, 3 sc, 2 ch, skip 2ch-sp, 1 sc; rep from * 3 more times, slst in first st to join, turn. (52 sts)

Round 8: Change to colour 1, 1 ch, *1 sc, 1 mdc, 2 ch, skip 1 st, 2 sc, 2 ch, skip 1 st, (1 sc, 2 ch, 1 sc) in 2ch-sp, 2 ch, skip 1 st, 2 sc, 2 ch, skip 1 st, 1 mdc, 1 sc, 2 ch, skip 1 st; rep from * 3 more times, slst in first st to join, turn. (60 sts)

Round 9: 1 ch, *[2 ch, skip 2ch-sp, 2 sc] twice, 2 ch, skip 2ch-sp, 1 sc, (1 sc, 2 ch, 1 sc) in 2ch-sp, 1 sc, [2 ch, skip 2ch-sp, 2 sc] twice; rep from * 3 more times, slst in first st, turn. (68 sts)

Round 10: Change to colour 2, 1 ch, *[2 ch, skip 1 st, 1 sc, 1 mdc] twice, 2 ch, skip 1 st, 1 sc, (1 sc, 2 ch, 1 sc) in 2ch-sp, 1 sc, [2 ch, skip 1 st, 1 mdc, 1 sc] twice, 2 ch, skip 1 st, 1 mdc; rep from * 3 more times, slst in 2ch-sp to join, turn. (76 sts)

Round 11: 1 ch, *[1 sc, 2 ch, skip 2ch-sp, 1 sc] 3 times, 1 sc, (1 sc, 2 ch, 1 sc) in 2ch-sp, 1 sc, [1 sc, 2 ch, skip 2ch-sp, 1 sc] twice, 1 sc, 2 ch, skip 2ch-sp; rep from * 3 more times, slst in first st, turn. (84 sts)

Round 12: Change to colour 1, 1 ch, *[1 mdc, 2 ch, skip 1 st, 1 sc] 3 times, 1 sc, (1 sc, 2 ch, 1 sc) in 2ch-sp, 1 sc, [1 sc, 2 ch, skip 1 st, 1 mdc] 3 times, 1 sc; rep from * 3 more times, slst in first st to join, turn. (92 sts)

Round 13: 1 ch, *[2 sc, 2 ch, skip 2ch-sp] 3 times, 3 sc, (1 sc, 2 ch, 1 sc) in 2ch-sp, 3 sc, [2 ch, skip 2ch-sp, 2 sc] twice, 2 ch, skip 2ch-sp, 1 sc; rep from * 3 more times, slst in first st, turn. (100 sts)

Round 14: Change to colour 2, 1 ch, *[1 sc, 1 mdc, 2 ch, skip 1 st] 3 times, 2 sc, 2 ch, skip 1 st, (1 sc, 2 ch, 1 sc) in 2ch-sp, 2 ch, skip 1 st, 2 sc, [2 ch, skip 1 st, 1 mdc, 1 sc] 3 times, 2 ch, skip 1 st; rep from * 3 more times, slst in first st to join, turn. (108 sts)

Round 15: 1 ch, *[2 ch, skip 2ch-sp, 2 sc] 4 times, 2 ch, skip 2ch-sp, 1 sc, (1 sc, 2 ch, 1 sc) in 2ch-sp, 1 sc, [2 ch, skip 2ch-sp, 2 sc] 4 times; rep from * 3 more times, slst in first st, turn. (116 sts)

Round 16: Change to colour 1, 1 ch, *[2 ch, skip 1 st, 1 sc, 1 mdc] 4 times, 2 ch, skip 1 st, 1 sc, (1 sc, 2 ch, 1 sc) in 2ch-sp, 1 sc, [2 ch, skip 1 st, 1 mdc, 1 sc] 4 times, 2 ch, skip 1 st, 1 mdc; rep from * 3 more times, slst in first st to join, turn. (124 sts)

Round 17: 1 ch, *[1 sc, 2 ch, skip 2ch-sp, 1 sc] 5 times, 1 sc, (1 sc, 2 ch, 1 sc) in 2ch-sp, 1 sc, [1 sc, 2 ch, skip 2ch-sp, 1 sc] 4 times, 1 sc, 2 ch, skip 2ch-sp; rep from * 3 more times, slst in first st to join, turn. (132 sts)

Round 18: Change to colour 2, 1 ch, *[1 mdc, 2 sc] 5 times, 1 sc, (1 sc, 2 ch, 1 sc) in 2ch-sp, 1 sc, [2 sc, 1 mdc] 5 times, 1 sc; rep from * 3 more times, slst in first st to join, turn. (140 sts)

Round 19: 1 ch, *sc in each st to 2ch-sp, (1 sc, 2 ch, 1 sc) in 2ch-sp; rep from * 3 more times, 1 sc in each st to end, slst in first st to join. (148 sts)

Fasten off and weave in ends.

Chart shows one quarter of square; it should be repeated four times on each round. Note that the starting/finishing position of each round is as shown by the black line. Turn after every round.

Each square represents one stitch on one round.

In this pattern even numbered rounds are RS rounds and are worked in a clockwise direction. Odd numbered rounds are WS rounds and are worked in an anti-clockwise direction.

Start with magic ring of 8 sc using colour 1, then chart starts at Round 2 using colour 2 working in clockwise direction.

KEY

- ▨ Colour 1
- ☐ Colour 2
- ○ chain (ch)
- ✕ mosaic double crochet (mdc)

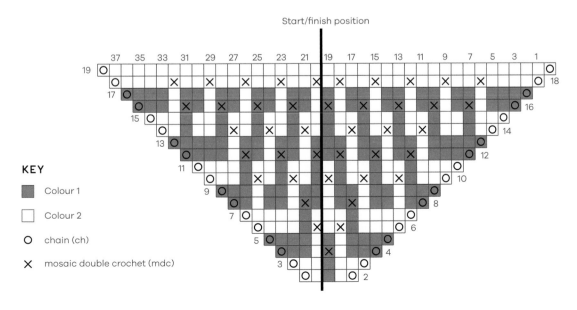

ON A SLANT

DESIGNER: CAROL IBBETSON

YARN

Lion Brand 24/7 Cotton, worsted (aran), in foll shades:

Colour 1: Black (153)
Colour 2: Goldenrod (158)

HOOK

US size E/4 (3.5mm) hook.

GAUGE (TENSION)

A single motif measures approx 8in (20cm) using a US size E/4 (3.5mm) hook.

SPECIAL ABBREVIATION

mdc, double crochet worked in skipped st three rounds below

NOTES

Motif is worked in inset mosaic crochet in rounds.
Two rounds are worked in each colour and work is turned after EACH round.
Carry unused yarn across WS of work.
In st counts each 3ch-sp counts as 2 sts.

PATTERN

Using E/4 hook and colour 1, make a magic ring.

Round 1 (RS): 4 sc in ring, slst in first sc to join, turn. (4 sc)

Round 2 (WS): 1 ch (does not count as st throughout), 1 sc, *(1 sc, 2 ch, 1 sc) in next st; rep from * twice more, 1 sc, 2 ch, slst in first st from back to front to join, turn. (8 sts)

Round 3: Change to colour 2, slst in corner 2ch-sp, (2 ch, 1 sc) in same 2ch-sp, *2 sc, (1 sc, 2 ch, 1 sc) in 2ch-sp; rep from * twice more, 2 sc, 1 sc in corner 2ch-sp, slst in first 2ch-sp to join, turn. (16 sts)

Round 4: 1 ch, 1 sc in corner 2ch-sp, *4 sc, (1 sc, 2 ch, 1 sc) in 2ch-sp; rep from * twice more, 4 sc, (1 sc, 2 ch) in corner 2ch-sp, slst in first st from back to front to join, turn. (24 sts)

Round 5: Change to colour 1, slst in corner 2ch-sp, (2 ch, 1 sc) in same 2ch-sp, *2 sc, 3 ch, skip 2 sts, 2 sc, (1 sc, 2 ch, 1 sc) in 2ch-sp; rep from * twice more, 2 sc, 3 ch, skip 2 sts, 2 sc, 1 sc in corner 2ch-sp, slst in first 2ch-sp to join, turn. (32 sts)

Round 6: 1 ch, 1 sc in corner 2ch-sp, *3 sc, 3 ch, skip 3ch-sp, 3 sc, (1 sc, 2 ch, 1 sc) in 2ch-sp; rep from * twice more, 3 sc, 3 ch, skip 3ch-sp, 3 sc, (1 sc, 2 ch) in corner 2ch-sp, slst in first st from back to front to join, turn. (40 sts)

Round 7: Change to colour 2, slst in corner 2ch-sp, (2 ch, 1 sc) in same 2ch-sp, 2 sc, 3 ch, skip 2 sts, 2 mdc, 4 sc, (1 sc, 2 ch, 1 sc) in 2ch-sp, 4 sc, 2 mdc, 3 ch, skip 2 sts, 2 sc, (1 sc, 2 ch, 1 sc) in 2ch-sp, 2 sc, 3 ch, skip 2 sts, 2 mdc, 4 sc, (1 sc, 2 ch, 1 sc) in 2ch-sp, 4 sc, 2 mdc, 3 ch, skip 2 sts, 2 sc, 1 sc in corner 2ch-sp, slst in first 2ch-sp to join, turn. (48 sts)

Round 8: 1 ch, 1 sc in corner 2ch-sp, 3 sc, 3 ch, skip 3ch-sp, 7 sc, (1 sc, 2 ch, 1 sc) in 2ch-sp, 7 sc, 3 ch, skip 3ch-sp, 3 sc, (1 sc, 2 ch, 1 sc) in 2ch-sp, 3 sc, 3 ch, skip 3ch-sp, 7 sc, (1 sc, 2 ch, 1 sc) in 2ch-sp, 7 sc, 3 ch, skip 3ch-sp, 3 sc, (1 sc, 2 ch) in corner 2ch-sp, slst in first st from back to front to join, turn. (56 sts)

Round 9: Change to colour 1, slst in corner 2ch-sp, (2 ch, 1 sc) in same 2ch-sp, 2 sc, 3 ch, skip 2 sts, 2 mdc, 4 sc, 3 ch, skip 2 sts, 2 sc, (1 sc, 2 ch, 1 sc) in 2ch-sp, 2 sc, 3 ch, skip 2 sts, 4 sc, 2 mdc, 3 ch, skip 2 sts, 2 sc, (1 sc, 2 ch, 1 sc) in 2ch-sp, 2 sc, 3 ch, skip 2 sts, 2 mdc, 4 sc, 3 ch, skip 2 sts, 2 sc, (1 sc, 2 ch, 1 sc) in 2ch-sp, 2 sc, 3 ch, skip 2 sts, 4 sc, 2 mdc, 3 ch, skip 2 sts, 2 sc, 1 sc in corner 2ch-sp, slst in first 2ch-sp to join, turn. (64 sts)

Round 10: 1 ch, 1 sc in corner 2ch-sp, 3 sc, 3 ch, skip 3ch-sp, 6 sc, 3 ch, skip 3ch-sp, 3 sc, (1 sc, 2 ch, 1 sc) in 2ch-sp, 3 sc, 3 ch, skip 3ch-sp, 6 sc, 3 ch, skip 3ch-sp, 3 sc, (1 sc, 2 ch, 1 sc) in 2ch-sp, 3 sc, 3 ch, skip

3ch-sp, 6 sc, 3 ch, skip 3ch-sp, 3 sc, (1 sc, 2 ch, 1 sc) in 2ch-sp, 3 sc, 3 ch, skip 3ch-sp, 6 sc, 3 ch, skip 3ch-sp, 3 sc, (1 sc, 2 ch) in corner 2ch-sp, slst in first st from back to front to join, turn. (72 sts)

Round 11: Change to colour 2, slst in corner 2ch-sp, (2 ch, 1 sc) in same 2ch-sp, 2 sc, [3 ch, skip 2 sts, 2 mdc, 4 sc] twice, (1 sc, 2 ch, 1 sc) in 2ch-sp, [4 sc, 2 mdc, 3 ch, skip 2 sts] twice, 2 sc, (1 sc, 2 ch, 1 sc) in 2ch-sp, 2 sc, [3 ch, skip 2 sts, 2 mdc, 4 sc] twice, (1 sc, 2 ch, 1 sc) in 2ch-sp, [4 sc, 2 mdc, 3 ch, skip 2 sts] twice, 2 sc, 1 sc in corner 2ch-sp, slst in first 2ch-sp, turn. (80 sts)

Round 12: 1 ch, 1 sc in corner 2ch-sp, 3 sc, [3 ch, skip 3ch-sp, 6 sc] twice, 1 sc, (1 sc, 2 ch, 1 sc) in 2ch-sp, 1 sc, [6 sc, 3 ch, skip 3ch-sp] twice, 3 sc, (1 sc, 2 ch, 1 sc) in 2ch-sp, 3 sc, [3 ch, skip 3ch-sp, 6 sc] twice, 1 sc, (1 sc, 2 ch, 1 sc) in 2ch-sp, 1 sc, [6 sc, 3 ch, skip 3ch-sp] twice, 3 sc, (1 sc, 2 ch) in corner 2ch-sp, slst in first st from back to front to join, turn. (88 sts)

Round 13: Change to colour 1, slst in corner 2ch-sp, (2 ch, 1 sc) in same 2ch-sp, 2 sc, [3 ch, skip 2 sts, 2 mdc, 4 sc] twice, 3 ch, skip 2 sts, 2 sc, (1 sc, 2 ch, 1 sc) in 2ch-sp, 2 sc, 3 ch, skip 2 sts, [4 sc, 2 mdc, 3 ch, skip 2 sts] twice, 2 sc, (1 sc, 2 ch, 1 sc) in 2ch-sp, 2 sc, [3 ch, skip 2 sts, 2 mdc, 4 sc] twice, 3 ch, skip 2 sts, 2 sc, (1 sc, 2 ch,

1 sc) in 2ch-sp, 2 sc, 3 ch, skip 2 sts, [4 sc, 2 mdc, 3 ch, skip 2 sts] twice, 2 sc, 1 sc in corner 2ch-sp, slst in first 2ch-sp to join, turn. (96 sts)

Round 14: 1 ch, 1 sc in corner 2ch-sp, 3 sc, [3 ch, skip 3ch-sp, 6 sc] twice, 3 ch, skip 3ch-sp, 3 sc, (1 sc, 2 ch, 1 sc) in 2ch-sp, 3 sc, [3 ch, skip 3ch-sp, 6 sc] twice, 3 ch, skip 3ch-sp, 3 sc, (1 sc, 2 ch, 1 sc) in 2ch-sp, 3 sc, [3 ch, skip 3ch-sp, 6 sc] twice, 3 ch, skip 3ch-sp, 3 sc, (1 sc, 2 ch, 1 sc) in 2ch-sp, 3 sc, [3 ch, skip 3ch-sp, 6 sc] twice, 3 ch, skip 3ch-sp, 3 sc, (1 sc, 2 ch) in corner 2ch-sp, slst in first st from back to front to join, turn. (104 sts)

continued on next page >

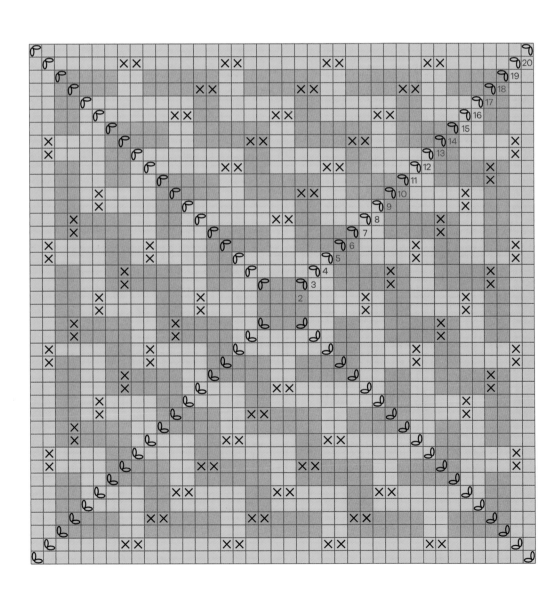

KEY

Colour 1

Colour 2

2 chain (2 ch)

mosaic double crochet (mdc)

Each square represents one stitch on one round.

Odd numbered (RS) rounds are worked in an anti-clockwise direction. Even numbered (WS) rounds are worked in a clockwise direction. Turn after every round.

Chart starts with magic ring of 4 sc using colour 1 (middle 4 squares in colour 1 count as Round 1 on chart), then start Round 2 using colour 1 working in clockwise direction.

Round 15: Change to colour 2, slst in corner 2ch-sp, (2 ch, 1 sc) in same 2ch-sp, 2 sc, [3 ch, skip 2 sts, 2 mdc, 4 sc] 3 times, (1 sc, 2 ch, 1 sc) in 2ch-sp, [4 sc, 2 mdc, 3 ch, skip 2 sts] 3 times, 2 sc, (1 sc, 2 ch, 1 sc) in 2ch-sp, 2 sc, [3 ch, skip 2 sts, 2 mdc, 4 sc] 3 times, (1 sc, 2 ch, 1 sc) in 2ch-sp, [4 sc, 2 mdc, 3 ch, skip 2 sts] 3 times, 2 sc, 1 sc in corner 2ch-sp, slst in first 2ch-sp to join, turn. (112 sts)

Round 16: 1 ch, 1 sc in corner 2ch-sp, 3 sc, [3 ch, skip 3ch-sp, 6 sc] 3 times, 1 sc, (1 sc, 2 ch, 1 sc) in 2ch-sp, 1 sc, [6 sc, 3 ch, skip 3ch-sp] 3 times, 3 sc, (1 sc, 2 ch, 1 sc) in 2ch-sp, 3 sc, [3 ch, skip 3ch-sp, 6 sc] 3 times, 1 sc, (1 sc, 2 ch, 1 sc) in 2ch-sp, 1 sc, [6 sc, 3 ch, skip 3ch-sp] 3 times, 3 sc, (1 sc, 2 ch) in corner 2ch-sp, slst in first st from back to front to join, turn. (120 sts)

Round 17: Change to colour 1, slst in corner 2ch-sp, (2 ch, 1 sc) in same 2ch-sp, 2 sc, [3 ch, skip 2 sts, 2 mdc, 4 sc] 3 times, 3 ch, skip 2 sts, 2 sc, (1 sc, 2 ch, 1 sc) in 2ch-sp, 2 sc, 3 ch, skip 2 sts, [4 sc, 2 mdc, 3 ch, skip 2 sts] 3 times, 2 sc, (1 sc, 2 ch, 1 sc) in 2ch-sp, 2 sc, [3 ch, skip 2 sts, 2 mdc, 4 sc] 3 times, 3 ch, skip 2 sts, 2 sc, (1 sc, 2 ch, 1 sc) in 2ch-sp, 2 sc, 3 ch, skip 2 sts, [4 sc, 2 mdc, 3 ch, skip 2 sts] 3 times, 2 sc, 1 sc in corner 2ch-sp, slst in first 2ch-sp to join, turn. (128 sts)

Round 18: 1 ch, 1 sc in corner 2ch-sp, 3 sc, [3 ch, skip 3ch-sp, 6 sc] 3 times, 3 ch, skip 3ch-sp, 3 sc, (1 sc, 2 ch, 1 sc) in 2ch-sp, 3 sc, [3 ch, skip 3ch-sp, 6 sc] 3 times, 3 ch, skip 3ch-sp, 3 sc, (1 sc, 2 ch, 1 sc) in 2ch-sp, 3 sc, [3 ch, skip 3ch-sp, 6 sc] 3 times, 3 ch, skip 3ch-sp, 3 sc, (1 sc, 2 ch, 1 sc) in 2ch-sp, 3 sc, [3 ch, skip 3ch-sp, 6 sc] 3 times, 3 ch, skip 3ch-sp, 3 sc, (1 sc, 2 ch) in corner 2ch-sp, slst in

first st from back to front to join, turn. (136 sts)

Round 19: Change to colour 2, slst in corner 2ch-sp, (2 ch, 1 sc) in same 2ch-sp, *4 sc, [2 mdc, 6 sc] 3 times, 2 mdc, 4 sc, (1 sc, 2 ch, 1 sc) in 2ch-sp; rep from * twice more, 4 sc, [2 mdc, 6 sc] 3 times, 2 mdc, 4 sc, 1 sc in corner 2ch-sp, slst in first 2ch-sp to join, turn. (144 sts)

Round 20: 1 ch, 1 sc in corner 2ch-sp, *1 sc in each st to 2ch-sp, (1 sc, 2 ch, 1 sc) in 2ch-sp; rep from * twice more, 1 sc in each st to 2ch-sp, (1 sc, 2 ch) in corner 2ch-sp, slst in first st from back to front to join, turn. (152 sts)

Fasten off and weave in ends.

TILED BRICKS

DESIGNER: CAROL IBBETSON

YARN

Lion Brand 24/7 Cotton, worsted (aran), in foll shades:
Colour 1: Denim (108)
Colour 2: Aqua (102)

HOOK

US size E/4 (3.5mm) hook

GAUGE (TENSION)

A single motif measures approx 8in (20cm) using a US size E/4 (3.5mm) hook.

SPECIAL ABBREVIATION

mdc, double crochet worked in skipped st three rows below

NOTES

Motif is worked in inset mosaic crochet in rows.
Two rows are worked in each colour.
Carry unused yarn across right-hand side of work.

PATTERN

Using E/4 hook and colour 1, 34 ch.

Row 1 (RS): 1 sc in 2nd ch from hook and each ch to end, turn. (33 sts)

Rows 2 to 4: 1 ch (does not count as st throughout), 1 sc in each st to end, turn.

Row 5: Using colour 2, 1 ch, 4 sc, *[2 ch, skip 1 st, 1 sc] 3 times, 2 sc, rep from * twice more, [2 ch, skip 1 st, 1 sc] twice, 1 sc, turn.

Row 6: 1 ch, 1 sc, [1 sc, 2 ch, skip 2ch-sp] twice, *2 sc, [1 sc, 2 ch, skip 2ch-sp] 3 times, rep from * twice more, 4 sc, turn.

Row 7: Using colour 1, 1 ch, 4 sc, *[1 mdc, 2 ch, skip 1 st] twice, 1 mdc, 3 sc; rep from * twice more, [1 mdc, 2 ch, skip 1 st] twice, 1 sc, turn.

Row 8: 1 ch, 1 sc, [2 ch, skip 2ch-sp, 1 sc] twice, *4 ch, [2 ch, skip 2ch-sp, 1 sc] twice, rep from * twice more, 4 sc, turn.

Row 9: Using colour 2, 1 ch, 4 sc, *[2 ch, skip 1 st, 1 mdc] twice, 2 ch, skip 1 st, 3 sc, rep from * twice more, [2 ch, skip 1 st, 1 mdc] twice, 1 sc, turn.

Row 10: 1 ch, 1 sc, [1 sc, 2 ch, skip 2ch-sp] twice, *2 sc, [1 sc, 2 ch, skip 2ch-sp] 3 times, rep from * twice more, 4 sc, turn.

Row 11: Using colour 1, 1 ch, 4 sc, *[1 mdc, 1 sc] twice, 1 mdc, 3 sc; rep from * twice more, 1 mdc, 1 sc, 1 mdc, 2 sc, turn.

Row 12: 1 ch, 1 sc in each st, turn.

Row 13: Using colour 2, 1 ch, 2 sc, 2 ch, skip 1 st, 1 sc, *2 ch, skip 1 st, 3 sc, [2 ch, skip 1 st, 1 sc] twice, rep from * twice more, 2 ch, skip 1 st, 4 sc, turn.

Row 14: 1 ch, 4 sc, 2 ch, skip 2ch-sp, *[1 sc, 2 ch, skip 2ch-sp] twice, 3 sc, 2 ch, skip 2ch-sp, rep from * twice more, 1 sc, 2 ch, skip 2ch-sp, 2 sc, turn.

Row 15: Using colour 1, 1 ch, 1 sc, 2 ch, skip 1 st, 1 mdc, 2 ch, skip 1 st, *1 mdc, 3 sc, [1 mdc, 2 ch, skip 1 st] twice; rep from * twice more, 1 mdc, 4 sc, turn.

Row 16: 1 ch, 5 sc, *[2 ch, skip 2ch-sp, 1 sc] twice, 4 sc, rep from * twice more, [2 ch, skip 2ch-sp, 1 sc] twice, turn.

Row 17: Using colour 2, 1 ch, 1 sc, 1 mdc, 2 ch, skip 1 st, 1 mdc, *2 ch, skip 1 st, 3 sc, [2 ch, skip 1 st, 1 mdc] twice, rep from * twice more, 2 ch, skip 1 st, 4 sc, turn.

Row 18: As Row 14.

Row 19: Using colour 1, 1 ch, 2 sc, 1 mdc, 1 sc, *1 mdc, 3 sc, [1 mdc, 1 sc] twice; rep from * twice more, 1 mdc, 4 sc, turn.

Row 20: 1 ch, 1 sc in each st, turn.

Rows 21 to 36: As Rows 5 to 20.

Rows 37 to 44: As Rows 5 to 12.

Rows 45 and 46: As Rows 3 and 4.

Fasten off and weave in ends.

Each square represents one stitch and two rows.

Odd numbered (RS) rows are worked from right to left. Even numbered (WS) rows are worked from left to right.

RS row numbers are on right-hand side and WS row numbers on left. Remember that every chart row represents two rows worked in same colour.

Work section within red lines number of times stated.

KEY

■ Colour 1

□ Colour 2

✗ mosaic double crochet (mdc)

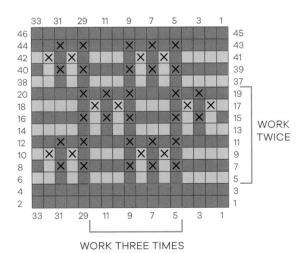

WORK THREE TIMES

WORK TWICE

TUNNEL VISION

DESIGNER: CAROL IBBETSON

YARN

Lion Brand 24/7 Cotton, worsted (aran), in foll shades:
Colour 1: Red (113)
Colour 2: White (100)

HOOK

US size E/4 (3.5mm) hook

GAUGE (TENSION)

A single motif measures approx 8in (20cm) using a US size E/4 (3.5mm) hook.

SPECIAL ABBREVIATION

mdc, double crochet worked in skipped st three rows below

NOTES

Motif is worked in inset mosaic crochet in rows.
Two rows are worked in each colour, work is turned after EACH row.
Carry unused yarn across right-hand side of work.

PATTERN

Using E/4 hook and colour 1, 34 ch.

Row 1 (RS): 1 sc in 2nd ch from hook and in each ch to end, turn. (33 sts)

Row 2 (WS): 1 ch [does not count as st throughout], 1 sc in each st to end, turn.

Row 3: Using colour 2, 1 ch, [1 sc, 2 ch, skip 1 st] 3 times, 5 sc, 2 ch, skip 1 st, [1 sc, 2 ch, skip 1 st] 5 times, 5 sc, [2 ch, skip 1 st, 1 sc] 3 times, turn.

Row 4: 1 ch, [1 sc, 2 ch, skip 2ch-sp] 3 times, 5 sc, 2 ch, skip 2ch-sp, [1 sc, 2 ch, skip 2ch-sp] 5 times, 5 sc, [2 ch, skip 2ch-sp, 1 sc] 3 times, turn.

Row 5: Using colour 1, 1 ch, 1 sc, [1 mdc, 2 ch, skip 1 st] twice, 1 mdc, 5 sc, [1 mdc, 2 ch, skip 1 st] 5 times, 1 mdc, 5 sc, [1 mdc, 2 ch, skip 1 st] twice, 1 mdc, 1 sc, turn.

Row 6: 1 ch, 1 sc, [1 sc, 2 ch, skip 2ch-sp] twice, 7 sc, 2 ch, skip 2ch-sp, [1 sc, 2 ch, skip 2ch-sp] 4 times, 7 sc, [2 ch, skip 2ch-sp, 1 sc] twice, 1 sc, turn.

Row 7: Using colour 2, 1 ch, 1 sc, [2 ch, skip 1 st, 1 mdc] twice, 7 sc, [1 mdc, 2 ch, skip 1 st] 4 times, 1 mdc, 7 sc, [1 mdc, 2 ch, skip 1 st] twice, 1 sc, turn.

Row 8: 1 ch, [1 sc, 2 ch, skip 2ch-sp] twice, 9 sc, 2 ch, skip 2ch-sp, [1 sc, 2 ch, skip 2ch-sp] 3 times, 9 sc, [2 ch, skip 2ch-sp, 1 sc] twice, turn.

Row 9: Using colour 1, 1 ch, 1 sc, 1 mdc, 2 ch, skip 1 st, 1 mdc, 9 sc, [1 mdc, 2 ch, skip 1 st] 3 times, 1 mdc, 9 sc, 1 mdc, 2 ch, skip 1 st, 1 mdc, 1 sc, turn.

Row 10: 1 ch, 2 sc, 2 ch, skip 2ch-sp, 11 sc, 2 ch, skip 2ch-sp, [1 sc, 2 ch, skip 2ch-sp] twice, 11 sc, 2 ch, skip 2ch-sp, 2 sc, turn.

Row 11: Using colour 2, 1 ch, 1 sc, 2 ch, skip 1 st, 1 mdc, 11 sc, [1 mdc, 2 ch, skip 1 st] twice, 1 mdc, 11 sc, 1 mdc, 2 ch, skip 1 st, 1 sc, turn.

Row 12: 1 ch, 1 sc, 2 ch, skip 2ch-sp, 13 sc, 2 ch, skip 2ch-sp, 1 sc, 2 ch, skip 2ch-sp, 13 sc, 2 ch, skip 2ch-sp, 1 sc, turn.

Row 13: Using colour 1, 1 ch, [1 sc, 1 mdc, 13 sc, 1 mdc] twice, 1 sc, turn.

Row 14: 1 ch, 1 sc in each st to end, turn.

Row 15: Using colour 2, 1 ch, [1 sc, 2 ch, skip 1 st] 7 times, 1 sc, 4 ch, skip 3 sts, [1 sc, 2 ch, skip 1 st] 7 times, 1 sc, turn.

Row 16: 1 ch, [1 sc, 2 ch, skip 2ch-sp] 7 times, 1 sc, 4 ch, skip 4ch-sp, [1 sc, 2 ch, skip 2ch-sp] 7 times, 1 sc, turn.

Row 17: Using colour 1, 1 ch, 1 sc, [1 mdc, 2 ch, skip 1 st] 7 times, 3 mdc, [2 ch, skip 1 st, 1 mdc] 7 times, 1 sc, turn.

Row 18: 1 ch, 1 sc, [1 sc, 2 ch, skip 2ch-sp] 7 times, 4 ch, skip 4ch-sp, [1 sc, 2 ch, skip 2ch-sp] 7 times, 1 sc, turn.

Row 19: Using colour 2, 1 ch, 2 sc, [1 mdc, 2 ch, skip 1 st] 6 times, 1 mdc, 3 sc, [1 mdc, 2 ch, skip 1 st] 6 times, 1 mdc, 2 sc, turn.

Row 20: 1 ch, 3 sc, [2 ch, skip 2ch-sp, 1 sc] 6 times, 3 sc, [1 sc, 2 ch, skip 2ch-sp] 6 times, 3 sc, turn.

Row 21: Using colour 1, 1 ch, 3 sc, [1 mdc, 2 ch, skip 1 st] 5 times, 1 mdc, 5 sc, 1 mdc, [2 ch, skip 1 st, 1 mdc] 5 times, 3 sc, turn.

Row 22: 1 ch, 4 sc, [2 ch, skip 2ch-sp, 1 sc] 5 times, 5 sc, [1 sc, 2 ch, skip 2ch-sp] 5 times, 4 sc, turn.

Row 23: Using colour 2, 1 ch, 4 sc, [1 mdc, 2 ch, skip 1 st] 4 times, 1 mdc, 7 sc, [1 mdc, 2 ch, skip 1 st] 4 times, 1 mdc, 4 sc, turn.

Row 24: 1 ch, 5 sc, [2 ch, skip 2ch-sp, 1 sc] 4 times, 7 sc, [1 sc, 2 ch, skip 2ch-sp] 4 times, 5 sc, turn.

Row 25: Using colour 1, 1 ch, 5 sc, [1 mdc, 2 ch, skip 1 st] 3 times, 1 mdc, 9 sc, 1 mdc, [2 ch, skip 1 st, 1 mdc] 3 times, 5 sc, turn.

Row 26: 1 ch, 6 sc, [2 ch, skip 2ch-sp, 1 sc] 3 times, 9 sc, [1 sc, 2 ch, skip 2ch-sp] 3 times, 6 sc, turn.

Row 27: Using colour 2, 1 ch, 6 sc, [1 mdc, 2 ch, skip 1 st] twice, 1 mdc, 11 sc, [1 mdc, 2 ch, skip 1 st] twice, 1 mdc, 6 sc, turn.

Row 28: 1 ch, 7 sc, [2 ch, skip 2ch-sp, 1 sc] twice, 11 sc, [1 sc, 2 ch, skip 2ch-sp] twice, 7 sc, turn.

Row 29: Using colour 1, 1 ch, 7 sc, 1 mdc, 2 ch, skip 1 st, 1 mdc, 13 sc, 1 mdc, 2 ch, skip 1 st, 1 mdc, 7 sc, turn.

Row 30: 1 ch, 1 sc in each st to end, turn.

Row 31: Using colour 2, 1 ch, [1 sc, 2 ch, skip 1 st] 3 times, 1 sc, 4 ch, skip 3 sts, [1 sc, 2 ch, skip 1 st] 6 times, 1 sc, 4 ch, skip 3 sts, [1 sc, 2 ch, skip 1 st] 3 times, 1 sc, turn.

Row 32: 1 ch, [1 sc, 2 ch, skip 2ch-sp] 3 times, 1 sc, 4 ch, skip 4ch-sp, [1 sc, 2 ch, skip 2ch-sp] 6 times, 1 sc, 4 ch, skip 4ch-sp, [1 sc, 2 ch, skip 2ch-sp] 3 times, 1 sc, turn.

Row 33: Using colour 1, 1 ch, 1 sc, [1 mdc, 2 ch, skip 1 st] 3 times, 3 mdc, [2 ch, skip 1 st, 1 mdc] 6 times, 2 ch, skip 1 st, 3 mdc, [2 ch, skip 1 st, 1 sc] 3 times, 1 sc, turn.

Row 34: 1 ch, 1 sc, [1 sc, 2 ch, skip 2ch-sp] 3 times, 3 sc, [2 ch, skip 2ch-sp, 1 sc] 6 times, 2 ch, skip 2ch-sp, 3 sc, [2 ch, skip 2ch-sp, 1 sc] 3 times, 1 sc, turn.

Row 35: Using colour 2, 1 ch, [1 sc, 2 ch, skip 1 st] 3 times, 1 mdc, 3 sc, 1 mdc, 2 ch, skip 1 st, [1 sc, 2 ch, skip 1 st] 5 times, 1 mdc, 3 sc, 1 mdc, [2 ch, skip 1 st, 1 sc] 3 times, turn.

Rows 36 to 46: As Rows 4 to 14.

Fasten off and weave in ends.

Each square represents one stitch and two rows.

Odd numbered (RS) rows are worked from right to left. Even numbered (WS) rows are worked from left to right.

RS row numbers are on right-hand side and WS row numbers on left. Remember that every chart row represents two rows worked in same colour.

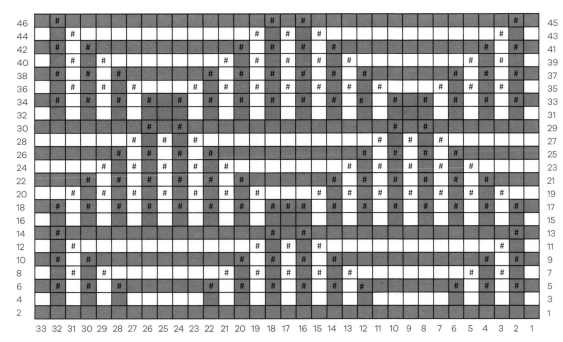

KEY

█ Colour 1

□ Colour 2

\# mosaic double crochet (mdc)

OFFSET SQUARES

DESIGNER: CAROL IBBETSON

· · · · · · · · · · · · · · · · ·

YARN

Lion Brand 24/7 Cotton, worsted (aran), in foll shades:

Colour 1: Black (153)

Colour 2: Mint (156)

HOOK

US size E/4 (3.5mm) hook

GAUGE (TENSION)

A single motif measures approx 8in (20cm) using a US size E/4 (3.5mm) hook.

SPECIAL ABBREVIATION

mdc, double crochet worked in skipped st three rows below

NOTES

Motif is worked in inset mosaic crochet in rows.

Two rows are worked in each colour.

Carry unused yarn across right-hand side of work.

PATTERN

Using E/4 hook and colour 1, 34 ch.

Row 1 (RS): 1 sc in 2nd ch from hook and each ch to end, turn. (33 sts)

Row 2 (WS): 1 ch [does not count as st throughout], 1 sc in each st to end, turn.

Row 3: Using colour 2, 1 ch, 7 sc, 2 ch, skip 1 st, 1 sc, 2 ch, skip 1 st, 13 sc, 2 ch, skip 1 st, 1 sc, 2 ch, skip 1 st, 7 sc, turn.

Row 4: 1 ch, 7 sc, 2 ch, skip 2ch-sp, 1 sc, 2 ch, skip 2ch-sp, 13 sc, 2 ch, skip 2ch-sp, 1 sc, 2 ch, skip 2ch-sp, 7 sc, turn.

Row 5: Using colour 1, 1 ch, 7 sc, [1 mdc, 2 ch, skip 1 st] twice, 11 sc, [2 ch, skip 1 st, 1 mdc] twice, 7 sc, turn.

Row 6: 1 ch, 8 sc, 2 ch, skip 2ch-sp, 1 sc, 2 ch, skip 2ch-sp, 11 sc, 2 ch, skip 2ch-sp, 1 sc, 2 ch, skip 2ch-sp, 8 sc, turn.

Row 7: Using colour 2, 1 ch, 8 sc, [1 mdc, 2 ch, skip 1 st] twice, 9 sc, [2 ch, skip 1 st, 1 mdc] twice, 8 sc, turn.

Row 8: 1 ch, 9 sc, 2 ch, skip 2ch-sp, 1 sc, 2 ch, skip 2ch-sp, 9 sc, 2 ch, skip 2ch-sp, 1 sc, 2 ch, skip 2ch-sp, 9 sc, turn.

Row 9: Using colour 1, 1 ch, 9 sc, [1 mdc, 2 ch, skip 1 st] twice, 7 sc, [2 ch, skip 1 st, 1 mdc] twice, 9 sc, turn.

Row 10: 1 ch, 10 sc, 2 ch, skip 2ch-sp, 1 sc, 2 ch, skip 2ch-sp, 7 sc, 2 ch, skip 2ch-sp, 1 sc, 2 ch, skip 2ch-sp, 10 sc, turn.

Row 11: Using colour 2, 1 ch, 9 sc, [2 ch, skip 1 st, 1 mdc] twice, 2 ch, skip 1 st, 5 sc, [2 ch, skip 1 st, 1 mdc] twice, 2 ch, skip 1 st, 9 sc, turn.

Row 12: 1 ch, 9 sc, [2 ch, skip 2ch-sp, 1 sc] twice, 2 ch, skip 2ch-sp, 5 sc, [2 ch, skip 2ch-sp, 1 sc] twice, 2 ch, skip 2ch-sp, 9 sc, turn.

Row 13: Using colour 1, 1 ch, 9 sc, [1 mdc, 2 ch, skip 1 st] twice, 1 mdc, 5 sc, 1 mdc, [2 ch, skip 1 st, 1 mdc] twice, 9 sc, turn.

Row 14: As Row 10.

Row 15: Using colour 2, 1 ch, 9 sc, [2 ch, skip 1 st, 1 mdc] twice, 7 sc, [1 mdc, 2 ch, skip 1 st] twice, 9 sc, turn.

Row 16: As Row 8.

Row 17: Using colour 1, 1 ch, 8 sc, [2 ch, skip 1 st, 1 mdc] twice, 9 sc, [1 mdc, 2 ch, skip 1 st] twice, 8 sc, turn.

Row 18: As Row 6.

Row 19: Using colour 2, 1 ch, 7 sc, [2 ch, skip 1 st, 1 mdc] twice, 11 sc, [1 mdc, 2 ch, skip 1 st] twice, 7 sc, turn.

Row 20: As Row 4.

Row 21: Using colour 1, 1 ch, 6 sc, [2 ch, skip 1 st, 1 mdc] twice, 13 sc, [1 mdc, 2 ch, skip 1 st] twice, 6 sc, turn.

Row 22: 1 ch, 6 sc, 2 ch, skip 2ch-sp, sc, 2 ch, skip 2ch-sp, 15 sc, 2 ch, skip 2ch-sp, sc, 2 ch, skip 2ch-sp, 6 sc, turn.

Row 23: Using colour 2, 1 ch, 5 sc, [2 ch, skip 1 st, 1 mdc] twice, 2 ch, skip 1 st, 13 sc, [2 ch, skip 1 st, 1 mdc] twice, 2 ch, skip 1 st, 5 sc, turn.

Row 24: 1 ch, 5 sc, [2 ch, skip 2ch-sp, sc] twice, 2 ch, skip 2ch-sp, 13 sc, [2 ch, skip 2ch-sp, sc] twice, 2 ch, skip 2ch-sp, 5 sc, turn.

Row 25: Using colour 1, 1 ch, 5 sc, [1 mdc, 2 ch, skip 1 st] twice, 1 mdc, 13 sc, [1 mdc, 2 ch, skip 1 st] twice, 1 mdc, 5 sc, turn.

Row 26: As Row 22.

Row 27: Using colour 2, 1 ch, 6 sc, [1 mdc, 2 ch, skip 1 st] twice, 13 sc, [2 ch, skip 1 st, 1 mdc] twice, 6 sc, turn.

Row 28: As Row 4.

Rows 29 to 44: As Rows 5 to 20.

Row 45: Using colour 1, 1 ch, 7 sc, 1 mdc, 1 sc, 1 mdc, 13 sc, 1 mdc, 1 sc, 1 mdc, 7 sc, turn.

Row 46: 1 ch, 1 sc in each st to end.

Fasten off and weave in ends.

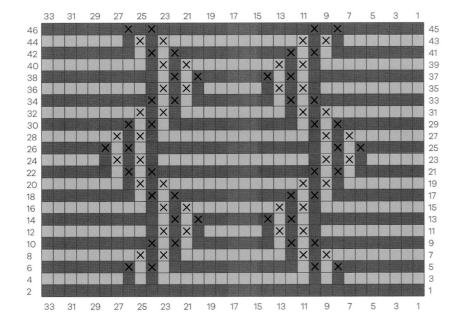

KEY

■ Colour 1

□ Colour 2

✕ mosaic double crochet (mdc)

Each square represents one stitch and two rows.

Odd numbered (RS) rows are worked from right to left. Even numbered (WS) rows are worked from left to right.

RS row numbers are on right-hand side and WS row numbers on left. Remember that every chart row represents two rows worked in same colour.

GRECIAN

DESIGNER: SARAH SHRIMPTON

YARN

Rico Creative Cotton Aran, worsted (aran), in foll shades:
Colour 1: Royal (39)
Colour 2: White (80)

HOOK

US size G/6 (4mm) hook

GAUGE (TENSION)

A single motif measures approx 5¾in (14.5cm) using a US size G/6 (4mm) hook.

SPECIAL ABBREVIATION

mdc, double crochet worked in skipped st three rows below

NOTES

Motif is worked in inset mosaic in rows. Two rows are worked in each colour. Except on first row, change colour at beg of every odd row and carry unused yarn up back of motif.
From Row 5 onward work odd number rows as given, but in even rows work an sc in place of each mdc.

PATTERN

Using G/6 hook and colour 1, 24 ch.

Rows 1 and 2: 1 ch (does not count as st throughout), 1 sc in each st across, turn. (24 sts)

Rows 3 and 4: Using colour 2, 1 ch, 7 sc, [2 ch, skip 2 sts, 2 sc] 3 times, 5 sc, turn.

Rows 5 and 6: Using colour 1, 1 ch, 1 sc, 2 ch, skip 2 sts, 4 sc, [2 mdc, 2 ch, skip 2 sts] twice, 2 mdc, 4 sc, 2 ch, skip 2 sts, 1 sc, turn.

Rows 7 and 8: Using colour 2, 1 ch, 1 sc, 2 mdc, 2 ch, skip 2 sts, 4 sc, 2 mdc, 2 ch, skip 2 sts, 2 mdc, 4 sc, 2 ch, skip 2 sts, 2 mdc, 1 sc, turn.

Rows 9 and 10: Using colour 1, 1 ch, 3 sc, 2 mdc, 2 ch, skip 2 sts, 4 sc, 2 mdc, 4 sc, 2 ch, skip 2 sts, 2 mdc, 3 sc, turn.

Rows 11 and 12: Using colour 2, 1 ch, 5 sc, 2 mdc, 2 ch, skip 2 sts, 6 sc, 2 ch, skip 2 sts, 2 mdc, 5 sc, turn.

Rows 13 and 14: Using colour 1, 1 ch, 7 sc, 2 mdc, 2 ch, skip 2 sts, 2 sc, 2 ch, skip 2 sts, 2 mdc, 7 sc, turn.

Rows 15 and 16: Using colour 2, 1 ch, 7 sc, 2 ch, skip 2 sts, 2 mdc, 2 sc, 2 mdc, 2 ch, skip 2 sts, 7 sc, turn.

Rows 17 and 18: Using colour 1, 1 ch, 5 sc, 2 ch, skip 2 sts, 2 mdc, 6 sc, 2 mdc, 2 ch, skip 2 sts, 5 sc, turn.

Rows 19 and 20: Using colour 2, 1 ch, 3 sc, 2 ch, skip 2 sts, 2 mdc, 4 sc, 2 ch, skip 2 sts, 4 sc, 2 mdc, 2 ch, skip 2 sts, 3 sc, turn.

Rows 21 and 22: Using colour 1, 1 ch, 1 sc, 2 ch, skip 2 sts, 2 mdc, 4 sc, 2 ch, skip 2 sts, 2 mdc, 2 ch, skip 2 sts, 4 sc, 2 mdc, 2 ch, skip 2 sts, 1 sc, turn.

Rows 23 and 24: Using colour 2, 1 ch, 1 sc, 2 mdc, 4 sc, 2 ch, skip 2 sts, 2 mdc, 2 ch, skip 2 sts, 2 mdc, 2 ch, skip 2 sts, 4 sc, 2 mdc, 1 sc, turn.

EDGING

Round 1 (RS): Join colour 1 to right edge of Row 1, 24 sc evenly along edge, 1 ch (corner), turn work 90 degrees, 1 sc in same st, 7 sc, 2 mdc, 2 sc, 2 mdc, 2 sc, 2 mdc, 7 sc, 1 ch (corner), turn work 90 degrees, 1 sc in same st, 23 sc evenly along left edge, 1 ch (corner), sl st in next st.

Fasten off colour 1.

Round 2 (RS): Join colour 1 to bottom-right edge, work sc around three sides (not bottom edge).

Fasten off.

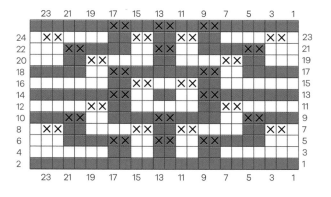

KEY

■ Colour 1

□ Colour 2

✕ mosaic double crochet (mdc)

Each square represents one stitch and two rows.

Odd numbered (RS) rows are worked from right to left.

Even numbered (WS) rows are worked from left to right.

RS row numbers are on left-hand side and WS row numbers on right. Remember that every chart row represents two rows worked in same colour.

WILDFLOWER

DESIGNER: CATHERINE NORONHA

YARN

Stylecraft Special DK, light worsted (DK), in foll shades:

Colour 1: Boysenberry (1828)
Colour 2: Mustard (1823)
Colour 3: Petrol (1708)
Colour 4: Cream (1005)

HOOK

US size E/4 (3.5mm) hook

GAUGE (TENSION)

A single motif measures approx 8in (20cm) using a US size E/4 (3.5mm) hook.

NOTES

Motif is worked in tapestry crochet in rounds.

Change to next colour on last yoh of prev st. Carry unused yarn across work and crochet over except when you make a FPdc, in which case carry unused yarn across WS (behind FPdc). Make joining slst at end of each round around unused yarn to carry it up ready for next round. Each round of motif starts with 3 ch (apart from Round 1 which starts with 4 ch), which counts as 1 dc, 1 ch. This is final dc of one side of motif, plus 1 ch to form first corner ch-sp. Other corner ch-sps are formed of 2 ch.

PATTERN

Change colour foll chart.

Using E/4 hook and colour 1, make a magic ring.

Round 1 (RS): Working in ring, 4 ch (counts as 1 dc, 1 ch), [3 dc, 2 ch] 3 times, 2 dc, slst in 3rd ch of beg 4-ch to join, slst in ch-sp. (12 dc, 1 x 1ch-sp corner, 3 x 2ch-sp corners)

Round 2: 3 ch (counts as 1 dc, 1 ch throughout), 2 dc in ch-sp, *1 dcBLO, 1 FPdc, 1 dcBLO, (2 dc, 2 ch, 2 dc) in 2ch-sp; rep from * twice more; 1 dcBLO, 1 FPdc, 1 dcBLO, 1 dc in ch-sp, slst in 2nd ch of beg 3-ch to join, slst in ch-sp. (28 dc, 1 x 1ch-sp corner, 3 x 2ch-sp corners)

Round 3: 3 ch, 2 dc in ch-sp, *3 dcBLO, 1 FPdc, 3 dcBLO, (2 dc, 2 ch, 2 dc) in 2ch-sp; rep from * twice more; 3 dcBLO, 1 FPdc, 3 dcBLO, 1 dc in ch-sp, slst in 2nd ch of beg 3-ch to join, slst in ch-sp. (44 dc, 1 x 1ch-sp corner, 3 x 2ch-sp corners)

Round 4: 3 ch, 2 dc in ch-sp, *5 dcBLO, 1 FPdc, 5 dcBLO, (2 dc, 2 ch, 2 dc) in 2ch-sp; rep from * twice more; 5 dcBLO, 1 FPdc, 5 dcBLO, 1 dc in ch-sp, slst in 2nd ch of beg 3-ch to join, slst in ch-sp. (60 dc, 1 x 1ch-sp corner, 3 x 2ch-sp corners)

continued on next page >

Chart shows one side of square; it should be repeated four times on each round.

Read chart from bottom to top, right to left.

Each square represents one stitch.

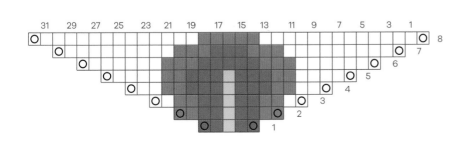

KEY

- Colour 1
- Colour 2
- Colour 3
- Colour 4
- O chain (ch)

Round 5: 3 ch, 2 dc in ch-sp, *7 dcBLO, 1 FPdc, 7 dcBLO, (2 dc, 2 ch, 2 dc) in 2ch-sp; rep from * twice more; 7 dcBLO, 1 FPdc, 7 dcBLO, 1 dc in ch-sp, slst in 2nd ch of beg 3-ch to join, slst in ch-sp. (76 dc, 1 x 1ch-sp corner, 3 x 2ch-sp corners)

Round 6: 3 ch, 2 dc in ch-sp, *19 dcBLO, (2 dc, 2 ch, 2 dc) in 2ch-sp; rep from * twice more; 19 dcBLO, 1 dc in ch-sp, slst in 2nd ch of beg 3-ch to join, slst in ch-sp. (92 dc, 1 x 1ch-sp corner, 3 x 2ch-sp corners)

Round 7: 3 ch, 2 dc in ch-sp, *23 dcBLO, (2 dc, 2 ch, 2 dc) in 2ch-sp; rep from * twice more; 23 dcBLO, 1 dc in ch-sp, slst in 2nd ch of beg 3-ch to join, slst in ch-sp. (108 dc, 1 x 1ch-sp corner, 3 x 2ch-sp corners)

Round 8: 3 ch, 2 dc in ch-sp, *27 dcBLO, (2 dc, 2 ch, 2 tr) in 2ch-sp; rep from * twice more; 27 dcBLO, 1 dc in ch-sp, slst in 2nd ch of beg 3-ch to join. (124 dc, 1 x 1ch-sp corner, 3 x 2ch-sp corners)

Fasten off and weave in ends.

IRIDESCENT

DESIGNER: CATHERINE NORONHA

YARN

Stylecraft Special DK, light worsted (DK), in foll shades:
Colour 1: Cypress (1824)
Colour 2: Boysenberry (1828)
Colour 3: Petrol (1708)

HOOK

US size E/4 (3.5mm) hook

GAUGE (TENSION)

A single motif measures approx 7in (18cm) using a US size E/4 (3.5mm) hook.

NOTES

Motif is worked in tapestry crochet from Round 2 onward.
Change to next colour on last yoh of prev st. Carry unused yarn across work, and crochet over. Make joining slst at end of round around unused yarns to carry them up for next round.
Each round starts with 3 ch (apart from Round 1 which starts with 4 ch), which counts as 1 dc, 1 ch. This is final dc of one side of motif, plus 1 ch to form first corner ch-sp. Other corner ch-sps are formed of 2 ch.

PATTERN

Change colour foll chart.

Using E/4 hook and colour 1, make a magic ring.

Round 1 (RS): Working into ring, 4 ch (counts as 1 dc, 1 ch), [3 dc, 2 ch] 3 times, 2 dc, slst in 3rd ch of beg 4-ch, slst in ch-sp to join. (12 dc, 1 x 1ch-sp corner, 3 x 2ch-sp corners)

Round 2: 3 ch (counts as 1 dc, 1 ch throughout), 2 dc in ch-sp, *3 dcBLO, (2 dc, 2 ch, 2 dc) in 2ch-sp; rep from * 2 more times, 3 dcBLO, 1 dc in ch-sp, slst in 2nd ch of beg 3-ch, slst in ch-sp to join. (28 dc, 1 x 1ch-sp corner, 3 x 2ch-sp corners)

Round 3: 3 ch, 2 dc in ch-sp, *7 dcBLO, (2 dc, 2 ch, 2 dc) in 2ch-sp; rep from * 2 more times, 7 dcBLO, 1 dc in ch-sp, slst in 2nd ch of beg 3-ch, slst in ch-sp to join. (44 dc, 1 x 1ch-sp corner, 3 x 2ch-sp corners)

Round 4: 3 ch, 2 dc in ch-sp, *11 dcBLO, (2 dc, 2 ch, 2 dc) in 2ch-sp; rep from * 2 more times, 11 dcBLO, 1 dc in ch-sp, slst in 2nd ch of beg 3-ch, slst in ch-sp to join. (60 dc, 1 x 1ch-sp corner, 3 x 2ch-sp corners)

Round 5: 3 ch, 2 dc in ch-sp, *15 dcBLO, (2 dc, 2 ch, 2 dc) in 2ch-sp; rep from * 2 more times, 15 dcBLO, 1 dc in ch-sp, slst in 2nd ch of beg 3-ch, slst in ch-sp to join. (76 dc, 1 x 1ch-sp corner, 3 x 2ch-sp corners)

Round 6: 3 ch, 2 dc in ch-sp, *19 dcBLO, (2 dc, 2 ch, 2 dc) in 2ch-sp; rep from * 2 more times, 19 dcBLO, 1 dc in ch-sp, slst in 2nd ch of beg 3-ch, slst in ch-sp to join. (92 dc, 1 x 1ch-sp corner, 3 x 2ch-sp corners)

Round 7: 3 ch, 2 dc in ch-sp, *23 dcBLO, (2 dc, 2 ch, 2 dc) in 2ch-sp; rep from * 2 more times; 23 dcBLO, 1 dc in ch-sp, slst in 2nd ch of beg 3-ch to join. (108 dc, 1 x 1ch-sp corner, 3 x 2ch-sp corners)

Fasten off and weave in ends.

KEY

Colour 1

Colour 2

Colour 3

O   chain (ch)

Chart shows one side of square; it should be repeated four times on each round.

Read chart from bottom to top, right to left.

Each square represents one stitch.

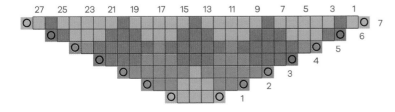

DEEP SPACE

DESIGNER: CATHERINE NORONHA

YARN

Stylecraft Special DK, light worsted (DK), in foll shades:
Colour 1: Midnight (1011)
Colour 2: Petrol (1708)
Colour 3: Cypress (1824)
Colour 4: Cream (1005)

HOOK

US size E/4 (3.5mm) hook

GAUGE (TENSION)

A single motif measures approx 8in (20cm) using a US size E/4 (3.5mm) hook.

NOTES

Motif is worked in tapestry crochet from Round 2 onward.
Change to next colour on last yoh of prev st. Carry unused yarn across work, and crochet over. Make joining slst at end of round around unused yarns to carry them up for next round.
Each round starts with 3 ch (apart from Round 1 which starts with 4 ch), which counts as 1 dc, 1 ch. This is final dc of one side of motif, plus 1 ch to form first corner ch-sp. Other corner ch-sps are 2 ch.

PATTERN

Change colour foll chart.

Using E/4 hook and colour 1, make a magic ring.

Round 1 (RS): Working into ring, 4 ch (counts as 1 dc, 1 ch), [3 dc, 2 ch] 3 times, 2 dc, slst in 3rd ch of beg 4 ch, slst in ch-sp. (12 dc, 1 x 1ch-sp corner, 3 x 2ch-sp corners)

continued on next page >

Round 2: 3 ch (counts as 1 dc, 1 ch throughout), 2 dc in ch-sp, *3 dcBLO, (2 dc, 2 ch, 2 dc) in 2ch-sp; rep from * twice more; 3 dcBLO, 1 dc in ch-sp, slst in 2nd ch of beg 3-ch to join, slst in ch-sp. (28 dc, 1 x 1ch-sp corner, 3 x 2ch-sp corners)

Round 3: 3 ch, 2 dc in ch-sp, *7 dcBLO, (2 dc, 2 ch, 2 dc) in 2ch-sp; rep from * twice more; 7 dcBLO, 1 dc in ch-sp, slst in 2nd ch of beg 3-ch to join, slst in ch-sp. (44 dc, 1 x 1ch-sp corner, 3 x 2ch-sp corners)

Round 4: 3 ch, 2 dc in ch-sp, *11 dcBLO, (2 dc, 2 ch, 2 dc) in 2ch-sp; rep from * twice more; 11 dcBLO, 1 dc in ch-sp, slst in 2nd ch of beg 3-ch to join, slst in ch-sp. (60 dc, 1 x 1ch-sp corner, 3 x 2ch-sp corners)

Round 5: 3 ch, 2 dc in ch-sp, *15 dcBLO, (2 dc, 2 ch, 2 dc) in 2ch-sp; rep from * twice more; 15 dcBLO, 1 dc in ch-sp, slst in 2nd ch of beg 3-ch to join, slst in ch-sp. (76 dc, 1 x 1ch-sp corner, 3 x 2ch-sp corners)

Round 6: 3 ch, 2 dc in ch-sp, *19 dcBLO, (2 dc, 2 ch, 2 dc) in 2ch-sp; rep from * twice more; 19 dcBLO, 1 dc in ch-sp, slst in 2nd ch of beg 3-ch to join, slst in ch-sp. (92 dc, 1 x 1ch-sp corner, 3 x 2ch-sp corners)

Round 7: 3 ch, 2 dc in ch-sp, *23 dcBLO, (2 dc, 2 ch, 2 dc) in 2ch-sp; rep from * twice more; 23 dcBLO, 1 dc in ch-sp, slst in 2nd ch of beg 3-ch to join, slst in ch-sp. (108 dc, 1 x 1ch-sp corner, 3 x 2ch-sp corners)

Round 8: 3 ch, 2 dc in ch-sp, *27 dcBLO, (2 dc, 2 ch, 2 dc) in 2ch-sp; rep from * twice more; 27 dcBLO, 1 dc in ch-sp, slst in 2nd ch of beg 3-ch to join. (124 dc, 1 x 1ch-sp corner, 3 x 2ch-sp corners)

Fasten off and weave in ends.

Chart shows one side of square; it should be repeated four times on each round.

Read chart from bottom to top, right to left.

Each square represents one stitch.

KEY

- ▨ Colour 1
- ▨ Colour 2
- ▨ Colour 3
- ☐ Colour 4
- ◯ chain (ch)

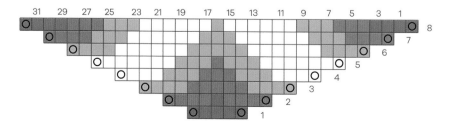

ABSTRACT DAISY

DESIGNER: LYNNE ROWE

YARN

Scheepjes Stone Washed, sport (4ply), in foll shade:

Colour 1: Nile (944)

Scheepjes River Washed, sport (4ply), in foll shade:

Colour 2: Amazonite (813)

HOOK

US size E/4 (3.5mm) hook

GAUGE (TENSION)

A single motif measures approx 6½in (16.5cm) using a US size E/4 (3.5mm) hook

SPECIAL ABBREVIATIONS

sc/dc2tog, insert hook in next st, yoh, pull through, yoh, insert hook in next st, yoh, pull through, yoh, pull through first 2 loops, yoh, pull through all rem loops

dc/sc2tog, yoh, insert hook in next st, yoh, pull through, yoh, pull through first 2 loops, insert hook in next st, yoh, pull through, yoh and pull through all rem loops

NOTES

Motif is worked in tapestry crochet in rounds.

Change to next colour on last yoh of prev st. Carry unused yarn across work and crochet over, holding slightly to back of working st.

At beg of round (1 sc, 2 ch) replaces dc for neater st.

PATTERN

Change colour foll chart.

Using E/4 hook and colour 1, make a magic ring.

Round 1 (RS): 1 ch (does not count as st, throughout), 8 sc in ring, do not join round. (8 sc)

Round 2: 2 sc in each st, slst in first st to join. (16 sc)

Round 3: 1 ch, (1 sc, 2 ch, 1 dc) in same st, 1 dc, *2 dc in next st, 1 dc; rep from * to end, slst in top of 2-ch to join. (24 dc)

Round 4: 1 ch, (1 sc, 2 ch) in same st, 2 dc in next st, 2 dc in next st, *1 dc, 2 dc in next st, 2 dc in next st; rep from * to end, slst in top of 2-ch to join. (40 dc)

Round 5: 1 ch, (1 sc, 2 ch, 1 dc) in same st, 1 dc, 2 dc in next st, 2 dc, *2 dc in next st, 1 dc, 2 dc in next st, 2 dc; rep from * to end, slst in top of 2-ch to join. (56 dc)

continued on next page >

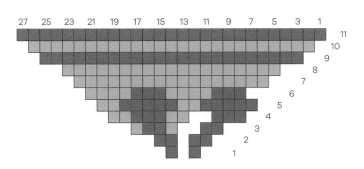

KEY

■ Colour 1

■ Colour 2

Chart shows one side of square; it should be repeated four times on each round.

Read chart from bottom to top, right to left.

Each square represents one stitch.

Round 6: 1 ch, starting in first st, *1 sc/dc2tog over next 2 sts, 1 dc, 1 dc/sc2tog over next 2 sts, 2 dc in next 2 sts; rep from * to end, slstBLO in first st to join. (56 dc)

Fasten off colour 1 and cont using colour 2 only.

Round 7: 1 ch, 1 scBLO in same st, 1 scBLO, *1 hdcBLO, 1 dc, (1 dc, 1 tr) in next st, 1 tr in sp before next st (for corner st), (1 tr, 1 dc) in next st, 1 dc, 1 hdcBLO, 2 scBLO, 4 sc, 2 scBLO; rep from * 3 times more omitting last 2 sts, slst in first sc to join. (68 sts)

Fasten off colour 2.

Round 8: Rejoin colour 2 in any corner st, 4 ch (counts as first tr), 2 tr in same st, *1 dc in each st to next corner st, 3 tr in corner st; rep from * to end omitting last corner, slst in top of beg 4-ch to join. (76 sts)

Fasten off colour 2.

Round 9: Join colour 1 in a corner st, 1 ch, *(2 sc, 1 dc, 2 sc) in same st, 1 sc in each st to next corner; rep from * to end, slst in top of first sc to join. (92 sts)

Fasten off colour 1, rejoin colour 2 in any corner st.

Round 10: As Round 8. (100 sts)

Fasten off colour 2, rejoin colour 1 in any corner st.

Round 11: As Round 8. (108 sts)

Fasten off and weave in ends.

ART DECO SUNSET

DESIGNER: LYNNE ROWE

YARN

Sirdar Happy Cotton DK, light worsted (DK), in foll shades:
Colour 1: Lippy (789)
Colour 2: Juicy (792)
Colour 3: Liquorice (775)
Colour 4: Wicket (781)

HOOK

US size E/4 (3.5mm) hook

GAUGE (TENSION)

A single motif measures approx 6¾in (17cm) using a US size E/4 (3.5mm) hook

NOTES

Motif is worked in tapestry crochet in rounds.
Change to next colour on last yoh of prev st. Carry unused yarn across work and crochet over, holding slightly to back of working st.

PATTERN

Change colour foll chart.

Using E/4 hook and colour 1, make a magic ring.

Round 1 (RS): 4 ch (counts as 1 tr throughout), 2 dc in ring, [2 tr in ring, 2 dc in ring] 3 times, 1 tr in ring, slst in top of beg 4-ch to join. (16 sts)

Round 2: 4 ch, 2 dc in same st at base of 4-ch, *1 dc, 1 dc, (2 dc, 1 tr) in next st**, (1 tr, 2 dc) in next st; rep from * 3 more times, ending last rep at **, slst in top of beg 4-ch to join. (32 sts)

Round 3: 4 ch, 2 dc in same st at base of 4-ch, *3 dc, 3 dc, (2 dc, 1 tr) in next st**, (1 tr, 2 dc) in next st; rep from * 3 more times, ending last rep at **, slst in top of beg 4-ch to join. (48 sts)

Round 4: 4 ch, 1 dc in same st at base of 4-ch, *5 dc, 5 dc, (1 dc, 1 tr) in next st**, (1 tr, 1 dc) in next st; rep from * 3 more times, ending last rep at **, slst in top of beg 4-ch to join. (56 sts)

Round 5: 4 ch, 1 dc in same st at base of 4-ch, *6 dc, 6 dc, (1 dc, 1 tr) in next st**, (1 tr, 1 dc) in next st; rep from * 3 more times, ending last rep at **, slst in top of beg 4-ch to join. (64 sts)

Fasten off both colours.

Round 6: Join colour 3 in first tr of prev round (top of beg 4-ch), 4 ch, 1 dc in same st at base of 4-ch, *1 dc in each st to first tr of next corner, (1 dc, 1 tr) in next st**, (1 tr, 1 dc) in next st; rep from * 3 more times, ending last rep at **, slst in top of beg 4-ch to join. (72 sts)

Round 7: 1 ch (does not count as st), (1 hdc, 2 sc) in same st at base of 1-ch, *1 sc in each st to first tr of next corner, (2 sc, 1 hdc) in next st**, (1 hdc, 2 sc) in next st; rep from * 3 more times, ending last rep at **, slst in first hdc to join. (88 sts)

Fasten off colour 3.

Round 8: Join colour 4 in space between 2 corner hdc, 4 ch, 2 dc in space at base of 4-ch, *1 dc in each st to next space between corner hdc, (2 dc, 1 tr, 2 dc) in space; rep from * around omitting last tr and 2 dc, slst in top of beg 4-ch to join. (108 sts)

Fasten off colour 4.

Round 9: Join colour 3 in any corner tr, 1 ch (does not count as st), 3 sc in same st, *1 sc in each st to next corner st, 3 sc in corner st; rep from * around omitting last 3 sc, slst in first sc to join. (116 sts)

Round 10: 1 ch (does not count as st), 3 hdc in same st, *1 hdc in each st to next corner st, 3 hdc in corner st; rep from * around omitting last 3 hdc, slst in first hdc to join. (124 sts)

Fasten off and weave in ends.

Chart shows one side of square; it should be repeated four times on each round.

Read chart from bottom to top, right to left.

Each square represents one stitch.

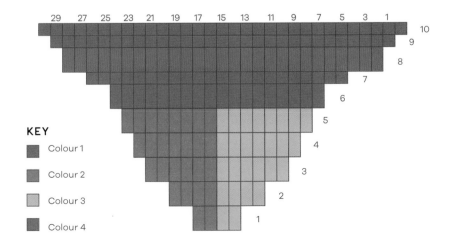

KEY

- Colour 1
- Colour 2
- Colour 3
- Colour 4

TOTTENHAM COURT ROAD

DESIGNER: STEFFI GLAVES

YARN

Cygnet DK, light worsted (DK), in foll shades:

Colour 1: Cloud (2033)
Colour 2: White (208)
Colour 3: Fuchsia (676)
Colour 4: Apple (6711)
Colour 5: Sunshine (184)
Colour 6: Black (217)
Colour 7: Red (1206)
Colour 8: Burnt Orange (4888)

HOOK

US size B/1 or C/2 (2.5mm) hook

GAUGE (TENSION)

A single motif measures approx 7in (18cm) using a US size B/1 or C/2 (2.5mm) hook.

SPECIAL ABBREVIATIONS

5dc-PC, popcorn of 5 dc in back loop only
4dc-PC, popcorn of 4 dc

NOTES

Motif is worked in tapestry crochet in rounds.
Change to new colour on last yoh of prev st.
Rounds 3 to 15 are only worked around two sides of initial square.

PATTERN

Change colour foll chart.

Using B/1 or C/2 hook and colour 1, make a magic ring.

Round 1: Working in ring, 3 ch (counts as 1 hdc throughout), 2 hdc, [3 ch, 3 hdc] 3 times, 1 ch, 1 dc in top of beg 3-ch to join. (12 sts, 4 x 3ch-sp corners)

continued on next page >

Fasten off colour 1.

Round 2: Using colour 2, slst in 2nd ch st on corner, 3 ch, 1 hdc in next ch, *3 hdcBLO, 1 hdc in ch, [1 hdc, 3 ch, 1 hdc] in 2nd ch; rep from * 3 more times ending 1 ch, 1 hdc in top of beg 3-ch to join. (28 sts, 4 x 3ch-sp corners)

Fasten off colour 2.

Round 3: Join colour 4 with slst in 2nd corner ch, 3 ch, 1 hdc in next ch, *7 hdcBLO, 1 hdc in ch, [1 hdc, 3 ch, 1 hdc] in 2nd ch; rep from * on next side only ending 1 hdc in next 2 ch. (22 sts, 1 x 3ch-sp corner)

Fasten off colour 4.

Round 4: Join colour 5 with slst in top of beg 3-ch from Round 3, 3 ch, 10 hdcBLO, 5dc-PC in same st as 10th hdcBLO just made, 4 ch, 5dc-PC in 2nd ch, 4 ch, 5dc-PC in first st of next side, 1 hdcBLO in same st, 10 dcBLO. (22 hdc, 2 PC, 4ch-sp + PC + 4ch-sp corner)

Fasten off colour 5.

Round 5: Join colour 1 with slst in top of beg 3-ch from Round 4, 3 ch, 10 hdcBLO, 3 tr in 4ch-sp, 3 ch, 3 tr in 4ch-sp, 11 hdcBLO. (28 sts, 1 x 3ch-sp corner)

Fasten off colour 1.

Round 6: Join colour 6 with slst in top of beg 3-ch from Round 5, 3 ch, 11 hdcBLO, 5dc-PC, 1 hdcBLO, 1 hdc in ch, 1 ch, 5dc-PC in 2nd ch, 1 ch, 1 hdc in 3rd ch, 1 hdcBLO, 5dc-PC, 12 hdcBLO. (28 sts, 2 PC, 1ch-sp + PC + 1ch-sp corner)

Fasten off colour 6.

Round 7: Join colour 7 with slst in top of beg 3-ch from Round 6, 3 ch, 15 hdcBLO working in all sts inc PC and ch, 3 ch, 16 hdcBLO on next side, turn. (32 sts, 1 x 3ch-sp corner)

Round 8 (WS): 3 ch, 15 FLhdc, 1 hdc in ch, [1 hdc 3 ch, 1 hdc] in 2nd ch, 1 hdc in 3rd ch, 16 FLhdc, turn. (36 sts, 1 x 3ch-sp corner)

Fasten off colour 7.

Round 9 (RS): Join colour 8 with slst in BLO of last st of Round 8, 3 ch, 2 hdcBLO, skip 1 st, 13 hdcBLO, skip 1 st, 1 hdc in ch, [1 hdc, 3 ch, 1 hdc] in 2nd ch, 1 hdc in 3rd ch, skip 1 st, 14 hdcBLO, skip 1 st, 2 hdcBO. (36 sts, 1 x 3ch-sp corner)

Fasten off colour 8.

Round 10: Join colour 4 with slst in BLO of first st of Round 9, 3 ch, 17 hdcBLO, 1 hdc in ch, [1 hdc, 3 ch, 1 hdc] in 2nd ch, 1 hdc in 3rd ch, 18 hdcBLO. (40 sts, 1 x 3ch-sp corner)

Fasten off colour 4.

Round 11: Join colour 4 with slst in BLO of first st of Round 10, 3 ch, 19 hdcBLO, 1 hdc in ch, [1 hdc, 3 ch, 1 hdc] in 2nd ch, 1 hdc in 3rd ch, 20 hdcBLO, slst. (44 sts, 1 x 3ch-sp corner)

Fasten off colour 4.

Round 12: Join colour 6 with slst in BLO of first st of Round 11, 3 ch, 21 hdcBLO, 3 ch, 4dc-PC in corner sp, 3 ch, 22 hdcBLO on next side. (44 sts, 2 x 3ch-sp, PC corner)

Fasten off colour 6.

Round 13: Join colour 2 with slst in BLO of first st of Round 12, 3 ch, 2 hdcBLO, 1 dcFLO in Round 11 st, [3 hdcBLO in Round 12 sts, 1 dcFLO in Round 11 st] 4 times, 2 hdcBLO, 2 hdc in 3ch-sp, 4 ch, 2 hdc in next ch-sp, 2 hdcBLO, [1 dcFLO in Round 11 st, 3 hdcBLO in Round 12 sts] 5 times. (48 sts, 1 x 4ch-sp corner)

Fasten off colour 2.

Round 14: Join colour 4 with slst in BLO of first st of Round 13, 3 ch, [1 dcFLO in Round 12 st, 3 hdcBLO in Round 13 sts] 5 times, 1 dcFLO in Round 12 st, 2 hdcBLO, [2 tr, 3 ch, 2 tr] in Round 12 PC, 2 hdcBLO, [1 dcFLO in Round 12 st, 3 hdcBLO in Round 13 sts] 5 times, 1 dcFLO in Round 12 st, 1 hdcBLO. (52 sts, 1 x 3ch-sp corner)

Fasten off colour 4.

Round 15: Join colour 8 with slst in BLO of first st of Round 14, 3 ch, 2 hdcBLO, 1 dcFLO in Round 13 st, [3 hdcBLO in Round 13 sts, 1 dcFLO in Round 14 st] 6 times, 2 hdcBLO, 2 hdc in 3 ch sp, [1 hdc, 2ch, 1 hdc] in 2nd ch, 2 hdc in 3 ch sp, 2 hdcBLO, [1 dcFLO in Round 13 st, 3 hdcBLO in Round 14 sts] 6 times. (56 sts, 1 x 3ch-sp corner)

BORDER

Work around all 4 sides.

Round 16: Join colour 3 with slst in BLO of first st of Round 14, 28 scBLO, 1 sc in ch, [1 sc, 2 ch, 1 sc] in second ch, 1 sc in third ch, 27 scBLO down next side, (1 scBLO, 2 ch, 1 scBLO) in last st, 27 sc evenly down side, 1 sc in ch, [1 sc, 2 ch, 1 sc] in second ch, 1 sc in third ch, 27 sc evenly down side, [1 sc, 2 ch] in last row, slst in first st to join. (120 sts, 4 x 2ch-sp corners)

Round 17: Join colour 2 with slst in corner sp, *[1 sc, 2 ch, 1 sc] in corner sp, 30 sc; rep from * 3 more times, slst in beg st to join. (128 sts, 4 x 2ch-sp corners)

Fasten off and weave in ends.

KEY

- Colour 1
- Colour 2
- Colour 3
- Colour 4
- Colour 5
- Colour 6
- Colour 7
- Colour 8
- ∞ chain (ch)
- popcorn (PC)

Begin chart in bottom left corner. Read Rounds 3 to 7 and 9 to 15 in an anti-clockwise direction, and Round 8 in a clockwise direction.

Each square represents one stitch.

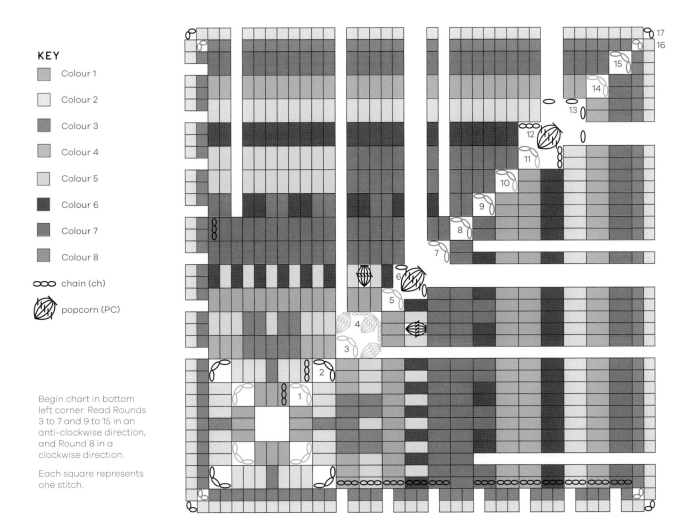

- 119 -

KINGS CROSS

DESIGNER: STEFFI GLAVES

YARN

Cygnet DK, light worsted (DK), in foll
shades:

Colour 1: White (208)

Colour 2: Cloud (2033)

Colour 3: Red (1206)

Colour 4: Sunshine (184)

Colour 5: Emerald (377)

HOOK

US size D/3 (3mm) hook

GAUGE (TENSION)

A single motif measures approx 7in
(18cm) using a US size D/3 (3mm) hook.

NOTES

*Motif is worked in tapestry crochet in
rounds.*

*Change to next colour on last yoh of
prev st. Carry unused yarn across work
and crochet over. Make joining st at end
of each round around unused yarn to
carry it up for next round.*

*All sts on corners are hdc worked in 3 ch
sts and not st sps, for crisper edges on
colour changes.*

PATTERN

Change colour foll chart.

Using D/3 hook and colour 1, make a
magic ring.

Round 1: 3 ch (counts as 1 hdc
throughout), 2 hdc, [3 ch, 3
hdc] 3 times, 1 ch, 1 hdcBLO in
top of beg 3-ch to join. (12 sts,
4 x 3ch-sp corners)

Round 2: 3 ch, [4 hdcBLO, skip ch st,
(1 hdcBLO, 3 ch, 1 hdcBLO) in corner
ch] 4 times ending 1 ch, 1 hdcBLO in
top of beg 3-ch to join. (24 sts, 4 x
3ch-sp corners)

Round 3: 3 ch, 1 hdcBLO on side of
connecting hdc from Round 2, [6
hdcBLO, 1 hdc in first ch st (1 hdc,
1 ch, 1 hdc) in 2nd ch st, 1 hdc in next
ch st] 4 times ending (1 ch, 1 hdc) in
top of beg 3-ch to join. (40 sts, 4 x
1ch-sp corners)

Round 4: 3 ch, 1 hdcBLO on side of
connecting hdc from Round 3, [10
hdcBLO, (2 hdc, 1 ch, 2 hdc) in ch] 4
times ending (1 ch, 1 hdc) in ch, 1 hdc
in top of beg 3-ch to join. (56 sts, 4 x
1ch-sp corners)

Round 5: 3 ch, 1 hdcBLO on side of
connecting hdc from Round 4, [14
hdcBLO, (2 hdc, 3 ch, 2 hdc) in ch] 4
times ending (1 ch, 1 hdc) in ch, 1 hdc
in top of beg 3-ch to join. (72 sts, 4 x
3ch-sp corners)

Round 6: 3 ch, 1 hdcBLO on side
of connecting hdc from Round 5,
[18 hdcBLO, 1 hdc in ch st (1 hdc,
3 ch, 1 hdc) in next ch st, 1 hdc
in next ch st] 4 times ending (1
ch, 1 hdc) in top of beg 3-ch to
join. (88 sts, 4 x 3ch-sp corners)

Round 7: 3 ch, 1 hdcBLO on side
of connecting hdc from Round 6,
[22 hdcBLO, 1 hdc in ch st (1 hdc,
3 ch, 1 hdc) in next ch st, 1 hdc
in next ch st] 4 times ending
(1 ch, 1 hdc) in top of beg 3-ch to
join. (104 sts, 4 x 3ch-sp corners)

Round 8: 3 ch, 1 hdcBLO on side of
connecting hdc from Round 7, [26
hdcBLO, 1 hdc in ch st (1 hdc, 3 ch,
1 hdc) in next ch st, 1 hdc in next ch
st] 4 times ending (1 ch, 1 hdc) in top
of beg 3-ch to join. (120 sts, 4 x 3ch-
sp corners)

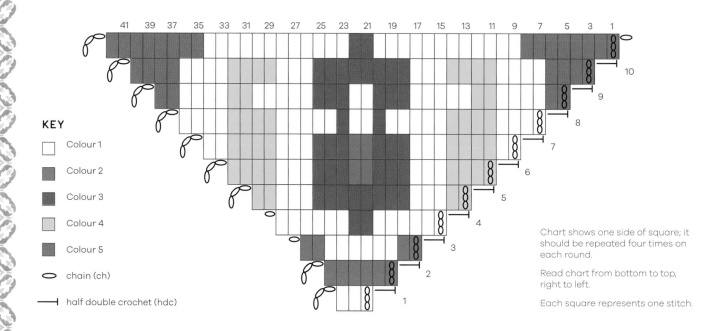

KEY

☐ Colour 1

◼ Colour 2

◼ Colour 3

◻ Colour 4

◼ Colour 5

⬭ chain (ch)

⊢ half double crochet (hdc)

Chart shows one side of square; it
should be repeated four times on
each round.

Read chart from bottom to top,
right to left.

Each square represents one stitch.

Round 9: 3 ch, 1 hdcBLO on side of connecting hdc from Round 8, [30 hdcBLO, 1 hdc in ch st (1 hdc, 3 ch, 1 hdc) in next ch st, 1 hdc in next ch st] 4 times ending (1 ch, 1 hdc) in top of beg 3-ch to join. (136 sts, 4 x 3ch-sp corners)

Round 10: 3 ch, 1 hdcBLO on side of last hdc from Round 9, [34 hdcBLO, 1 hdc in ch st (1 hdc, 3 ch, 1 hdc) in next ch st, 1 hdc in next ch st] 4 times ending (1 ch, 1 hdcBLO) in top of beg 3-ch to join. (152 sts, 4 x 3ch-sp corners)

Round 11: 3 ch, 1 hdcBLO on side of last hdc from Round 9, [38 hdcBLO, 1 hdc in ch st (1 hdc, 3 ch, 1 hdc) in next ch st, 1 hdc in next ch st] 4 times, 3 ch, slst in top of beg 3-ch to join. (168 sts, 4 x 3ch-sp corners)

Fasten off and weave in ends.

RUSSELL SQUARE

DESIGNER: STEFFI GLAVES

YARN

Cygnet DK, light worsted (DK), in foll shades:
Colour 1: Light Grey (195)
Colour 2: Emerald (337)
Colour 3: Black (217)
Colour 4: White (208)

HOOK

US size D/3 (3mm) hook

GAUGE (TENSION)

A single motif measures approx 7½ x 7in (19 x 18cm) using a US size D/3 (3mm) hook.

NOTES

Motif is worked in tapestry crochet in rows. Change to next colour on last yoh of prev st. Carry unused yarn and crochet over.

PATTERN

Change colour foll chart.

Using D/3 hook and colour 1, 37 ch.

Row 1: 1 sc in 2nd ch from hook, 1 sc in each st to end. (36 sts)

Row 2: 1 ch (does not count as st throughout), 1 sc in each st to end, turn.

Fasten off colour 1.

Row 3: Join colour 2 with a slst, 1 ch, 36 sc, turn.

Row 4: 1 ch, 36 sc, turn.

Fasten off colour 2.

continued on next page >

Row 5: Using colour 3, as Row 3.

Row 6: As Row 4.

Row 7: Using colour 2, as Row 3.

Row 8: As Row 4.

Row 9: Join colour 4 with a slst, 3 ch (does not count as st throughout), 36 dc, turn.

Rows 10 to 17: 3 ch, 36 dc, turn.

Rows 18 to 23: As Rows 3 to 8.

Rows 24 and 25: As Rows 2 and 3.

Fasten off and weave in ends.

KEY

	Colour 1
	Colour 2
	Colour 3
	Colour 4
∞	chain (ch)

Read chart from bottom to top, odd numbered (RS) rows are read right to left, even numbered (WS) rows are read left to right.

Each square represents one stitch.

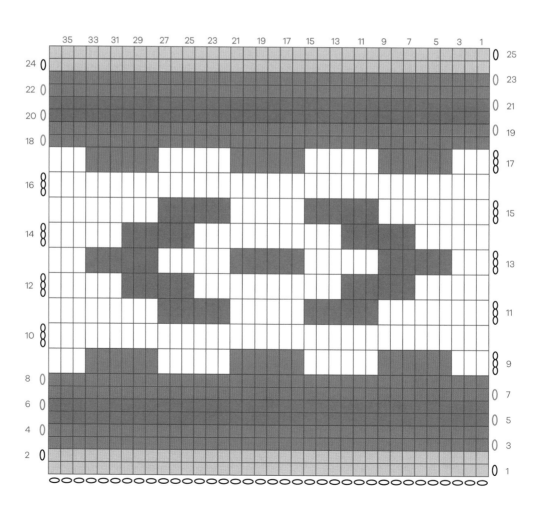

NORTHERN AND CENTRAL LINES

DESIGNER: STEFFI GLAVES

YARN

Cygnet DK, light worsted (DK), in foll shades:
Colour 1: Red (1206)
Colour 3: Black (217)
Stylecraft Special DK, light worsted (DK), in foll shade:
Colour 2: Parchment (1218)

HOOK

US size B/1 or C/2 (2.5mm) hook

GAUGE (TENSION)

A single motif measures approx 6¾in (17cm) using a US size B/1 or C/2 (2.5mm) hook.

NOTES

Motif is worked in tapestry crochet in rounds.
Change to next colour on last yoh of prev st. Carry unused yarn across work and crochet over. Make joining st at end of each round around unused yarn to carry it up for next round.
All sts on corners are sc worked in 3 ch sts and not st sps, for crisper edges on colour changes.

PATTERN

Change colour foll chart.

Using B/1 or C/2 hook and colour 1, make a magic ring.

Round 1: Working into ring, 1 ch, [2 sc, 2 ch] 4 times, 1 sc in side of first st to join. (8 sts, 4 x 2ch-sp corners)

Round 2: 1 ch, 1 sc in corner sp, 3 scBLO, 2 ch (makes corner), [4 scBLO, 2 ch] twice, 4 scBLO, 1 sc in side of first st to join, change to colour 2 on this st. (16 sts, 4 x 2ch-sp corners)

Round 3: 1 ch, [6 scBLO, 2 ch] 4 times, working 1 ch on last rep, 1 sc in side of first st to join. (24 sts, 4 x 2ch-sp corners)

continued on next page >

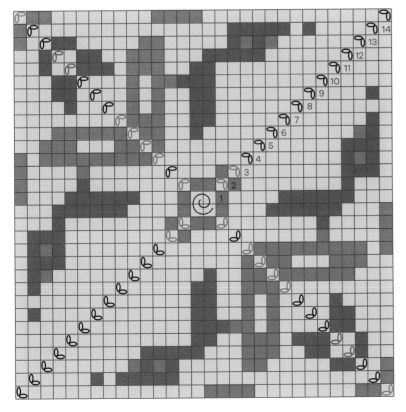

KEY

- ■ Colour 1
- □ Colour 2
- ■ Colour 3
- ✍ 2 chain (2 ch)

Read chart from centre outward.

Each square represents one stitch on one round.

Round 4: 1 ch, 8 scBLO, [2 ch, 8 scBLO] 3 times, 1 ch, 1 sc in side of first st to join. (32 sts, 4 x 2ch-sp corners)

Round 5: 1 ch, [10 scBLO, 2 ch] 3 times, 10 scBLO, 1 ch, 1 sc in side of first st to join. (40 sts, 4 x 2ch-sp corners)

Round 6: 1 ch, [12 scBLO, 2 ch] 3 times, 12 scBLO, 1 ch, 1 sc in side of first st to join. (48 sts, 4 x 2ch-sp corners)

Round 7: 1 ch, [14 scBLO, 2 ch] 3 times, 14 scBLO, 1 ch, 1 sc in side of first st to join. (56 sts, 4 x 2ch-sp corners)

Round 8: 1 ch, [16 scBLO, 2 ch] 3 times, 16 scBLO, 1 ch, 1 sc in side of first st to join. (64 sts, 4 x 2ch-sp corners)

Round 9: 1 ch, [18 scBLO, 2 ch] 3 times, 18 scBLO, 1 ch, 1 sc in side of first st to join. (72 sts, 4 x 2ch-sp corners)

Round 10: 1 ch, [20 scBLO, 2 ch] 3 times, 20 scBLO, 1 ch, 1 sc in side of first st to join. (80 sts, 4 x 2ch-sp corners)

Round 11: 1 ch, [22 scBLO, 2 ch] 3 times, 22 scBLO, 1 ch, 1 sc in side of first st to join. (88 sts, 4 x 2ch-sp corners)

Round 12: 1 ch, [24 scBLO, 2 ch] 3 times, 24 scBLO, 1 ch, 1 sc in side of first st to join. (96 sts, 4 x 2ch-sp corners)

Round 13: 1 ch, [26 scBLO, 2 ch] 3 times, 26 scBLO, 1 ch, 1 sc in side of first st to join. (104 sts, 4 x 2ch-sp corners)

Round 14: 1 ch, [28 scBLO, 2 ch] 3 times, 28 scBLO, 1 ch, 1 sc in side of first st to join, slst in first st to join. (112 sts, 4 x 2ch-sp corners)

Fasten off and weave in ends.

PORTO ROOFTOPS

DESIGNER: STEFFI GLAVES

YARN

Stylecraft Special DK, light worsted (DK), in foll shade:
Colour 1: Waterfall (1125)
Rico Essentials Acrylic Antipilling DK, light worsted (DK), in foll shades:
Colour 2: Berry (002)
Colour 3: Burgundy (003)

HOOK

US size B/1 or C/2 (2.5mm) hook

GAUGE (TENSION)

A single motif measures approx 6¾in (17cm) using a US size B/1 or C/2 (2.5mm) hook.

NOTES

Motif is worked in tapestry crochet in rounds.
Change to next colour on last yoh of prev st. Carry unused yarn across work and crochet over. Make joining st at end of each round around unused yarn to carry it up for next round.

PATTERN

Change colour foll chart.

Using B/1 or C/2 hook and colour 1, make a magic ring.

Round 1: Working into ring, 3 ch (counts as 1 dc throughout), 2 dc, [3 ch, 3 dc] 3 times, 1 ch, 1 dc in top of beg 3-ch to join, change to colour 2 last yoh. (12 sts, 4 x 3ch-sp corners)

Round 2: 3 ch, 1 dc in corner sp, *3 dc, (2 dc, 3 ch, 2 dc) in corner sp; rep from * 3 more times ending 2 dc in corner sp, 1 ch, 1 dc in top of beg 3-ch to join. (28 sts, 4 x 3ch-sp corners)

Round 3: 3 ch, 1 dc in corner sp, *3 dc, 1 FPdc, 3 dc, [2 dc, 3 ch, 2t r] in corner sp; rep from * 3 more times ending 2 dc in corner sp, 1 ch, 1 dc in top of beg 3-ch to join. (44 sts, 4 x 3ch-sp corners)

Round 4: 3 ch, 1 dc in corner sp, *5 dc, 1 FPdc, 5 dc, (2 dc, 3 ch, 2 dc) in corner sp; rep from * 3 more times ending 2 dc in corner sp, 1 ch, 1 dc in top of beg 3-ch to join. (60 sts, 4 x 3ch-sp corners)

Round 5: 3 ch, 1 dc in corner sp, *7 dc, 1 FPdc, 7 dc, (2 dc, 3 ch, 2 dc) in corner sp; rep from * 3 more times ending 2 dc in corner sp, 1 ch, 1 dc in top of beg 3-ch to join. (76 sts, 4 x 3ch-sp corners)

Round 6: 3 ch, 1 dc in corner sp, *8 dc, skip 1 st, 3 dc in colour 2 st from

Round 5, skip 1 st, 8 dc, (2 dc, 3 ch, 2 dc) in corner sp; rep from * 3 more times ending 2 dc in corner sp, 1 ch, 1 dc in top of beg 3-ch to join. (92 sts, 4 x 3ch-sp corners)

Round 7: 3 ch, 1 dc in corner sp, *23 dc, (2 dc, 3 ch, 2 dc) in corner sp; rep from * 3 more times ending 2 dc in corner sp, 1 ch, 1 dc in top of beg 3-ch to join. (108 sts, 4 x 3ch-sp corners)

Round 8: 3 ch, 1 dc in corner sp, *27 dc, (2 dc, 3 ch, 2 dc) in corner sp; rep from * 3 more times ending 2 dc in corner sp, 1 ch, 1 dc in 1 dc in top of beg 3-ch to join. (124 sts, 4 x 3ch-sp corners)

Fasten off and weave in ends.

PORT DROPS

DESIGNER: STEFFI GLAVES

YARN

Stylecraft Special DK, light worsted (DK), in foll shade:
Colour 1: Pale Rose (1080)
Rico Essentials Acrylic Antipilling DK, light worsted (DK), in foll shade:
Colour 2: Burgundy (003)
Cygnet DK, light worsted (DK), in foll shade:
Colour 3: Jam (1910)

HOOK

US size B/1 or C/2 (2.5mm) hook

GAUGE (TENSION)

A single motif measures approx 6¾in (17cm) using a US size B/1 or C/2 (2.5mm) hook.

NOTES

Motif is worked in tapestry crochet in rounds. Change to next colour on last yoh of prev st. Carry unused yarn across work and crochet over. Make joining st at end of each round around unused yarn to carry it up for next round.

PATTERN

Change colour foll chart.

Using B/1 or C/2 hook and colour 1, make a magic ring.

continued on next page >

KEY

- ▨ Colour 1
- ▨ Colour 2
- ▨ Colour 3
- ○ chain (ch)
- ⊢ double crochet (dc)

Chart shows one side of square; it should be repeated four times on each round.

Read chart from bottom to top, right to left.

Each square represents one stitch.

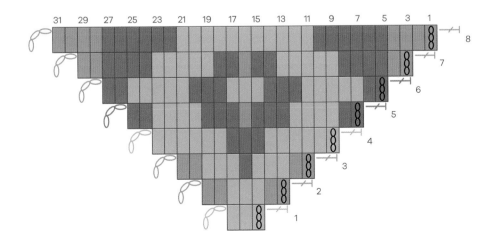

Round 1: Working into ring, 3 ch (counts as 1 dc throughout), 2 dc, [3 ch, 3 dc] 3 times, 1 ch, 1 dc in top of beg 3-ch to join, changing to colour 2 on this st. (12 sts, 4 x 3ch-sp corners)

Round 2: 3 ch, 1 dc in corner sp, *3 dc, (2 dc, 3 ch, 2 dc) in corner sp; rep from * 3 more times ending 2 dc in corner sp, 1 ch, 1 dc in top of beg 3-ch to join. (28 sts, 4 x 3ch-sp corners)

Round 3: 3 ch, 1 dc in corner sp, *7 dc, (2 dc, 3 ch, 2 dc) in corner sp; rep from * 3 more times ending 2 dc in corner sp, 1 ch, 1 dc in top of beg 3-ch to join. (44 sts, 4 x 3ch-sp corners)

Round 4: 3 ch, 1 dc in corner sp, *11 dc, (2 dc, 3 ch, 2 dc) in corner sp; rep from * 3 more times ending 2 dc in corner sp, 1 ch, 1 dc in top of beg 3-ch to join. (60 sts, 4 x 3ch-sp corners)

Round 5: 3 ch, 1 dc in corner sp, *6 dc, skip 1 st, 3 FPtr in middle st of Round 4, skip 1 st, 6 dc, (2 dc, 3 ch, 2 dc) in corner sp; rep from * 3 more times ending 2 dc in corner sp, 1 ch, 1 dc in top of beg 3-ch to join. (76 sts, 4 x 3ch-sp corners)

Round 6: 3 ch, 1 dc in corner sp, *19 dc, (2 dc, 3 ch, 2 dc) in corner sp; rep from * 3 more times ending 2 dc in corner sp, 1 ch, 1 dc in top of beg 3-ch to join. (92 sts, 4 x 3ch-sp corners)

Round 7: 3 ch, 1 dc in corner sp, *23 dc, (2 dc, 3 ch, 2 dc) in corner sp; rep from * 3 more times ending 2 dc in corner sp, 1 ch, 1 dc in top of beg 3-ch to join. (108 sts, 4 x 3ch-sp corners)

Round 8: 3 ch, 1 dc in corner sp, *27 dc, (2 dc, 3 ch, 2 dc) in corner sp; rep from * 3 more times ending 2 dc in corner sp, 1 ch, 1 dc in top of beg 3-ch to join. (124 sts, 4 x 3ch-sp corners)

Fasten off and weave in ends.

KEY

☐	Colour 1
☐	Colour 2
☐	Colour 3
⦵	chain (ch)
⊢	double crochet (dc)

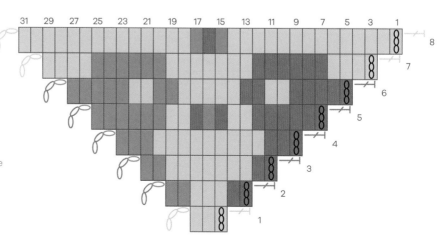

Chart shows one side of square; it should be repeated four times on each round.

Read chart from bottom to top, right to left.

Each square represents one stitch.

PORTO TRAIN STATION

DESIGNER: STEFFI GLAVES

YARN

Stylecraft Special DK, light worsted (DK), in foll shade:

Colour 1: Waterfall (1125)

James C Brett Baby Twinkle DK, light worsted (DK), in foll shade:

Colour 2: Cream (BT6)

HOOK

US size B/1 or C/2 (2.5mm) hook

GAUGE (TENSION)

A single motif measures approx 6¾in (17cm) using a US size B/1 or C/2 (2.5mm) hook.

NOTES

Motif is worked in tapestry crochet in rounds.
Change to next colour on last yoh of prev st. Carry unused yarn across work and crochet over. Make joining st at end of each round around unused yarn to carry it up for next round.

PATTERN

Change colour foll chart.

Using B/1 or C/2 hook and colour 1, make a magic ring.

Round 1: Working into ring, 3 ch (counts as 1 dc throughout), 2 dc, [3 ch, 3 dc] 3 times, 1 ch, 1 dc in top of beg 3-ch to join. (12 sts, 4 x 3ch-sp corners)

Round 2: 3 ch, 1 dc in corner sp, *1 dc, 1 FPtr, 1 dc, 2 dc in corner sp, 1 ch, 1 FPtr around 3rd and 4th dc sts tog on corner, 1 ch, 2 dc in corner sp; rep from * 3 more times ending 1 FPtr around 3rd and 4th dc sts tog on corner, 1 dc in top of beg 3-ch to join. (28 sts, 4 x 1ch-sp + FPtr + 1ch-sp corners)

Round 3: 3 ch, 1 dc in corner sp, *2 dc, skip 1 st, 3 dc in FP st from Round 2, skip 1 st, 2 dc, 2 dc in corner sp, 1 ch, 1 FPtr in FP st of Round 2, 1 ch, 2 dc in corner sp; rep from * 3 more times ending 1 FPtr in FP st of Round 2, 1 dc in top of beg 3-ch to join. (44 sts, 4 x 1ch-sp + FPtr + 1ch-sp corners)

Round 4: 3 ch, 1 dc in corner sp, *3 dc, 2 dc in next st, dc3tog, 2 dc in next st, 3 dc, 2 dc in corner sp, 1 ch, 1 FPtr in FP st of Round 3, 1 ch, 2 dc in corner sp; rep from * 3 more times ending 1 FPtr in FP st of Round 3, 1 dc in top of beg 3-ch to join. (60 sts, 4 x 1ch-sp + FPtr + 1ch-sp corners)

continued on next page >

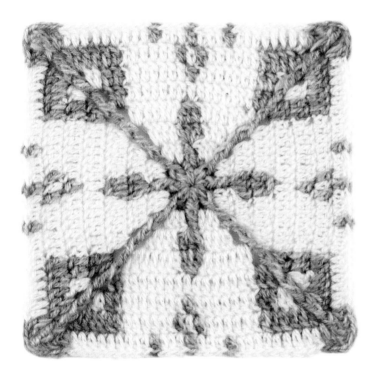

KEY

▨	Colour 1
☐	Colour 2
⌀	chain (ch)
⊢	double crochet (dc)

Chart shows one side of square; it should be repeated four times on each round.

Read chart from bottom to top, right to left.

Each square represents one stitch.

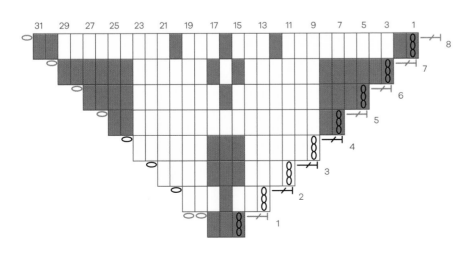

Round 5: 3 ch, 1 dc in corner sp, *15 dc, 2 dc in corner sp, 1 ch, 1FPtr in FP st of Round 4, 1 ch, 2 dc in corner sp; rep from * 3 more times ending 1 FPtr in FP st of Round 4, 1 dc in top of beg 3-ch to join. (76 sts, 4 x 1ch-sp + FPtr + 1ch-sp corners)

Round 6: 3 ch, 1 dc in corner sp, *19 dc, 2 dc in corner sp, 1 ch, 1FPtr in FP st of Round 5, 1 ch, 2 dc in corner sp; rep from * 3 more times ending 1 FPtr in FP st of Round 5, 1 dc in top of beg 3-ch to join. (92 sts, 4 x 1ch-sp + FPtr + 1ch-sp corners)

Round 7: 3 ch, 1 dc in corner sp, *23 dc, 2 dc in corner sp, 1 ch, 1FPtr in FP st of Round 6, 1 ch, 2 dc in corner sp; rep from * 3 more times ending 1 FPtr in FP st of Round 6, 1 dc in top of beg 3-ch to join. (108 sts, 4 x 1ch-sp + FPtr + 1ch-sp corners)

Round 8: 3 ch, 1 dc in corner sp, *27 dc, 2 dc in corner sp, 1 ch, 1 FPtr in FP st of Round 7, 1 ch, 2 dc in corner sp; rep from * 3 more times ending 1 FPtr in FP st of Round 3, 1 dc in top of beg 3-ch to join. (134 sts, 4 x 1ch-sp + FPtr + 1ch-sp corners)

Fasten off and weave in ends.

PRAÇA DE RIBEIRA 1

DESIGNER: STEFFI GLAVES

YARN

Cygnet DK, light worsted (DK), in foll shade:
Colour 1: Juniper (1348)
Stylecraft Special DK, light worsted (DK), in foll shade:
Colour 2: Parchment (1218)
Rico Essentials Acrylic Antipilling DK, light worsted (DK), in foll shades:
Colour 3: Burgundy (003)
Colour 4: Berry (002)

HOOK

US size B/1 or C/2 (2.5mm) hook

GAUGE (TENSION)

A single motif measures approx 6¾in (17cm) using a US size B/1 or C/2 (2.5mm) hook.

NOTES

Motif is worked in tapestry crochet in rounds.
Change to next colour on last yoh of prev st. Carry unused yarn across work and crochet over. Make joining st at end of each round around unused yarn to carry it up for next round.

PATTERN

Change colour foll chart.

Using B/1 or C/2 hook and colour 1, make a magic ring.

Round 1: Working into ring, 3 ch (counts as 1 dc throughout), 2 dc,

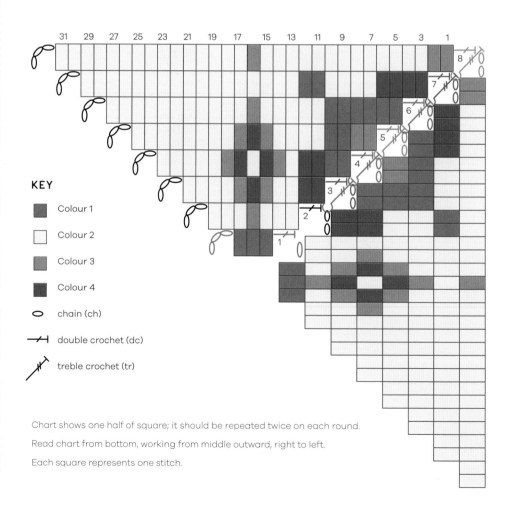

KEY

- ■ Colour 1
- □ Colour 2
- ■ Colour 3
- ■ Colour 4
- ⬯ chain (ch)
- ⊢ double crochet (dc)
- ⚹ treble crochet (tr)

Chart shows one half of square; it should be repeated twice on each round.

Read chart from bottom, working from middle outward, right to left.

Each square represents one stitch.

[3 ch, 3 dc] 3 times, 1 ch, 1 dc in top of beg 3-ch to join. (12 sts)

Round 2: 3 ch, 1 dc in corner sp, *3 dc, [2 dc, 3 ch, 2 dc] in corner sp; rep from * 3 more times ending 1 ch, 1 dc in top of beg 3-ch to join. (28 sts, 4 x 3ch-sp corners)

Round 3: 3 ch, 1 dc in corner sp, *7 dc, [2 dc, 2 ch, 2 dc] in corner sp, 7 dc, [2 dc, 1 FPtrtog around 2 corner dc in Round 2, 2 ch, 2 dc] in corner sp; rep from * twice more, 1 ch, 1 dc in top of beg 3-ch to join. (44 sts, 2 x 3ch-sp corners, 2 x 2ch-sp + FPtrtog + 2ch-sp corners)

Round 4: 3 ch, 1 dc in corner sp, *11 dc, [2 dc, 3 ch, 2 dc] in corner sp, 11 dc, 2 dc in corner sp, 2 ch, 1 FPtr around Round 3 FP st, 2 ch, 2 dc in corner ch sp; rep from * twice more omitting final 2 ch and 2 dc, 1 dc in top of beg 3-ch to join. (60 sts, 2 x 3ch-sp corners, 2 x 2ch-sp + FPtrtog + 2ch-sp corners)

Round 5: 3 ch, 1 dc in corner sp, *15 dc, [2 dc, 3 ch, 2 dc] in corner sp, 15 dc, 2 dc in corner sp, 2 ch, 1 FPtr around Round 4 FP st, 2 ch, 2 dc in corner sp; rep from * twice more omitting final 2 ch and 2 dc, 1 dc in top of beg 3-ch to join. (76 sts, 2 x 3ch-sp corners, 2 x 2ch-sp + FPtrtog + 2ch-sp corners)

Round 6: 3 ch, 1 dc in corner sp, *19 dc, [2 dc, 3 ch, 2 dc] in corner sp, 19 dc, 2 dc in corner sp, 2 ch, 1 FPtr around Round 5 FP st, 2 ch, 2 dc in corner sp; rep from * twice more omitting final 2 ch and 2 dc, 1 dc in top of beg 3-ch to join. (92 sts, 2 x 3ch-sp corners, 2 x 2ch-sp + FPtrtog + 2ch-sp corners)

Round 7: 3 ch, 1 dc in corner sp, *23 dc, [2 dc, 3 ch, 2 dc] in corner ch sp, 23 dc, 2 dc in corner sp, 2 ch, 1 FPtr around Round 6 FP st, 2 ch, 2 dc in corner sp; rep from * twice more omitting final 2 ch and 2 dc, 1 dc in top of beg 3-ch to join. (108 sts, 2 x 3ch-sp corners, 2 x 2ch-sp + FPtrtog + 2ch-sp corners)

Round 8: 3 ch, 1 dc in corner sp, *27 dc, [2 dc, 3 ch, 2 dc] in corner sp, 27 dc, 2 dc in corner sp, 2 ch, 1 FPtr around Round 7 FP st, 2 ch, 2 dc in corner sp; rep from * twice more omitting final 2 ch and 2 dc, 1 dc in top of beg 3-ch to join. (124 sts, 2 x 3ch-sp corners, 2 x 2ch-sp + FPtrtog + 2ch-sp corners)

Fasten off and weave in ends.

PRAÇA DE RIBEIRA 2

DESIGNER: STEFFI GLAVES

YARN

Rico Essentials Acrylic Antipilling DK, light worsted (DK), in foll shades:
Colour 1: Berry (002)
Colour 2: Teal (014)
Cygnet DK, light worsted (DK), in foll shade:
Colour 3: Juniper (1348)

HOOK

US size B/1 or C/2 (2.5mm) hook

GAUGE (TENSION)

A single motif measures approx 7in (18cm) using a US size B/1 or C/2 (2.5mm) hook.

NOTES

*Motif is worked in tapestry crochet in rounds.
Change to next colour on last yoh of prev st. Carry unused yarn across work and crochet over. Make joining st at end of each round around unused yarn to carry it up for next round.*

PATTERN

Change colour foll chart.

Using B/1 or C/2 hook and colour 1, make a magic ring.

Round 1: Working into ring, 3 ch (counts as first dc throughout), 2 dc, [3 ch, 3 dc] 3 times, 1 ch, 1 dc in top of beg 3-ch to join, change to colour 2 on last yoh. (12 sts, 4 x 3ch-sp corners)

continued on next page >

Round 2: 3 ch, 1 dc in corner sp, *1 dc, 1 FPtr, 1 dc, [2 dc, 3 ch, 2 dc] in corner sp; rep from * 3 more times ending 2 dc in corner sp, 1 ch, 1 dc in top of beg 3-ch to join. (28 sts, 4 x 3ch-sp corners)

Round 3: 3 ch, 1 dc in corner sp, *3 dc, 1 FPdc, 3 dc, [2 dc, 3 ch, 2 dc] in corner sp; rep from * 3 more times ending 2 dc in corner sp, 1 ch, 1 dc in top of beg 3-ch to join. (44 sts, 4 x 3ch-sp corners)

Round 4: 3 ch, 1 dc in corner sp, *5 dc, 1 FPdc, 5 dc, [2 dc, 3 ch, 2 dc] in corner sp; rep from * 3 more times ending 2 dc in corner sp, 1 ch, 1 dc in top of beg 3-ch to join. (60 sts, 4 x 3ch-sp corners)

Round 5: 3 ch, 1 dc in corner sp, *5 dc, 1 FPtr around middle FP st, 5 dc, 1 FPtr around middle FP st, 5 dc, [2 dc, 3 ch, 2 dc] in corner sp; rep from * 3 more times ending 2 dc in corner sp, 1 ch, 1 dc in top of beg 3-ch to join. (84 sts, 4 x 3ch-sp corners)

Round 6: 3 ch, 1 dc in corner sp, *10 dc, 1 FPtr around right FP st from Round 5, 1 FPtr around left FP st, skip 1 st, 10 dc, [2 dc, 3 ch, 2 dc] in corner sp; rep from * 3 more times ending 2 dc in corner sp, 1 ch, 1 dc in top of beg 3-ch to join. (104 sts, 4 x 3ch-sp corners)

Round 7: 3 ch, 1 dc in corner sp, *12 dc, 1 FPtrtog around 2 FP sts from Round 6, 12 dc, [2 dc, 3 ch, 2 dc] in corner sp; rep from * 3 more times ending 2 dc in corner sp, 1 ch, 1 dc in top of beg 3-ch to join. (116 sts, 4 x 3ch-sp corners)

Round 8: 3 ch, 1 dc in corner sp, *14 dc, 1 FPtr, 14 dc, [2 dc, 3 ch, 2 dc] in corner sp; rep from * 3 more times ending 2 dc in corner sp, 1 ch, 1 dc in top of beg 3-ch to join. (132 sts, 4 x 3ch-sp corners)

Fasten off and weave in ends.

KEY

- ▥ Colour 1
- ▨ Colour 2
- ▧ Colour 3
- ○ chain (ch)
- ⊢ double crochet (dc)

Chart shows one side of square; it should be repeated four times on each round.

Read chart from bottom to top, right to left.

Each square represents one stitch.

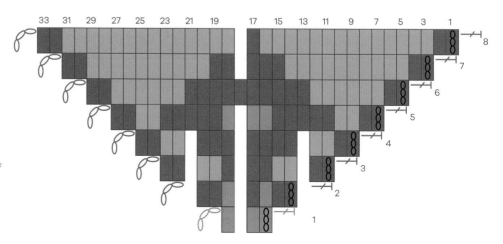

SAO BENTO

DESIGNER: STEFFI GLAVES

YARN

Stylecraft Special DK, light worsted (DK), in foll shade:
Colour 1: Parchment (1218)
Cygnet DK, light worsted (DK), in foll shade:
Colour 2: Juniper (1348)

HOOK

US size B/1 or C/2 (2.5mm) hook

GAUGE (TENSION)

A single motif measures approx 6¾in (17cm) using a US size B/1 or C/2 (2.5mm) hook.

SPECIAL ABBREVIATION

5dc-PC, popcorn of 5 dc

NOTES

Motif is worked in tapestry crochet in rounds.
Change to next colour on last yoh of prev st. Carry unused yarn across work and crochet over. Make joining st at end of each round around unused yarn to carry it up for next round..

PATTERN

Change colour foll chart.

Using B/1 or C/2 hook and colour 1, make a magic ring.

Round 1: Working into ring, 3 ch (counts as 1 dc throughout), 2 dc, [3 ch, 3 dc] 3 times, 1 ch, 1 dc in top of beg 3-ch to join. (12 sts, 4 x 3ch-sp corners)

Round 2: 3 ch, 1 dc in corner sp, *1 dc, 5dc-PC, 1 dc, (2 dc, 3 ch, 2 dc) in corner sp; rep from * 3 more times ending 2 dc in corner sp, 1 ch, 1 dc in top of beg 3-ch to join. (28 sts, 4 x 3ch-sp corners)

Round 3: 3 ch, 1 dc in corner sp, *1 dc, 1 FPtr in PC from Round 2, 5dc, 1 FPtr in same PC, 1 dc, [2 dc, 3 ch, 2 dc] in corner sp; rep from * 3 more times ending 2 dc in corner sp, 1 ch, 1 dc in top of beg 3-ch to join. (52 sts, 4 x 3ch-sp corners)

Round 4: 3 ch, 1 dc in corner sp, *3 dc, 1 FPtr in FP st, skip 1 st, 3 dc, skip 1 dc, 1 FPtr in FP st, 3 dc, (2 dc, 3 ch, 2 dc) in corner sp; rep from * 3 more times ending 2 dc in corner sp, 1 ch, 1 dc in top of beg 3-ch to join. (60 sts, 4 x 3ch-sp corners)

continued on next page >

KEY

☐	Colour 1
■	Colour 2
⬭	chain (ch)
⊢	double crochet (dc)

Chart shows one side of square; it should be repeated four times on each round.

Read chart from bottom to top, right to left.

Each square represents one stitch.

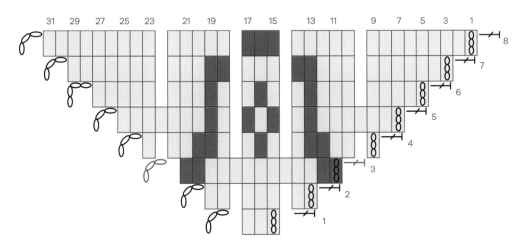

Round 5: 3 ch, 1 dc in corner sp, *2 dc, 1 FPdtr in FP st, 11 dc, 1 FPdtr in FP st, 2 dc, (2 dc, 3 ch, 2 dc) in corner sp; rep from * 3 more times ending 2 dc in corner sp, 1 ch, 1 dc in top of beg 3-ch to join. (84 sts, 4 x 3ch-sp corners)

Round 6: 3 ch, 5dc-PC in corner sp, *4 dc, 1 FPtr in FP st, 11 dc, 1 FPtr in FP st, 4 dc, (5dc-PC, 4 ch, 5dc-PC) in corner sp; rep from * 3 more times ending 2 dc in corner sp, 1 ch, 1 dc in top of beg 3-ch to join. (92 sts, 4 x 4ch-sp corners)

Round 7: 3 ch, 2 dc in corner sp, *1 dc in PC, 2 dc, 1 FPdtr in FP st, skip 1st, 13 dc, 1 FPdtr in FP st, skip 1st, 2 dc, 1 dc in PC, (3 dc, 3 ch, 3 dc) in corner sp; rep from * 3 more times ending 2 dc in corner sp, 1 ch, 1 dc in top of beg 3-ch to join. (108 sts, 4 x 3ch-sp corners)

Round 8: 3 ch, 1 dc in corner sp, *4 dc, 1 FPtr in FP st, 17 dc, 1 FPtr in FP post, 4 dc (2 dc, 3 ch, 2 dc) in corner sp; rep from * 3 more times ending 1 ch, 1 dc in top of beg 3-ch to join. (124 sts, 4 x 3ch-sp corners)

Fasten off and weave in ends.

BERRY HEARTS

DESIGNER: STEFFI GLAVES

YARN

Rico Essentials Acrylic Antipilling DK, light worsted (DK), in foll shades:
Colour 1: Berry (002)
Colour 4: Burgundy (003)
Stylecraft Special DK, light worsted (DK), in foll shade:
Colour 2: Parchment (1218)
Cygnet DK, light worsted (DK), in foll shade:
Colour 3: Jam (1910)

HOOK

US size B/1 or C/2 (2.5mm) hook

GAUGE (TENSION)

A single motif measures approx 6¾in (17cm) using a US size B/1 or C/2 (2.5mm) hook.

SPECIAL ABBREVIATION

5dc-PC, popcorn of 5 dc

NOTES

Motif is worked in tapestry crochet in rounds.
Change to next colour on last yoh of prev st. Carry unused yarn across work and crochet over. Make joining st at end of each round around unused yarn to carry it up for next round.

PATTERN

Change colour foll chart.

Using B/1 or C/2 hook and colour 1, make a magic ring.

Round 1: Working into ring, 3 ch (counts as 1 dc throughout), 2 dc, [3 ch, 3 dc] 3 times ending 1 ch, 1 dc in top of beg 3-ch to join. (12 sts, 4 x 3ch-sp corners)

Round 2: 3 ch, 1 dc in corner sp, *3 dc, [2 dc, 3 ch, 2 dc] in corner sp; rep from * 3 more times ending 1 ch, 1 dc in top of beg 3-ch to join. (28 sts, 4 x 3ch-sp corners)

Round 3: 3 ch, 1 dc in corner sp, *7 dc, [2 dc, 3 ch, 2 dc] in corner sp; rep from * 3 more times ending 1 ch, 1 dc in top of beg 3-ch to join. (44 sts, 4 x 3ch-sp corners)

Round 4: 3 ch, 1 dc in corner sp, *11 dc, [2 dc, 3 ch, 2 dc] in corner sp; rep from * 3 more times ending 1 ch, 1 dc in top of beg 3-ch to join. (60 sts, 4 x 3ch-sp corners)

Round 5: 3 ch, 1 dc in corner sp, *15 dc, 2 dc in corner sp, 2 ch, 1 FPtrtog around 2 sts either side of corner sp from Round 4, 2 ch, 2 dc in corner sp; rep from * 3 more times ending 1 FPtrtog around 2 sts either side of corner sp from Round 4, 1 dc in top of beg 3-ch to join. (76 sts, 4 x 2ch-sp + FPtrtog + 2ch-sp corners)

Round 6: 3 ch, 1 dc in corner sp, *1 FPdc around FP st from Round 5, skip st FP covers, 17 dc, 1 FPtr around FP st from Round 5, 2 dc in corner sp, 2 ch, 1 FPtr around same FP st from Round 5, 2 dc, 2 dc in corner sp; rep from * 3 more times ending 1 FPtr around same FP st from Round 5, 1 dc in top of beg 3-ch to join. (92 sts, 4 x 2ch-sp + FPtrtog + 2ch-sp corners)

Round 7: 3 ch, 1 dc in corner sp, *2 dc, 1 FPdc around FP st from Round 6, skip st FP covers, 17 dc, 1 FPtr around FP st from Round 6, skip st FP covers, 2 dc, 2 dc in corner sp, 2 ch, 1 FPtr around corner FP st from Round 6, 2 ch, 2 dc in corner sp; rep from * 3 more times ending 1 FPtr around corner FP st from Round 6, 1 dc in top of beg 3-ch to join. (108 sts, 4 x 2ch-sp + FPtrtog + 2ch-sp corners)

Round 8: 3 ch, complete 5dc-PC in corner sp, *27 dc, 5dc-PC in corner sp, 3 ch, 1 FPtr around corner FP st from Round 7, 3 ch, 5dc-PC in corner sp; rep from * 3 more times ending 1 FPtr around corner FP st from Round 7, 1 dc in top of beg 3-ch to join, slst. (108 sts, 8 PC, 4 x 3ch-sp + FPtrtog + 3ch-sp corners)

Fasten off and weave in ends.

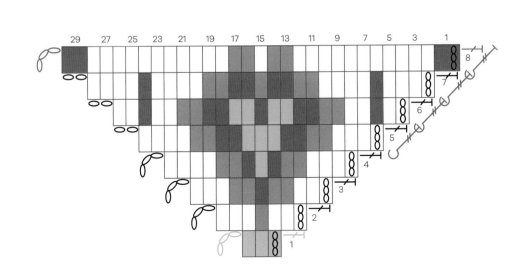

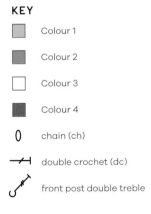

KEY

■ Colour 1

■ Colour 2

□ Colour 3

■ Colour 4

0 chain (ch)

⊢ double crochet (dc)

ſ front post double treble

Chart shows one side of square; it should be repeated four times on each round.

Read chart from bottom to top, right to left.

Each square represents one stitch.

WHITE AND YELLOW

DESIGNER: MEGHAN BALLMER

YARN

Bernat Softee Cotton, light worsted (DK), in foll shades:
Colour 1: Golden
Colour 2: Cotton

HOOK

US size F/5 (3.75mm) hook

GAUGE (TENSION)

A single motif measures approx 7in (18cm) using a US size F/5 (3.75mm) hook.

NOTES

Motif is worked in tapestry crochet from Row 2 onward.
Change to next colour on last yoh of prev st. Carry unused yarn and crochet over.

PATTERN

Change colour foll chart.

Using F/5 hook and colour 1, 32 ch.

Row 1 (RS): 1 sc in 2nd ch from hook, 1 sc in each ch to end. (31 sts)

Row 2 (WS): 1 ch (does not count as st), 1 sc in each st to end.

Rows 3 to 33: As Row 2.

Fasten off and weave in ends.

KEY

Colour 1

Colour 2

Read chart from bottom to top, odd numbered (RS) rows are read right to left, even numbered (WS) rows are read left to right.

Each square represents one stitch.

PAOLOZZI

DESIGNER: STEFFI GLAVES

YARN

Cygnet DK, light worsted (DK), in foll shades:

Colour 1: Fuchsia (676)

Colour 2: Cloud (2033)

Colour 3: Burnt Orange (4888)

Colour 4: Emerald (377)

Colour 5: Black (217)

Colour 6: Jam (1910)

Colour 7: Apple (6711)

Colour 8: White (208)

Colour 9: Red (1206)

Colour 10: Sunshine (184)

HOOK

US size B/1 or C/2 (2.5mm) hook

GAUGE (TENSION)

A single motif measures approx 7in (18cm) using a US size B/1 or C/2 (2.5mm) hook.

NOTES

Motif is worked in intarsia crochet in rows.
All rows are worked on RS right to left with no turning.
There is little carrying of yarns with colour changes.
To change colour, leave prev colour behind. When starting new row with prev colour, pick up yarn as you change colour and "crochet in" excess yarn between last st of prev row and new st of new row. The only times that carrying yarn over occurs is when 2 colours interchange frequently, such as in black and white chequered areas.

continued on next page >

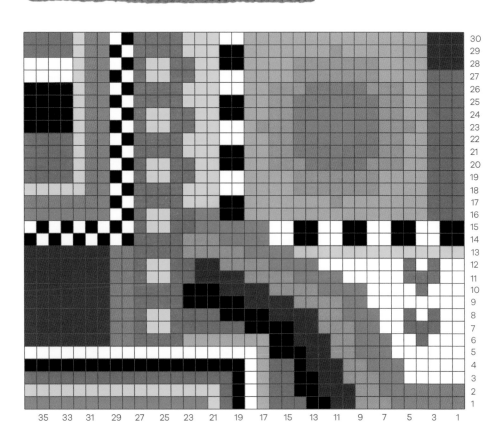

KEY

■ Colour 1

■ Colour 2

■ Colour 3

■ Colour 4

■ Colour 5

■ Colour 6

■ Colour 7

☐ Colour 8

■ Colour 9

■ Colour 10

Read the chart from bottom to top, odd numbered rows are read right to left, even numbered rows are read left to right.

Each square represents one stitch.

PATTERN

Change colour foll chart.

Using B/1 or C/2 hook and colour 1, 37 ch.

Row 1: 1 sc in 2nd ch from hook, 35 sc. (36 sts)

Fasten off colour 1.

Rows 2 to 30: 1 ch (does not count as st throughout), 36 scBLO. (36 sts)

BORDER

Round 1: Join colour 1 at beg of Row 30, 36 sc, 2 ch, 31 sc down left side, 2 ch, 36 sc along ch sts at bottom, 2 ch, 31 sc up right side, 1 ch, 1 sc in side of first border st to join. (36 sts on top and bottom, 31 sts on sides)

Round 2: 1 ch, 1 sc in corner sp, *36 sc, (1 sc, 2 ch, 1 sc) in 2ch-sp, 31 sc, (1 sc, 2 ch, 1 sc) in 2ch-sp; rep from * once working last 1 sc in side of first border st to join. (38 sts top and bottom, 33 sts on sides)

Round 3: As Round 2. (40 sts top and bottom, 35 sts on sides)

Fasten off and weave in ends.

CIRCE

DESIGNER: HATTIE RISDALE

YARN

Phildar Phil Coton 4, light worsted (DK), in foll shades:
Colour 1: Cyan (1362)
Colour 2: Craie (1937)
Colour 3: Rosee (1149)

HOOK

US size G/6 (4mm) hook

GAUGE (TENSION)

A single motif measures approx 6¾in (17cm) using a US size G/6 (4mm) hook.

SPECIAL ABBREVIATION

5tr-cl, cluster of 5 tr

PATTERN

Using G/6 hook and colour 1, make a magic ring.

Round 1: Working in ring, 4 ch (counts as 1 dc, 1 ch), *1 dc, 1 ch; rep from * 11 more times, slst in 3rd ch of beg 4-ch to join, do not fasten off. (12 dc, 12 ch)

Round 2: Slst in 1ch-sp, 1 ch (counts as 1 sc), 1 sc in same sp, 2 sc in each sp around, slst in beg 1-ch to join, do not fasten off. (24 sc)

Round 3: 3 ch (counts as first part of 5tr-cl) complete 5tr-cl in same sp, 3 ch, *skip 1 st, (5tr-cl, 3 ch) in next st; rep from * around, slst in top of beg 5tr-cl to join, do not fasten off. (12 x 5tr-cl, 12 x 3ch-sp)

Round 4: 1 ch (counts as 1 sc), *1 sc in first ch of 3-ch, 3 sc in ch-sp, 1 sc in top of 5tr-cl, rep from * around omitting sc in top of 5tr-cl on last rep, slst in beg 1-ch to join. (60 sc)

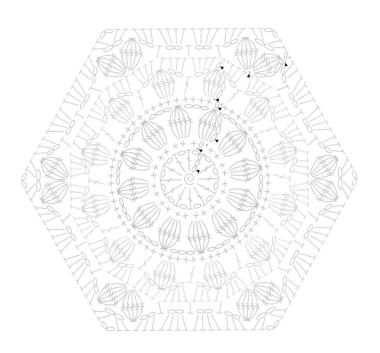

Fasten off colour 1.

Round 5: Join colour 2 with slst in top of any sc in first ch of 3-ch, 3 ch (counts as first part of 5tr-cl), complete 5tr-cl, 2 ch, (1 dc, 2 ch) in 3rd sc of 3 sc, *(5tr-cl, 2 ch) in first ch of 3-ch, (1 dc, 2 ch) in 3rd sc of 3 sc; rep from * around, slst in top of beg 5tr-cl to join, do not fasten off. (12 x 5tr-cl, 12 dc, 24 x 2ch-sp)

Round 6: 2 ch (counts as 1 hdc), *4 hdc in 2ch-sp after 5tr-cl, 3 hdc in next 2ch-sp, 1 hdc in top of 5tr-cl; rep from * around omitting hdc in top of 5tr-cl on last rep, slst in 2nd of beg 2-ch to join. (96 hdc)

Fasten off colour 2.

Round 7: Join colour 3 with slst in any sp between two sets of hdc (above 1-dc in Round 5), 3 ch (counts as first part of 5tr-cl), (complete 5tr-cl, 2 ch, 5tr-cl) in same sp, (2 ch, 1 hdc) in sp between two hdc groups (above 5tr-cl), [(2 ch, 1 hdc) in sp between next two hdc groups] twice, 2 ch, *(5tr-cl, 2 ch, 5tr-cl) in sp between next two hdc groups, [(2 ch, 1 hdc) in sp between two hdc groups] 3 times, 2 ch; rep from * around, slst in top of beg 5tr-cl to join, do not fasten off. (12 x 5tr-cl, 18 hdc, 30 x 2ch-sp)

Round 8: 2 ch (counts as 1 hdc), *(2 hdc, 2 ch, 2 hdc) in corner 2ch-sp, 3 hdc in next 2ch-sp, 4 hdc in next two 2ch-sp, 3 hdc in next 2ch-sp; rep from * around omitting final hdc on last rep, slst in top of beg 2-ch to join. (108 hdc, 6 x 2ch-sp)

Fasten off and weave in all ends.

IRIS

DESIGNER: HATTIE RISDALE

YARN

Paintbox Yarns Cotton DK, light worsted (DK), in foll shades:
Colour 1: Champagne White (403)
Colour 2: Marine Blue (434)
Colour 3: Candyfloss Pink (450)
Colour 4: Washed Teal (433)

HOOK

US size G/6 (4mm) hook

GAUGE (TENSION)

A single motif measures approx 6¾in (17cm) from point to point using a US size G/6 (4mm) hook.

SPECIAL ABBREVIATIONS

4dc-cl, cluster of 4 dc
4tr-cl, cluster of 4 tr

NOTE

In Round 7, first dc after dc3tog is worked in same st as last leg of dc3tog, and first leg of next dc3tog after 3-dc group is worked in same st as last dc of 3-dc group.

PATTERN

Using G/6 hook and colour 1, make a magic ring.

Round 1: 3 ch (counts 1 dc) 11 dc in ring, slst in 3rd ch of beg 3-ch to join. (12 dc)

Fasten off colour 1.

Round 2: Join colour 2 with slst in any sp between two dc, 1 ch (counts as 1 sc), 1 sc in same sp, 2 sc in each sp around, slst in beg 1-ch to join. (24 sc)

Fasten off colour 2.

continued on next page >

Round 3: Join colour 3 with slst in any sp between pairs of 2-sc, 2 ch (counts as first part of 4dc-cl), (complete 4dc-cl, 2 ch) in same sp, (4dc-cl, 2 ch) in each sp between pairs of 2-sc around, slst in first ch at top of first 4dc-cl to join. (12 x 4dc-cl, 12 x 2ch-sp)

Fasten off colour 3.

Round 4: Join colour 4 with slst in any 2ch-sp, (4 ch, 4tr-cl, 4 ch, slst) in same sp, *slst into next 2ch-sp, (4 ch, 4tr-cl, 4 ch, slst) in same sp; rep from * around, slst in beg 2-ch sp, slst in beg slst to join. (12 x 4tr-cl)

Fasten off colour 4.

Round 5: Join colour 2 with slst in space between sts in middle of any 4tr-cl, 1 ch (counts as 1 sc), (1 sc, 5 ch) in same sp, *(2 sc, 5 ch) in space between sts in middle of next 4tr-cl; rep from * around, slst in beg 1-ch to join. (24 sc, 12 x 5ch-sp)

Fasten off colour 2.

Round 6: Join colour 1 with slst in any 5ch-sp, 3 ch (counts as 1 dc), 6 dc in same sp, *7 dc in next 5ch-sp; rep from * around, slst in top of beg 3-ch to join, do not fasten off. (84 dc)

Round 7: 3 ch (counts as first part of dc3tog), complete dc3tog over 2nd and 3rd sts, 1 dc in 3rd st, 1 dc, 1 dc in 5th st, dc3tog over 5th, 6th and 7th sts, 2 ch, dc3tog over 8th, 9th and 10th sts, 1 dc in 10th st, 1 dc, 1 dc in 12th st, dc3tog beg in 12th st, 3 ch, [dc3tog, 1 dc in prev dc, 2 dc, dc3tog beg in prev dc, 2 ch, dc3tog, 1 dc in prev dc, 2 dc, dc3tog beg in prev dc, 3 ch] 5 times, slst in top of beg dc3tog to join, do not fasten off. (24 x dc3tog, 36 dc, 6 x 2ch-sp, 6 x 3ch-sp)

Round 8: 2 ch (counts as 1 hdc), 1 hdc in same st, *4 hdc, 2 hdc in 2ch-sp, 4 hdc, 2hdc in next st, (1 hdc, 2 ch, 1 hdc) in 3ch-sp (corner), 2 hdc in next sp; rep from * 5 more times omitting final 2 hdc on last rep, slst in top of beg 2-ch to join. (96 hdc, 6 x 2ch-sp corners)

Fasten off and weave in ends.

ATHENA

DESIGNER: HATTIE RISDALE

YARN

Paintbox Yarns Cotton DK, light worsted (DK), in foll shades:

Colour 1: Marine Blue (434)
Colour 2: Candyfloss Pink (450)
Colour 3: Champagne White (403)
Colour 4: Washed Teal (433)

HOOK

US size G/6 (4mm) hook

GAUGE (TENSION)

A single motif measures approx 7in (18cm) using a US size G/6 (4mm) hook.

SPECIAL ABBREVIATION

3dc-cl, cluster of 3 dc

PATTERN

Using G/6 hook and colour 1, make a magic ring.

Round 1: Working in ring, 2 ch (counts as part of 3dc-cl), complete 3dc-cl, 2 ch, *3dc-cl, 2 ch; rep from * 4 more times, slst in top of beg 3dc-cl to join. (6 clusters, 6 x 2ch-sp)

Fasten off colour 1.

Round 2: Join colour 2 with slst in any 2ch-sp, 3 ch (counts as 1 dc throughout), 5 dc in same ch-sp, *skip cluster, 6 dc in next ch-sp; rep from * around, slst in 3rd of beg 3-ch to join. (36 dc)

Fasten off colour 2.

Round 3: Join colour 1 with slst in any sp between two 6-dc groups, 3 ch, *(1 dc, 4 ch, 1 dc) in middle of 6-dc group, 2 dc in sp between two 6-dc groups; rep from * 4 more times, (1 dc, 4 ch, 1 dc) in middle of 6-dc group, 1 dc in beg ch-sp, slst in 3rd of beg 3-ch to join. (24 dc, 6 x 4ch-sp)

Fasten off colour 1.

Round 4: Join colour 3 with slst between 2 dc, *1 ch, (4 dc, 2 ch, 4 dc, 1 ch) in 4ch-sp, slst between 2 dc; rep from * around, with final slst in beg slst to join. (48 dc, 12 ch-sp, 6 x 2ch-sp)

Fasten off colour 3.

Round 5: Join colour 1 with slst in any 2ch-sp (at tip of petal), 2 ch (counts as 1 sc, 1 ch), *(3 tr, 3 ch) in 1ch-sp (at base of petal), (3 tr, 1 ch) in next 1ch-sp (at base of next petal), (2 sc, 1 ch) in 2ch-sp (at tip of petal); rep from * 4 more times, (3 tr, 3 ch) in 1ch-sp, (3 tr, 1 ch) in next 1ch-sp, 1 sc in last 2ch-sp, slst in first of beg 2-ch to join. (36 tr, 12 sc, 12 ch, 6 x 3ch-sp corners)

Fasten off colour 1.

continued on next page >

Round 6: Join colour 2 with slst in any 1ch-sp to right of 2-sc, 2 ch (counts as 1 hdc thoughout), (2 hdc, 1 ch) in same sp, (3 hdc, 1 ch) in next 1ch-sp, *(3 hdc, 1 ch, 3 hdc, 1 ch) in 3ch-sp, (3 hdc, 1 ch) in next two 1ch-sps; rep from * 4 more times, (3 hdc, 1 ch, 3 hdc, 1 ch) in final 3ch-sp, slst in 2nd of beg 2-ch. (72 hdc, 24 ch)

Fasten off colour 2.

Round 7: Join colour 4 with slst in any 1ch-sp to left of corner group, 2 ch, (2 hdc, 1 ch) in same sp, (3 hdc, 1 ch) in next two ch-sps, (2 hdc, 1 ch, 2 hdc, 1 ch) in corner sp, *(3 hdc, 1 ch) in next three ch-sps, (2 hdc, 1 ch, 2 hdc, 1 ch) in corner sp; rep from * 4 more times, slst in 2nd of beg 2-ch to join. (78 hdc, 30 ch)

Fasten off colour 4.

Round 8: Join colour 3 with slst in any 1ch-sp to left of corner, 3 ch, 2 dc in same sp, *4 dc in next two ch-sps, 3 dc in next sp, (2 dc, 2 ch, 2 dc) in corner sp; rep from * around, slst in 3rd of beg 3-ch to join. (108 dc, 6 x 2ch-sp corners)

Fasten off and weave in ends.

TALAVERA 2

DESIGNER: EMMA POTTER

YARN

Sirdar Snuggly DK, light worsted (DK), in foll shades:
Colour 1: White (251)
Colour 2: Pastel Blue (321)
Colour 3: Apricot (495)
Colour 4: Sunshine (500)

HOOK

US size G/6 (4mm) hook.

GAUGE (TENSION)

A single motif measures approx 5½in (14cm) using a US size G/6 (4mm) hook.

SPECIAL ABBREVIATION

3dc-cl, cluster of 3 dc
3dc-PC, popcorn of 3 dc

PATTERN

Using G/6 hook and colour 1, 4 ch, slst to join into a ring.

Round 1: 3 ch (counts as first dc throughout), complete 3dc-cl, 3 ch, [3dc-cl, 3 ch] 5 times, slst in top of beg 3-ch to join. (6 x 3dc-cl, 6 x 3ch-sp corners)

Fasten off colour 1.

Round 2: Join colour 2 in cluster, 3 ch, [5 dc in 3ch-sp, 1 dc in cluster] around, slst in top of beg 3-ch to join. (36 sts)

Fasten off colour 2.

Round 3: Join colour 3 in dc after join, 3 ch, 1 tr, 1 dtr, 1 tr, 1 dc, 2 ch, skip next st, [1 dc, 1 tr, 1 dtr, 1 tr, 1 dc, 2 ch, skip next st] around, join slst in top of beg 3-ch to join. (12 dc, 12 dtr, 24 tr, 6 x 2ch-sp)

Fasten off colour 3.

Round 4: Join colour 4 in first dc of Round 3, 1 ch (counts as first sc throughout), 4 sc, 3 tr in st below 2ch-sp, [5 sc, 3 tr in st below 2ch-sp] around, slst in beg 1-ch to join. (30 sc, 18 tr)

Round 5: 3 ch, 4 dc, (3 ch, 3dc-PC, 2 ch) in central tr, [5 dc, (3 ch, 3dc-PC, 3 ch) in central tr] around, slst in top of beg 3-ch to join. (6 PC, 30 dc, 12 x 3ch-sp)

Fasten off colour 4.

Round 6: Join colour 1 in first dc of Round 5, 1 ch, 4 sc, (3 dc in base, 1 sc in top, 3dc in base) of PC, [5 sc, (3 dc in base, 1 sc in top, 3 dc in base) of next PC] around, slst in beg 1-ch to join. (36 sc, 36 dc)

Round 7: 1 ch, 7 sc, (1 sc, 2 ch, 1 sc) in sc at top of PC, [11 sc, (1 sc, 2 ch, 1 sc) in sc at top of PC] around, 3 sc, slst in beg 1-ch to join. (78 sc, 6 x 2ch-sp)

Fasten off and weave in ends.

FLORAL HEXAGON

DESIGNER: RACHELE CARMONA

YARN

Scheepjes Stone Washed, sport (4ply), in foll shades:
Colour 1: Garnet (810)
Colour 2: Canada Jade (806)
Colour 3: New Jade (819)
Colour 4: Yellow Jasper (809)

HOOK

US size G/6 (4mm) hook

GAUGE (TENSION)

A single motif measures approx 6in (15cm) from top to bottom using a US size G/6 (4mm) hook.

SPECIAL ABBREVIATION

3ch-picot, picot with 3 ch

PATTERN

Using G/6 hook and colour 1, 3 ch, slst to join into a ring.

Round 1: 12 sc in ring, slst in first sc to join. (12 sc)

Round 2: (1 sc, 1 ch) in next st (counts as first dc throughout), 3 dc in same st, [1 ch, skip 1 st, 4 dc in next st] 5 times, 1 ch, slst in first dc to join. (24 dc, 6 x 1ch-sp corners)

Round 3: (1 sc, 2 ch) in same st as slst (counts as first tr), tr3tog, [3 ch, tr in ch-sp, 3ch-picot, 3 ch, tr4tog] 5 times, 3 ch, tr in ch-sp, 3ch-picot, 3 ch, slst in tr3tog. (6 x tr4tog, 6 picot, 6 tr, 12 x 3ch-sp)

Fasten off colour 1.

Round 4: Join colour 2 with slst in first 3ch-sp of Round 3, 1 sc in same sp, [5 ch, 1 sc in next ch-sp, 3 ch, 1 sc in next ch-sp] 6 times omitting final sc, slst in first sc to join. (12 sc, 6 x 5ch-sp, 6 x 3ch-sp)

Round 5: (1 sc, 1 ch) in first ch-sp, (2 dc, 1 ch, 3 dc) in same sp, *1 ch, 3 dc in next ch-sp, 1 ch, (3 dc, 1 ch, 3 dc) in next ch-sp, rep from * 4 times, 1 ch, 3dc in next ch-sp, 1 ch, slst in first dc to join. (54 dc, 18 ch-sp)

Fasten off colour 2.

Round 6: Join colour 3 with slst in first 1ch-sp, (1 sc, 1 ch, 1 dc, 1 ch, 2 dc) all in same sp, *[1 ch, 3 dc in next ch-sp] twice, 1 ch, (2 dc, 1 ch, 2 dc) in next ch-sp, rep from * 4 times, [1 ch, 3 dc in next ch-sp] twice, 1 ch, slst in first dc to join. (60 dc, 24 ch-sp)

Fasten off colour 3.

Round 7: Join colour 4 with slst in first ch-1 sp, (1 sc, 1 ch, 1 dc, 1 ch, 2dc) all in same sp, *[1 ch, 3 dc in next ch-sp] 3 times, 1 ch, (2 dc, 1 ch, 2 dc) in next ch-sp, rep from * 4 times, [1 ch, 3 dc in next ch-sp] 3 times, 1 ch, slst in first dc to join. (78 dc, 30 ch-sp)

Fasten off and weave in ends.

CRYSTAL RIPPLE

DESIGNER: RACHELE CARMONA

YARN

Scheepjes Stone Washed, sport (4ply), in foll shades:
Colour 1: Yellow Jasper (809)
Colour 2: Lepidolite (830)
Colour 3: Lilac Quartz (818)
Colour 4: Amazonite (813)
Colour 5: Turquoise (824)
Colour 6: Moon Stone (801)

HOOK

US size G/6 (4mm) hook

GAUGE (TENSION)

A single motif measures approx 6in (15cm) from flat top to bottom using a US size G/6 (4mm) hook.

SPECIAL ABBREVIATIONS

2tr-cl, cluster of 2 tr
3ch-picot, picot with 3 ch

NOTE

Treble sts in Round 2 make "bobbles" on RS of motif.

PATTERN

Using G/6 hook and colour 1, 3 ch, slst to join into a ring.

Round 1: (1 sc, 1 ch) in ring (counts as first dc throughout), 17 dc in ring, slst in first dc to join. (18 dc)

Fasten off colour 1.

Round 2: Join colour 2 with slst in any dc, (1 sc, 1 tr) in each st around, slst in first sc to join. (18 tr, 18 dc)

Fasten off colour 2.

Round 3: Join colour 3 with slst in any sc, (1 sc, 2 ch) in same st (counts as first tr), complete 2tr-cl in same st, [3 ch, 2tr-cl in next sc] 17 times, 3 ch, slst in 2nd tr to join. (18 x 2tr-cl, 18 x 3ch-sp)

Fasten off colour 3.

Round 4: Join colour 4 with slst in any ch-sp, 3 sc in same sp, [1 sc in 2tr-cl, 3 sc in next sp] 17 times, 1 sc in 2tr-cl, slst in first sc to join. (72 sc)

Round 5: (1 sc, 1 ch) in next st, 2 dc in same st, [1 ch, skip 3 sts, 3 dc in next st) 17 times, 1 ch, slst in first dc to join. (54 dc, 18 ch-sp)

Fasten off colour 4.

Round 6: Join colour 5 with slst in first sc of Round 5, 1 sc in same st, [1 FPdc in next st, 3ch-picot, 1 sc in next st, 1 ch, 1 sc in next sc] 18 times omitting final sc, slst in first sc to join. (18 FPdc, 18 picot, 36 sc, 18 ch-sp)

Fasten off colour 5.

Round 7: Join colour 6 with slst in any ch-sp, 1 sc in same sp, *[4 ch, sc in next ch-sp] twice, 6 ch, 1 sc in next ch-sp, rep from * 5 times omitting final sc, slst in first sc to join. (18 sc, 12 x 4ch-sp, 6 x 6ch-sp)

Round 8: [5 sc in next two 4ch-sps, 7 sc in next ch-sp] 6 times, slst in first sc to join. (102 sc)

Fasten off and weave in ends.

FLORAL BURST

DESIGNER: CATHERINE NORONHA

YARN

Stylecraft Special DK, light worsted (DK), in foll shades:

Colour 1: Mustard (1823)
Colour 2: Teal (1062)
Colour 3: Petrol (1708)
Colour 4: Boysenberry (1828)
Colour 5: Cream (1005)

HOOK

US size E/4 (3.5mm) hook

GAUGE (TENSION)

A single motif measures approx 7½in (19cm) from top to bottom using a US size E/4 (3.5mm) hook.

SPECIAL ABBREVIATION

2dc-cl, cluster of 2 dc

NOTES

Motif is worked in tapestry crochet from Round 3 onward.
Change to next colour on last yoh of prev st. Carry unused yarn and crochet over. Make joining slst at end of each round around unused yarn to carry it up for next round.

From Round 2 onward, each round starts with 3 ch, which counts as 1 dc, 1 ch. This is final dc of one side of motif, plus ch to form first corner ch-sp. Other corner ch-sps are formed of 2 ch.

PATTERN

Change colour foll chart.

Using E/4 hook and colour 1, make a magic ring.

Round 1 (RS): Working into ring, 2 ch, 1 dc (counts as 2dc-cl), 1 ch, [2dc-cl, 2 ch] 5 times, slst in beg dc to join. (6 x 2dc-cl, 1 x 1ch-sp corner, 5 x 2ch-sp corners)

Fasten off colour 1.

Round 2: Join colour 2 to any ch-sp, 3 ch (counts as 1 dc, 1 ch throughout), 1 dc in ch-sp, *1 dc, (1 dc, 2 ch, 1 dc) in 2ch-sp; rep from * 4 more times, 1 dc, slst in 2nd ch of beg 3-ch, slst in ch-sp to join. (18 dc, 1 x 1ch-sp corner, 5 x 2ch-sp corners)

Round 3: 3 ch, 1 dc in ch-sp, *3 dc, (1 dc, 2 ch, 1 dc) in 2ch-sp; rep from * 4 more times, 3 dc, slst in 2nd ch of beg 3-ch, slst in ch-sp to join. (30 dc, 1 x 1ch-sp corner, 5 x 2ch-sp corners)

Round 4: 3 ch, 1 dc in ch-sp, *5 dc, (1 dc, 2 ch, 1 dc) in 2ch-sp; rep from * 4 more times; 5 dc, slst in 2nd ch of beg 3-ch, slst in ch-sp to join. (42 dc, 1 x 1ch-sp corner, 5 x 2ch-sp corners)

Round 5: 3 ch, 1 dc in ch-sp, *7 dc, (1 dc, 2 ch, 1 dc) in 2ch-sp; rep from * 4 more times, 7 dc, slst in 2nd ch of beg 3-ch, slst in ch-sp to join. (54 dc, 1 x 1ch-sp corner, 5 x 2ch-sp corners)

Round 6: 3 ch, 1 dc in ch-sp, *9 dc, (1 dc, 2 ch, 1 dc) in 2ch-sp; rep from * 4 more times, 9 dc, slst in 2nd ch of beg 3-ch, slst in ch-sp to join. (66 dc, 1 x 1ch-sp corner, 5 x 2ch-sp corners)

Round 7: 3 ch, 1 dc in ch-sp, *11 dc, (1 dc, 2 ch, 1 dc) in 2ch-sp; rep from * 4 more times; 11 dc, slst in 2nd ch of beg 3-ch, slst in ch-sp to join. (78 dc, 1 x 1ch-sp corner, 5 x 2ch-sp corners)

Round 8: 1 ch (does not count as st), (1 sc, 2 dc, 1 sc) in ch-sp, *13 sc, (1 sc, 2 ch, 1 sc) in 2ch-sp; rep from * 4 more times, 13 sc, slst in beg sc to join. (90 sc, 1 x 1ch-sp corner, 5 x 2ch-sp corners)

Fasten off and weave in ends.

Chart illustrates one side of hexagon; it should be repeated six times on each round.

Each square represents one dc stitch, except in Round 1, where square represents one 2dc-cl, and in Round 8, where each square represents one sc stitch.

Read all chart rows from right to left.

KEY

- Colour 1
- Colour 2
- Colour 3
- Colour 4
- Colour 5
- O chain (ch)

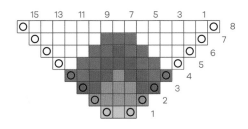

STARBURST

DESIGNER: CATHERINE NORONHA

YARN

Stylecraft Special DK, light worsted (DK), in foll shades:
Colour 1: Boysenberry (1828)
Colour 2: Cream (1005)

HOOK

US size E/4 (3.5mm) hook

GAUGE (TENSION)

A single motif measures approx 8in (20cm) from top to bottom using a US size E/4 (3.5mm) hook.

SPECIAL ABBREVIATION

2dc-cl, cluster of 2 dc

NOTES

Motif is worked in tapestry crochet from Round 4 onward.
Change to next colour on last yoh of prev st. Carry unused yarn and crochet over. Make joining slst at end of each round around unused yarn to carry it up for next round.
From Round 2 onward, each round starts with 3 ch, which counts as 1 dc, 1 ch. This is final dc of one side of motif, plus ch st to form first corner ch-sp. Other corner ch-sps are formed of 2 ch.

PATTERN

Change colour foll chart.

Using E/4 hook and colour 1, make a magic ring.

Round 1 (RS): Working into ring, 2 ch, 1 dc (counts as 2dc-cl), 1 ch, [2dc-cl, 2 ch] 5 times, slst in beg dc, slst in ch-sp to join. (6 x 2dc-cl, 1 x 1ch-sp corner, 5 x 2ch-sp corners)

Round 2: 3 ch (counts as 1 dc, 1 ch throughout), 1 dc in ch-sp, *1 dcBLO, (1 dc, 2 ch, 1 dc) in 2ch-sp; rep from * 4 more times, 1 dcBLO, slst in 2nd ch of beg 3-ch, slst in ch-sp to join. (18 dc, 1 x 1ch-sp corner, 5 x 2ch-sp corners)

Round 3: 3 ch, 1 dc in ch-sp, *3 dcBLO, (1 dc, 2 ch, 1 dc) in 2ch-sp; rep from * 4 more times; 3 dcBLO, slst in 2nd ch of beg 3-ch, slst in ch-sp to join. (30 dc, 1 x 1ch-sp corner, 5 x 2ch-sp corners)

Round 4: 3 ch, 1 dc in ch-sp, *5 dcBLO, (1 dc, 2 ch, 1 dc) in 2ch-sp; rep from * 4 more times; 5 dcBLO, slst in 2nd ch of beg 3-ch, slst in ch-sp to join. (42 dc, 1 x 1ch-sp corner, 5 x 2ch-sp corners)

Round 5: 3 ch, 1 dc in ch-sp, *7 dcBLO, (1 dc, 2 ch, 1 dc) in 2ch-sp; rep from * 4 more times; 7 dcBLO, slst in 2nd ch of beg 3-ch, slst in ch-sp to join. (54 dc, 1 x 1ch-sp corner, 5 x 2ch-sp corners)

Round 6: 3 ch, 1 dc in ch-sp, *9 dcBLO, (1 dc, 2 ch, 1 dc) in 2ch-sp; rep from * 4 more times; 9 dcBLO, slst in 2nd ch of beg 3-ch, slst in ch-sp to join. (66 dc, 1 x 1ch-sp corner, 5 x 2ch-sp corners)

Round 7: 3 ch, 1 dc in ch-sp, *11 dcBLO, (1 dc, 2 ch, 1 dc) in 2ch-sp; rep from * 4 more times; 11 dcBLO, slst in 2nd ch of beg 3-ch, slst in ch-sp to join. (78 dc, 1 x 1ch-sp corner, 5 x 2ch-sp corners)

Round 8: 3 ch, 1 dc in ch-sp, *13 dcBLO, (1 dc, 2 ch, 1 dc) in 2ch-sp; rep from * 4 more times; 13 dcBLO, slst in 2nd ch of beg 3-ch to join. (90 dc, 1 x 1ch-sp corner, 5 x 2ch-sp corners)

Fasten off and weave in ends.

Chart shows one side of hexagon; it should be repeated six times on each round.

Read chart from bottom to top, right to left.

Each square represents one stitch.

KEY

■ Colour 1

□ Colour 2

O chain (ch)

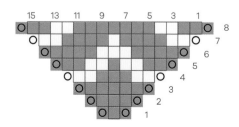

CLEMATIS

DESIGNER: CATHERINE NORONHA

YARN

Stylecraft Special DK, light worsted (DK), in foll shades:

Colour 1: Mustard (1823)

Colour 2: Cream (1005)

Colour 3: Boysenberry (1828)

Colour 4: Teal (1062)

HOOK

US size E/4 (3.5mm) hook

GAUGE (TENSION)

A single motif measures approx 8in (20cm) from top to bottom using a US size E/4 (3.5mm) hook.

SPECIAL ABBREVIATION

2dc-cl, cluster of 2 dc

NOTES

Motif is worked in tapestry crochet from Round 2 onward.

Change to next colour on last yoh of prev st. Carry unused yarn and crochet over except when you make a FPdc, in which case carry unused yarn across WS (behind FPdc). Make joining slst at end of each round around unused yarn to carry it up for next round.

From Round 2 onward, each round starts with 3 ch, which counts as 1 dc, 1 ch. This is final dc of one side of motif, plus ch to form first corner ch-sp. Other corner ch-sps are formed of 2 ch.

PATTERN

Change colour foll chart.

Using E/4 hook and colour 1, make a magic ring.

Round 1 (RS): Working into ring, 2 ch, 1 dc (counts as 2dc-cl), 1 ch, [2dc-cl, 2 ch] 5 times, slst in beg dc to join. (6 x 2dc-cl, 1 x 1ch-sp corner, 5 x 2ch-sp corners)

Fasten off colour 1.

Round 2: Join colour 2 to any ch-sp, 3 ch (counts as 1 dc, 1 ch throughout), 1 dc in ch-sp, *1 FPdc, (1 dc, 2 ch, 1 dc) in 2ch-sp; rep from * 4 more times, 1 FPdc, slst in 2nd ch of beg 3-ch, slst in ch-sp to join. (18 dc, 1 x 1ch-sp corner, 5 x 2ch-sp corners)

Round 3: 3 ch, 1 dc in ch-sp, *1 dc, 1 FPdc, 1 dc, (1 dc, 2 ch, 1 dc) in 2ch-sp; rep from * 4 more times, 1 dc, 1 FPdc, 1 dc, slst in 2nd ch of beg 3-ch, slst in ch-sp to join. (30 dc, 1 x 1ch-sp corner, 5 x 2ch-sp corners)

Round 4: 3 ch, 1 dc in ch-sp, *2 dc, 1 FPdc, 2 dc, (1 dc, 2 ch, 1 dc) in 2ch-sp; rep from * 4 more times, 2 dc, 1 FPdc, 2 dc, slst in 2nd ch of beg 3-ch, slst in ch-sp to join. (42 dc, 1 x 1ch-sp corner, 5 x 2ch-sp corners)

Round 5: 3 ch, 1 dc in ch-sp, *3 dc, 1 FPdc, 3 dc, (1 dc, 2 ch, 1 dc) in 2ch-sp; rep from * 4 more times, 3 dc, 1 FPdc, 3 dc, slst in 2nd ch of beg 3-ch, slst in ch-sp to join. (54 dc, 1 x 1ch-sp corner, 5 x 2ch-sp corners)

Round 6: 3 ch, 1 dc in ch-sp, *4 dc, 1 FPdc, 4 dc, (1 dc, 2 ch, 1 dc) in 2ch-sp; rep from * 4 more times, 4 dc, 1 FPdc, 4 dc, slst in 2nd ch of beg 3-ch, slst in ch-sp to join. (66 dc, 1 x 1ch-sp corner, 5 x 2ch-sp corners)

Round 7: 3 ch, 1 dc in ch-sp, *5 dc, 1 FPdc, 5 dc, (1 dc, 2 ch, 1 dc) in 2ch-sp; rep from * 4 more times; 5 dc, 1 FPdc, 5 dc, slst in 2nd ch of beg 3-ch, slst in ch-sp. (78 dc, 1 x 1ch-sp corner, 5 x 2ch-sp corners)

Round 8: 3 ch, 1 dc in ch-sp, *13 dc, (1 dc, 2 ch, 1 dc) in 2ch-sp; rep from * 4 more times, 13 dc, slst in 2nd ch of beg 3-ch to join. (90 dc, 1 x 1ch-sp corner, 5 x 2ch-sp corners)

Fasten off and weave in ends.

Chart shows one side of hexagon; it should be repeated six times on each round.

Read chart from bottom to top, right to left.

Each square represents one stitch.

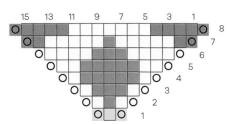

KEY

▨	Colour 1
☐	Colour 2
▓	Colour 3
▒	Colour 4
O	chain (ch)

OCTAGONAL FLOWER

DESIGNER: LYNNE ROWE

YARN

Ricorumi DK Cotton, light worsted (DK), in foll shades:
Colour 1: Light Blue (033)
Colour 2: Denim (034)
Colour 3: Cream (002)

HOOK

US size E/4 (3.5mm) hook.

GAUGE (TENSION)

A single motif measures approx 6½in (16.5cm) side to side using a US size E/4 (3.5mm) hook.

PATTERN

Using E/4 hook and colour 1, make a magic ring.

Round 1 (RS): Working in ring, 3 ch (counts 1 dc throughout), 1 dc, [1 ch, 2 dc] 7 times, 1 ch, slst in top of beg 3-ch to join. (16 dc, 8 ch)

Fasten off colour 1.

Round 2: Join colour 2 in any 1ch-sp, 3 ch, (1 dc, 1 ch, 2 dc) in same sp, *skip next 2 dc, (2 dc, 1 ch, 2 dc) in next 1ch-sp; rep from * 6 more times, skip last 2 dc, slst in top of beg 3-ch to join. (32 dc, 8 ch)

Round 3: Slst in next dc, slst in next 1ch-sp, 4 ch (counts as 1 tr), 6 tr in same sp, *2 ch, skip next 4 dc, 7 tr in next 1ch-sp; rep from * 6 more times, skip last 4 dc, slst in top of beg 4-ch to join. (8 x 7-tr petals, 8 x 2ch-sp)

Fasten off colour 2.

Round 4: Join colour 3 in BLO of first tr of any petal, 1 ch (does not count as st throughout), 1 scBLO in same st, 6 scBLO, 1 dc in sp between groups of 2-dc in Round 2 (working over 2ch-sp of Round 3), *7 scBLO, 1 dc in sp between groups of 2-dc in Round 2 (working over 2ch-sp of Round 3); rep from * 6 more times, slst in first sc to join. (56 scBLO, 8 dc)

Fasten off colour 3.

Round 5: Join colour 1 in middle sc of any petal (4th sc of 7-sc), 1 ch, 1 sc in same st, 2 hdc, 3 dc, 2 hdc, *1 sc, 2 hdc, 3 dc, 2 hdc; rep from * 6 more times, sl st in first sc to join. (64 sts)

Fasten off colour 1.

Round 6: Join colour 3 in any sc, 4 ch (counts as 1 dc, 1 ch), 1 dc in same st, 7 dc, *(1 dc, 1 ch, 1 dc) in sc, 7 dc; rep from * 6 more times, slst in 3rd ch of beg 4-ch to join. (72 dc, 8 x 1ch-sp corners)

Round 7: Slst in 1ch-sp, 4 ch (counts as 1 dc, 1 ch), 1 dc in same st, 9 dc, *(1 dc, 1 ch, 1 dc) in next 1ch-sp, 9 dc; rep from * 6 more times, slst in 3rd of beg 4-ch to join. (88 dc, 8 x 1ch-sp corners)

Fasten off colour 3.

Round 8: Join colour 1 to any 1ch-sp, 1 ch, (1 hdc, 1 ch, 1 hdc) in same 1ch-sp, 11 hdc, *(1 hdc, 1 ch, 1 hdc) in next 1ch-sp, 11 hdc; rep from * 6 more times, slst in 3rd ch of beg 4-ch to join. (104 hdc, 8 x 1ch-sp corners)

Fasten off and weave in ends.

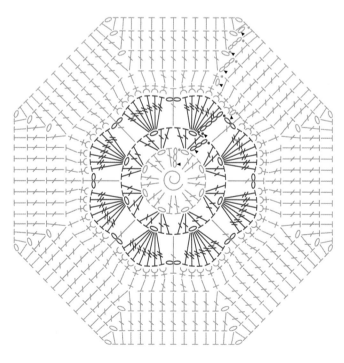

MARINE FLOWER

DESIGNER: ANNA NIKIPIROWICZ

YARN

Rowan Felted Tweed, light worsted (DK), in foll shades:
Colour 1: Fjord (218)
Colour 2: Duck Egg (173)
Colour 3: Clay (177)

HOOK

US size E/4 (3.5mm) hook

GAUGE (TENSION)

A single motif measures approx 7in (18cm) from point to point using a US size E/4 (3.5mm) hook.

SPECIAL ABBREVIATION

V-st, (1 dc, 2 ch, 1 dc) in same st

NOTE

Join yarn with standing sts unless otherwise indicated, and join round with invisible join in standing st.

PATTERN

Using E/4 hook and colour 1, make a magic ring.

Round 1: 1 ch (does not count as st), 8 hdc in ring, enclosing yarn end as you work, pull on yarn end to close opening, slst in first hdc to join. (8 hdc)

Round 2: 1 ch, 1 hdc, 1 ch, [1 hdc, 1 ch] 7 times, make invisible join in beg hdc. (8 hdc, 8 ch-sp)

Fasten off colour 1.

Round 3: Join colour 2, 1 stsc in first hdc, (1 hdc, 1 dc, 2 ch, 1 dc, 1 hdc) in 1ch-sp, *1 sc, (1 hdc, 1 dc, 2 ch, 1 dc, 1 hdc) in 1ch-sp, *rep from * to end. (16 hdc, 16 dc, 8 sc, 8 x 2ch-sp)

Fasten off colour 2.

Round 4: Join colour 3, 1 stdc in first sc, 2 ch, 1 dc in same st, skip next 2 sts, 1 sc in next 2ch-sp, skip next 2 sts, *V-st in next st, skip next 2 sts, 1 sc in next 2ch-sp, skip next 2 sts; rep from * to end. (8 V-sts, 8 sc)

Fasten off colour 3.

Round 5: Join colour 1, 1 sthdc in first 2ch-sp, (2 dc, 2 ch, 2 dc, 1 hdc) in same ch-sp, skip next st, 1 sc in sc, skip next st, *(1 hdc, 2 dc, 2 ch, 2 dc, 1 hdc) in next 2ch-sp, skip next st, 1 sc, skip next st; rep from * to end. (32 dc, 16 hdc, 8 sc, 8 x 2ch-sp

Fasten off colour 1.

Round 6: Join colour 3, 1 sttr in first sc, 5 ch, 1 tr in same st, skip next 3 sts, 1 sc in 2ch-sp, skip next 3 sts, *(1 tr, 5 ch, 1 tr) in next st, skip next 3 sts, 1 sc in 2ch-sp, skip next 3 sts; rep from * to end. (16 tr, 8 x 5ch-sp)

Fasten off colour 3.

Round 7: Join colour 2, 1 sthdc in first 5ch-sp, (1 hdc, 2 dc, 1 tr, 2 ch, 1 tr, 2 dc, 2 hdc) in same ch-sp, skip next st, 1 sc in sc, skip next st, *(2 hdc, 2 dc, 1 tr, 2 ch, 1 tr, 2 dc, 2 hdc) in 5ch-sp, skip next st, 1 sc in next sc, skip next st; rep from * to end. (32 hdc, 32 dc, 16 tr, 8 sc, 8 x 2ch-sp)

Fasten off colour 2.

continued on next page >

Round 8: Join colour 3, 1 stsc in first 2ch-sp, 2 ch, 1 sc in same sp, 3 ch, skip 2 sts, dc2tog working one leg in next st, skip 5 sts, work 2nd leg in 6th st, 3 ch, skip next 2 sts, *(1 sc, 2 ch, 1 sc) in 2ch-sp, 3 ch, skip 2 sts, dc2tog working one leg in next st, skip next 5 sts, work 2nd leg in 6th st, 3 ch, skip next 2 sts; rep from * to end. (16 x 3ch-sp, 16 sc, 8 dc, 8 x 2ch-sp corners)

Fasten off colour 3.

Round 9: Join colour 1, 1 stsc in first 2ch-sp, 2 ch, 1 sc in same sp, 1 sc, 5 sc in next 3ch-sp, 1 sc, 5 sc in next 3ch-sp, *1 sc, (1 sc, 2 ch, 1 sc) in next 2ch-sp, 1 sc, 5 sc in next 3ch-sp, 1 sc, 5 sc in next 3ch-sp; rep from * to last st, 1 sc. (120 sc, 8 x 2ch-sp corners)

Fasten off colour 1.

Round 10: Join colour 2, 1 stsc in first 2ch-sp, 2 ch, 1 sc in same sp, 6 sc, sc3tog, 6 sc, *(1 sc, 2 ch, 1 sc) in next 2ch-sp, 6 sc, sc3tog, 6 sc; rep from * to end. (120 sc, 8 x 2ch-sp corners)

Fasten off with invisible join, weave in all ends.

POPCORN ROUNDEL

DESIGNER: ANNA NIKIPIROWICZ

YARN

West Yorkshire Spinners ColourLab DK, light worsted (DK), in foll shades:

Colour 1: Pear Green (186)
Colour 2: Perfectly Plum (362)
Colour 3: Natural Cream (010)
Colour 4: Citrus Yellow (229)

HOOK

US size E/4 (3.5mm) hook

GAUGE (TENSION)

A single motif measures approx 7in (18cm) in diameter using a US size E/4 (3.5mm) hook.

SPECIAL ABBREVIATIONS

4dc-PC, popcorn of 4 dc
spike sc, single crochet worked in st two or more rows below
spike dc, double crochet worked in st two or more rows below

PATTERN

Using E/4 hook and colour 1, make a magic ring.

Round 1: 3 ch (counts as 1 dc), 10 dc in ring, slst in top of 3-ch and pull tight on tail to close ring. (11 dc)

Round 2: 1 ch (does not count as st throughout), 4dc-PC in st at base of 1-ch, [2 ch, 4dc-PC] 10 times, 2 ch, slst in top of first PC to join. (11 PC, 11 x 2ch-sp)

Change to colour 2.

Round 3: 1 ch (does not count as st throughout), 1 sc in top of first PC, [1 sc in next 2ch-sp, 1 spike dc in base of PC, 1 sc in same 2ch-sp, 1 sc in top of next PC] 11 times omitting last sc, slst in first sc to join. (44 sts)

Round 4: 1 ch, 2 sc in first st, 1 sc in each st to end, slst in first sc to join. (45 sc)

Change to colour 1.

Round 5: 1 ch, 4dc-PC in st at base of 1 ch, [3 ch, skip next 2 sts, 4dc-PC] 14 times, 3 ch, skip next 2 sts, slst in top of first PC to join. (15 PC, 15 x 3ch-sp)

Change to colour 2.

Round 6: 1 ch, 1 sc in top of first PC, [1 sc in 3ch-sp, 1 dc in skipped 2 sts in Round 4 (in front of 3-ch), 1 sc in same 3ch-sp, 1 sc in top of next PC] 15 times omitting last sc, slst in first sc to join. (45 sc, 30 dc)

Change to colour 3.

Round 7: 1 ch, 1 sc, 2 ch, skip next 2 sts, [1 sc, 2 ch, skip next 2 sts] 24 times, slst in first sc to join. (25 sc, 25 x 2ch-sp)

Change to colour 2.

Round 8: Slst in first 2ch-sp, 1 ch, 3 hdc in same 2ch sp, skip next st, [3 hdc in next 2ch-sp] 24 times, slst in first hdc to join. (75 hdc)

Change to colour 4.

Round 9: 4 ch (counts as 1 dc, 1 ch-sp throughout), 1 dc in same st, skip next st, *(1 dc, 1 ch, 1 dc) in next st, skip next st; rep from * to last 2 sts, skip last 2 sts, slst in 3rd of 4-ch to join. (74 dc, 37 ch)

Change to colour 1.

Round 10: Slst in first 1ch-sp, 4 ch, 1 dc in same ch-sp, *(1 dc, 1 ch, 1 dc) in next 1ch-sp; rep from * to end, slst in 3rd of 4-ch to join. (74 dc, 37 ch)

Change to colour 3.

Round 11: Slst in first 1ch-sp, 1 ch, 1 sc in same sp, 1 spike sc between two dc 2 rows below, *1 sc in next 1ch-sp, 1 spike sc between two dc 2 rows below; rep from * to end, slst in first st to join. (37 spike sc, 37 sc)

Change to colour 2.

Round 12: 1 ch, *1 spike sc in 1ch-sp 2 rows below, 1 sc; rep from * to end, slst in first st to join. (37 spike sc, 37 sc)

Fasten off and weave in ends.

FLOWER POWER

DESIGNER: RACHELE CARMONA

YARN

Scheepjes Colour Crafter, light worsted (DK), in foll shades:

Colour 1: Leeuwarden (1711)
Colour 2: Leek (1132)
Colour 3: Lelystad (1026)
Colour 4: Delfzijl (1822)
Colour 5: Goes (1820)

HOOK

US size G/6 (4mm) hook

GAUGE (TENSION)

A single motif measures approx 8in (20cm) from top point to bottom point using a US size G/6 (4mm) hook.

SPECIAL ABBREVIATIONS

2dc-cl, cluster of 2 dc
2tr-cl, cluster of 2 tr
4dc-PC, popcorn of 4 dc
3ch-picot, picot with 3 ch

continued on next page >

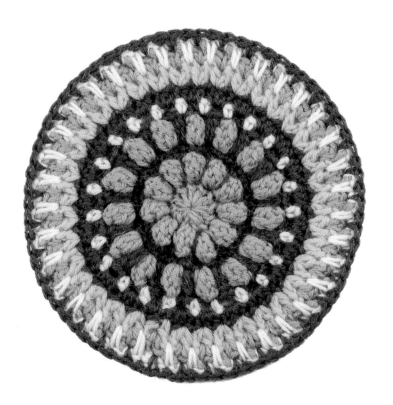

PATTERN

Using G/6 hook and colour 1, 3 ch, slst to join into a ring.

Round 1: (1 sc, 1 ch, 1 dc) in ring (counts as first 2dc-cl), [3 ch, 2dc-cl in ring] 5 times, 3 ch, slst in first 2dc-cl to join. (6 x 2dc-cl, 6 x 3ch-sp)

Fasten off colour 1.

Round 2: Join colour 2 with slst in any ch-sp, (1 sc, 1 ch, 3 dc) in first sp, remove loop from hook, insert hook in ch, grab loop, pull loop to front of work (counts as first 4dc-PC), 3 ch, 4dc-PC in same ch-sp, *(3 ch, 4dc-PC, 3 ch, 4dc-PC) in next ch-sp; rep from * 4 more times, 3 ch, slst in first 4dc-PC to join. (12 x 4dc-PC, 12 x 3ch-sp)

Fasten off colour 2.

Round 3: Join colour 3 with slst in first ch-sp from Round 2, (1 sc, 1 ch) in same ch-sp (counts as first dc), (1 ch, 2 dc, 3 ch, 2 dc) in next 11 ch-sps, (1 ch, 2 dc, 3 ch, 1 dc) in same ch-sp as first st of round, slst in first dc to join. (48 dc, 12 ch, 12 x 3ch-sp)

Round 4: *1 ch, (3 dc, 3ch-picot, 3 dc) in 3ch-sp; rep from * 11 more times, slst in first ch to join. (72 dc, 12 picot, 12 ch)

Fasten off colour 3.

Round 5: Join colour 4 with slst in both first ch-1 sps of Rounds 3 and 4, treating them as one ch-sp, (1 sc, 2 ch, 1 tr) in same sp (counts as first 2tr-cl), [6 ch, 2tr-cl in next 1ch-sps from Rounds 3 and 4, as before] 11 times, 6 ch, slst in first 2tr-cl to join. (12 x 2tr-cl, 12 x 6ch-sps)

Fasten off colour 4.

Round 6: Join colour 5 with slst in any ch-sp, [(3 sc, insert hook in back of sc used to close picot and under ch-sp and make sc to anchor picot to ch-sp, 3 sc) all in 6ch-sp] 12 times, slst in first sc to join. (84 sc)

Round 7: (1 sc, 1 ch) in next st (counts as first dc), *7 ch, skip 3 sts, 3 dc, 5 hdc, 4 dc, 2 dc in next st, 6 dc, 2 dc in next st, 6 dc, 2 dc in next st, 4 dc, 5 hdc, 3 dc; rep from * once more omitting last dc on final rep, slst in first dc to join. (64 dc, 20 hdc, 2 x 7ch-sps)

Round 8: (1 sc, 1 ch) in ch-sp (counts as first hdc), *(1 hdc, 2 dc, 2 tr, 5 ch, 2 tr, 2 dc, 2 hdc) in ch-sp, 2 hdc, 38 sc, 2 hdc, 1 hdc in ch-sp; rep from * once more omitting final hdc, slst in first hdc to join. (8 tr, 8 dc, 16 hdc, 76 sc, 2 x 5ch-sps)

Fasten off and weave in ends.

CLASSICAL OGEE

DESIGNER: RACHELE CARMONA

YARN

Scheepjes Softfun, light worsted (DK), in foll shades:
Colour 1: Crepe (2612)
Colour 2: Cyclamen (2534)
Colour 3: Lace (2426)

HOOK

US size G/6 (4mm) hook

GAUGE (TENSION)

A single motif measures approx 8in (20cm) from top point to bottom point using a US size G/6 (4mm) hook.

SPECIAL ABBREVIATIONS

2dc-cl, cluster of 2 dc
3dc-cl, cluster of 3 dc
4dc-cl, cluster of 4 dc

PATTERN

Round 1: Using G/6 hook and colour 1, 14 ch, 5 dc in 4th ch from hook (turning ch counts as first dc), 1 dc in next 10 ch, 6 dc in end of ch, 1 dc in bottom loop of next 10 ch, slst in first dc to join. (32 dc)

Fasten off colour 1.

Round 2: Join colour 2 with slst in first dc of Round 1, *(1 sc, 1 tr) in end 6 sts, [1 sc, 1 tr, skip next st] 5 times; rep from * once more, slst in first sc to join. (22 sc, 22 tr)

Note: Ensure tr sts pop out to form mini "bobbles" on RS of work on Round 2.

Fasten off colour 2.

Round 3: Join colour 3 with slst in first sc of Round 2, (1 sc, 1 ch, 1 dc) in same st, *[1 ch, (2dc-cl, 1 ch, 2dc-cl) in next sc, 1 ch, 2dc-cl in next sc] 3 times, [1 ch, 2dc-cl in next sc] 5 times; rep from * once more omitting final 2dc-cl, slst in first ch to join. (28 x 2dc-cl, 28 ch)

Fasten off colour 3.

Round 4: Join colour 1 with slst in final ch-sp of Round 3, (1 sc, 1 ch, 3dc-cl) in same sp, *1 ch, 4dc-cl in next ch-sp, [2 ch, 4dc-cl in next ch-sp] 8 times, [1 ch, 4dc-cl in next ch-sp] 5 times; rep from * once more omitting final 4dc-cl, slst in 3dc-cl to join. (28 x 4dc-cl, 12 ch, 16 x 2ch-sp)

Fasten off colour 1.

Round 5: Join colour 2 with slst in first 2ch-sp of Round 4, (1 sc, 1 ch, 2 dc) in same sp, *[1 ch, 3 dc in next ch-sp] 7 times, [1 ch, 2 dc in next 1ch-sp] 6 times, 1 ch, 3 dc in next ch-sp; rep from * once more, 1 ch, slst in first ch to join. (72 dc, 28 ch)

Fasten off colour 2.

TOP POINT

Row 1 (RS): Join colour 3 with slst in 4th ch-sp of Round 5, 1 sc in same ch-sp, 1 sc in next 13 sts/sps, turn. (14 sc)

Row 2: Slst in first st, 1 sc, 1 ch, 1 dc (these count as first dc2tog throughout), 7 dc, dc2tog, leave final st unworked, turn. (2 dc2tog, 7 dc)

Fasten off colour 3.

Row 3: Skip dc2tog, join colour 1 with slst in first dc, 1 sc in same st, 1 ch, 1 dc, 3 dc, dc2tog, turn. (2 dc2tog, 3 dc)

Row 4: Skip dc2tog, 1 sc, 1 ch, 1 dc, dc2tog, turn. (2 dc2tog)

Row 5: 1 sc, 1 ch, 1 dc. (dc2tog)

Fasten off colour 1.

BOTTOM POINT

With RS facing, join colour 3 in last ch-sp of Round 5.

Rows 1 to 5: Work as for Top Point.

Border round (RS): Join colour 3 in dc2tog of point, [5 sc in dc2tog, 11 sc evenly down point, 1 sc in 31 sts/sps, 11 sc evenly up point] twice, slst in first sc to join. (116 sc)

Fasten off and weave in ends.

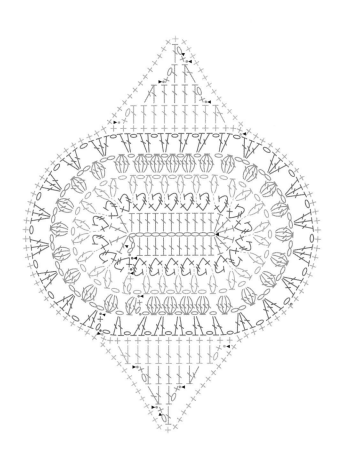

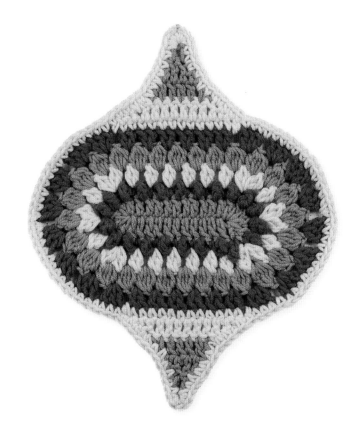

THE
PROJECTS

BABY WHEELS BLANKET

DESIGNER: ANA MORAIS SOARES

YARN

Rosários4 Bio Love (100% organic cotton), sport (4ply), 50g (191yd/175m), in foll shades:
Colour 1: Cream (02); 3 balls
Colour 2: Blue (10); 3 balls
Colour 3: Yellow (03); 2 balls
Colour 4: Beige (18); 2 balls

HOOK

US size C/2 or D/3 (3mm)

GAUGE (TENSION)

A single motif measures approx 7in (18cm) using US size C/2 or D/3 (3mm) hook.

FINISHED SIZE

Blanket measures approx 27½ x 34½in (70 x 88cm)

SPECIAL ABBREVIATION

5dc-cl, cluster worked with 5 double crochet

BLANKET

Make 20 Baby Wheels squares (five squares in each colour).

JOINING SQUARES

Squares are crocheted together through both loops of each stitch. First join squares together with horizontal seams across the width of the blanket, and then join the vertical seams, following the assembly diagram.

Horizontal seam row: Holding first two squares with RS together, work through corresponding sts from each square using colour 1, *1 sc in 2ch-sp corner, [1 ch, skip next st, 1 sc in next st] 21 times, 1 ch, skip next st, 1 sc in next 2ch-sp corner, 1 ch (connection between next set of squares), hold next two squares with RS together; rep from * 4 more times, ending last rep with 1 sc in next 2ch-sp corner.

Fasten off and weave in ends.

Rep horizontal seam row twice more so you have four rows of five squares.

Vertical seam row: Holding vertical rows with RS together each time, join as for horizontal row, with 1-ch connection going over horizontal 1-ch connection.

BORDER

Round 1: With RS of blanket facing and using colour 1, *(1 sc, 2 ch, 1 sc) in 2ch-sp corner (corner made), [43 scBLO, 1 sc in next 2ch-sp, 1 hdcBLO in joining st, 1 sc in next 2ch-sp] 3 times for short sides or 4 times for long sides, 43 scBLO; rep from * all around, slst in beg st to join. (183 sts each short side, 229 sts each long side, 4 x 2ch-sp corners)

Fasten off colour 1.

Round 2: Change to colour 2, *(1 sc, 2 ch, 1 sc) in 2ch-sp corner, 1 sc in every st to next corner; rep from * 3 more times, slst in beg st to join. (185 sts each short side, 231 sts each long side, 4 x 2ch-sp corners)

Fasten off colour 2.

Round 3: Change to colour 1, *(1 sc, 2 ch, 1 sc) in 2ch-sp corner, 1 sc in every st to next corner; rep from * 3 more times, slst in beg st to join. (187 sts each short side, 233 sts each long side, 4 x 2ch-sp corners)

FINISHING

Fasten off, weave in ends and block to size if required.

ASSEMBLY DIAGRAM

HAND-PAINTED TILES CUSHION

DESIGNER: ANA MORAIS SOARES

YARN

Rosários4 Meia (70% merino wool, 30% polyamide), sport (4ply), 50g (202yd/185m), in foll shade:
Colour 1: Dark Blue (12); 3 balls
Rosários4 Meia Print (70% merino wool, 30% polyamide), sport (4ply), 50g (202yd/185m), in foll shade:
Colour 2: Purples and Yellow (119); 3 balls

HOOK

US size C/2 or D/3 (3mm) hook

OTHER TOOLS AND MATERIALS

24 x 24in (60 x 60cm) cushion pad
24 x 24in (60 x 60cm) plain cushion cover with zipper
6in (15cm) wide piece of card

GAUGE (TENSION)

A single motif measures approx 7in (18cm) using a US size C/2 or D/3 (3mm) hook.

FINISHED SIZE

Cushion cover measures approx 24 x 24in (60 x 60cm)

FRONT

Make nine Hand-Painted squares. Crocheted panel is 3 x 3 squares and will be attached to front side of fabric cushion cover.

JOINING SQUARES

Squares are crocheted together through both loops of each st. First join squares together with horizontal seams across the width of the cushion, and then join the vertical seams.

Horizontal seam row: Holding first two squares with RS together, work through corresponding sts from each square using colour 1, *1 sc in 2ch-sp corner, [1 ch, skip next st, 1 sc in next st] 21 times, 1 ch, skip next st, 1 sc in next 2ch-sp corner, 1 ch (connection between next set of squares), hold next two squares with RS together; rep from * twice more, ending last rep with 1 sc in next 2ch-sp corner.

Fasten off and weave in ends.

Rep horizontal seam row once more so you have 3 rows of 3 squares.

Vertical seam row: Holding vertical rows with RS together, join as for horizontal row, with 1 ch connection going over horizontal 1-ch connection.

BORDER

Round 1: With RS facing and using colour 1, *(2 hdc, 2 ch, 2 hdc) in 2ch-sp corner (corner made), [43 hdc, 1 hdc in next 2ch-sp, 1 dcFLO in joining st, 1 hdc in next 2ch-sp] twice, 43 hdc; rep from * 3 more times, slst in first hdc to join. (139 sts each side, 4 x 2ch-sp corners)

Round 2: 1 ch (does not count as st throughout), 1 hdc in same st, 1 hdc in next st, *(2 hdc, 2 ch, 2 hdc) in next 2ch-sp corner, 139 hdc; rep from * 3 more times omitting last 2 hdc, slst in first hdc to join. (143 sts each side, 4 x 2ch-sp corners)

Round 3: 1 ch, 1 hdc in same st, 3 hdc, *(2 hdc, 2 ch, 2 hdc) in next 2ch-sp corner, 143 hdc; rep from * 3 more times omitting last 4 hdc, slst in first hdc to join. (147 sts each side, 4 x 2ch-sp corners)

Round 4: 1 ch, 1 hdc in same st, 5 hdc, *(1 hdc, 2 ch, 1 hdc) in next 2ch-sp corner, skip first st, 146 hdc; rep from * 3 more times omitting last 6 hdc, slst in first hdc to join. (148 sts each side, 4 x 2ch-sp corners)

Round 5: 1 ch, 1 hdc in same st, 6 hdc, *(1 hdc, 2 ch, 1 hdc) in next 2ch-sp corner, 148 hdc; rep from * 3 more times omitting last 7 hdc, slst in first hdc to join. (150 sts each side, 4 x 2ch-sp corners)

FINISHING

Fasten off, weave in all ends and block to size if required.

Hand sew crochet panel to front side of cushion cover with an invisible stitch.

TASSELS

(make 4)

Cut a piece of card 6in (15cm) wide. Cut a 118in (3m) strand of each colour yarn. Holding two strands together, wind around card. Cut another 20in (50cm) strand of colour 1 and slide this under all looped yarn strands at one edge of card. Tie tightly and knot twice to secure, then leave ends free at what will be top of tassel. Gently slide strands from card. Cut another 20in (50cm) strand of colour 1 and wrap it three times tightly around folded strands about one third down from top of tassel. Tie three knots at back of tassel to secure. Cut through strand loops at bottom of tassel and then trim to desired length.

ATTACHING TASSELS

Thread both tails of colour 1 strand at top of one tassel onto a needle. With RS of cushion facing, insert needle from back to front through centre hdc in corner of panel and then under colour 1 strand at top of tassel. Insert needle again into corner of panel, but this time from front to back. Separate colour 1 tails and weave them along either side of corner.

Rep for all four corners.

HEBE BLANKET

DESIGNER: HATTIE RISDALE

YARN

Paintbox Yarns Cotton DK (100% cotton),
light worsted (DK), 50g (137yd/125m), in
foll shades:
Colour 1: Champagne White (403); 5 balls
Colour 3: Candyfloss Pink (450); 2 balls
Colour 4: Marine Blue (434); 1 ball
Colour 5: Washed Teal (433); 1 ball
Sirdar Happy Cotton DK (100% cotton),
light worsted (DK), 20g (47yd/43m), in
foll shade:
Colour 2: Tea Time (751); 1 ball

HOOK

US size G/6 (4mm) hook

GAUGE (TENSION)

A single motif measures approx 7¼in
(18.5cm) using a US size G/6 (4mm) hook.

FINISHED SIZE

Blanket measures approx 29 x 29in
(74 x 74cm)

BLANKET

Make 16 Hebe squares.

JOINING SQUARES

Lay squares out in four rows of four squares. First join squares together horizontally, and then join them together vertically.

Horizontal joining row: Using G/6 hook and colour 1 and with first 2 tiles RS together, join with standing sc in corner 2ch-sp, then work 1 scBLO in corresponding sts of both squares along one side, 1 sc in each corner sp. Join next two squares in same way to make a row of 4.

Rep to join other 3 rows into strips of 4 squares.

Vertical joining row: Holding first two rows with RS together, join as for horizontal row.

Rep to add a third row and then to add the fourth row, so blanket is 4 x 4 squares.

BORDER

Round 1: Join colour 1 with sl st in first hdc after corner 2-ch, 2 ch (counts as 1 hdc), *[1 hdc in each st to join of two squares, (1 hdc, 1 ch) in ch-sp of each square] to corner, (2 hdc, 2 ch, 2 hdc, 1 ch) in corner; rep from * 3 times, slst in 2nd ch of beg 2-ch to join, do not fasten off.

Round 2: 4 ch (counts as 1 dc, 1 ch), *[skip 1 st, (1 dc, 1 ch) in next st] to corner, (2 dc, 2 ch, 2 dc, 1 ch) in corner; rep from * 3 times, slst in 3rd ch of beg 4-ch to join, do not fasten off.

Round 3: Sl st in 1ch-sp, 2 ch (counts as 1 hdc) 1 hdc in same sp, *2 hdc in each 1ch-sp to corner, (2 hdc, 2 ch, 2 hdc) in corner; rep 3 times, slst in 2nd ch of beg 2-ch to join.

FINISHING

Fasten off, weave in all ends and block to size if required.

PARTNERS CUSHION

DESIGNER: ROSINA PLANE

YARN

Stylecraft Special DK (100% acrylic),
light worsted (DK), 100g (322yd/295m),
in foll shades:
Colour 1: Grey (1099); 2 balls
Colour 2: Cream (1005); 1 ball
Colour 3: Buttermilk (1835); 1 ball
Colour 4: Dandelion (1856); 1 ball

HOOK

US size E/4 (3.5mm) hook

OTHER TOOLS AND MATERIALS

Stitch markers
4 buttons, 1⅙6in (18mm)
18 x 18in (45 x 45cm) cushion pad

GAUGE (TENSION)

Annie square measures 4in (10cm) after
Round 8 of patt using a US size E/4
(3.5mm) hook.
Samuel square measures 4in (10cm)
after Round 10 of patt using a US size
E/4 (3.5mm) hook.

FINISHED SIZE

A finished motif measures approx
9in (23cm)
Cushion measures approx 18 x 18in
(45 x 45cm)

NOTE

*A standing st is used at start of edging
so join looks seamless. At end of
round cut yarn, thread into tapestry
needle and work invisible join in top of
standing st.*

FRONT AND BACK

Make four Annie squares and four Samuel squares, substituting colours as given.

JOINING SQUARES

Using E/4 hook and colour 4 and holding two matching squares RS together, join with sc through every st along one edge of both squares tog, starting and ending with sc through corner ch-sps.

Rep for other two matching squares. Now join two pairs of squares in same way to make one large square. Rep with other four matching squares to make second large square.

EDGING

Join colour 4 with stsc in any corner 2ch-sp.

Round 1: *2 ch, 1 sc in same sp, skip 1 st (will be hidden within corner ch), 40 sc, 1 sc in each of central two ch-sp, skip 1 st (again is hidden), 40 sc, 1 sc in 2ch-sp; rep from * 3 more times omitting last sc on final rep. (84 sts each side, 4 x 2ch-sp corners)

Fasten off colour 4, sew to stsc with invisible join, weave in ends. Rep for second large square.

BUTTONHOLE BAND

(make 1)

Using colour 4, make 87 ch.

Row 1: 1 sc in 2nd ch from hook, 1 sc in each ch to end. Turn. (86 sts)

Rows 2 to 4: 1 ch (does not count as st here and throughout), 1 sc I each st to end. Turn. (86 sts)

Row 5 (buttonhole row): 1 ch, 18 sc, [2 ch, skip 2 sts, 14 sc] 4 times, 4 sc. Turn. (78 sts)

Row 6: 1 ch, 18 sc, [1 sc in each of next 2 ch, 14 sc] 4 times, 4 sc. Turn. (86 sts)

Rows 7 and 8: As Row 2.

Fasten off.

MAKING UP

Pin buttonhole band level with top edge of WS of back, making sure left and right edges of both pieces are aligned. Mark positions of buttons on back using st markers. Remove buttonhole band and attach buttons in marked positions.

Hold front and back WS tog, with RS of front facing you and buttons on top edge of back. Place buttonhole band between both parts, with final row at top, and join colour 4 with stsc through first corner 2ch-sp of front, first st of buttonhole band and first corner 2ch-sp of back. Make 2 more sc in same st/sps. Drop back, and work a row of sc through front and buttonhole band only. At end of row, pick up back again and work final sc through last 2ch-sp front and back, and final st of Buttonhole Band. Make 2 more sc in same st/sps.

Work sc around cushion, working through top loops of each st of front and back together, and taking care to also pick up side edge of buttonhole band as necessary. Work 3 sc in each corner 2ch-sp. At end of round join to stsc with invisible join.

FINISHING

Weave in all ends.

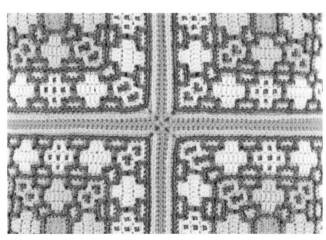

PETUNIA BAG

DESIGNER: ANA MORAIS SOARES

YARN

Rosários4 Damasco (70% cotton, 30% linen), 10-ply (aran), 100g (219yd/200m), in foll shades:
Colour 1: Cream (03); 2 balls
Colour 2: Yellow (33); 2 balls
Colour 3: Blue (35); 2 balls

HOOKS

US size E/4 (3.5mm) hook
US size G/6 (4mm) hook

OTHER TOOLS AND MATERIALS

Approx 19¾ x 29½in (50 x 75cm) cotton lining fabric

GAUGE (TENSION)

A single motif measures approx 7in (18cm) using a US size E/4 (3.5mm) hook.

FINISHED SIZE

Petunia motif with extension measures approx 8¾in (22cm)
Bag measures approx 17¾in (45cm) wide x 9½in (24cm) high

SPECIAL ABBREVIATION

3dc-cl, 3 double crochet cluster worked in same st or sp

SIDES AND BOTTOM

Make five Petunia squares, extending each as foll:

Round 13: Change to colour 2, *(2 dc, 2 ch, 2 dc) in 2ch-sp corner, 3 dc, [1 ch, skip next st, 3dc-cl in next st] 13 times, 1 ch, skip next st, 3 dc; rep from * 3 times, slst in first dc to join. (40 dc, 52 clusters, 56 ch-sp, 4 x 2ch-sp corners)

Fasten off colour 2.

Round 14: Change to colour 1, *(1 sc, 2 ch, 1 sc) in 2ch-sp corner, 5 sc, [1 sc in next ch-sp, FPsc around next 3dc-cl] 13 times, 1 sc in next ch-sp, 5 sc; rep from * 3 times, slst in first sc to join. (104 dc, 52 clusters, 4 x 2ch-sp corners)

Fasten off colour 1.

Round 15: Change to colour 3, *(2 hdc, 2 ch, 2 hdc) in 2ch-sp corner, 39 hdc; rep from * 3 times, slst in first hdc to join. (172 hdc, 4 x 2ch-sp corners)

Fasten off and weave in ends.

Use finished square to cut lining piece 1cm (⅜in) bigger all around than crochet square. Cut four lining pieces 1cm (⅜in) bigger on three sides and 2cm (¾in) bigger on one side for top border. Set aside.

JOINING SQUARES

Hold two squares with WS tog. Using G/6 hook and colour 1, join along one side by working 1 sc in 2ch-sp corner of both squares, 43 sc through sts of both squares, 1 sc in 2ch-sp corner of both squares. Add two more squares in same way to create a box open at bottom and top.

To join bottom square, work with RS of side squares facing you. Join 2ch-sp corner of bottom square to 2ch-sp corner of two side squares and joining seam as foll:

*Work 1 sc in 2ch-sp corner of right square and in 2ch-sp corner of bottom square, 1 sc in last st of joining seam and in 2ch-sp corner of bottom square, 1 sc in 2ch-sp corner of left square and 2ch-sp corner of bottom square, 43 sc through sts of both side and bottom squares; rep from * 3 times, slst in first sc to join.

While working sc in joining seam of two side squares be careful to catch front and back loops.

TOP BORDER

Round 1: With RS facing, using E/4 hook and colour 1, *work 43 sc along side, 1 sc in 2ch-sp corner, 1 sc in vertical joining seam, 1 sc in 2ch-sp corner; rep from * 3 times, slst in first sc to join. (184 sts)

Fasten off colour 1.

Round 2: As Round 1 using colour 2.

Round 3: As Round 1 using colour 1.

Round 4: As Round 1 using colour 3.

Round 5: As Round 1 using colour 1.

Fasten off and weave in ends.

HANDLES

(make 2)

All rows are worked with RS facing. Never turn work.

Using E/4 hook and colour 1, 101 ch.

Row 1: 1 sc in 2nd ch from hook, 1 sc in each st to end. (100 sc)

Fasten off colour 1.

Row 2: Join colour 2, 1 sc in each st to end. (100 sts)

Fasten off colour 2.

Row 3: Join colour 1, 1 sc in base of each ch, in same place where Row 2 sts were placed – not in lower loops of starting ch. (100 sts)

Fasten off colour 1.

Row 4: Join colour 3, 1 sc in every st of Row 3. (100 sts)

Fasten off colour 3.

Edging: Join colour 1, 3 sc in first st of Row 2, 98 sc, 3 sc in last st of Row 2, 1 sc in last st of Row 1, 1 sc in first st of Row 3, 3 sc in first st of Row 4, 98 sc, 3 sc in last st of Row 4, 1 sc in last st of Row 3, 1 sc in first st of Row 1, slst in first sc to join. (212 sts)

Fasten off and weave in ends.

FLOWERS

(make 2 in each of colours 2 and 3)

Using E/4 hook and colour 2 or 3, make a magic ring.

Round 1: 1 ch (does not count as st), 12 sc in ring, slst in first sc to join. Do not cut yarn. (12 sc)

Round 2: *3 ch (counts as 1 dc), 2 dc, 3 ch (counts as 1 dc), slst in next st; rep from * 3 more times, slst to base of first 3-ch to join. (16 dc)

Fasten off, leaving long tail for sewing.

Attach both ends of each handle to same square; handles do not cross over body of bag. Sew flower first to handle and then both to bag to secure handles in place.

LINING

Sew four larger panels together down one side with RS facing and 1cm (⅜in) seam to make a box open at bottom and top. Sew smaller panel into bottom in same way. Insert lining bag inside crochet bag with WS together. Fold over top edge of lining by 2cm (¾in) and hand sew to crochet around top.

POINSETTIA WALL PANEL

DESIGNER: CAITIE MOORE

YARN

Nurturing Fibres Eco-Cotton (100% cotton), light worsted (DK), 50g (136yd/125m), in foll shades:

Colour 1: Sunglow; 1 ball
Colour 2: Persian; 1 ball
Colour 3: Baltic; 1½ balls
Colour 4: Vanilla; 1 ball
Colour 5: Aventurine; 1 ball

HOOK

US size G/6 (4mm) hook

OTHER TOOLS AND MATERIALS

Wooden stick/dowel at least 6¼in (16cm) long
6in (15cm) wide piece of card

GAUGE (TENSION)

A single motif measures approx 5½in (14cm) using a US size G/6 (4mm) hook.

FINISHED SIZE

Wall panel measures approx 25¼in (64cm) long excl tassel x 6in (15cm) wide

NOTES

Join yarn with standing sts unless otherwise indicated. At the end of the rounds cut the yarn, thread in tapestry needle and work an invisible join in the top of the standing stitch.

WALL PANEL

Make three Mandalita squares, using following colour substitutions:

Round 1: Colour 1
Round 2: Colour 2
Round 3: Colour 3
Round 4: Colour 4
Round 5: Colour 5
Round 6: Colour 1
Round 7: Colour 4
Round 8: Colour 5
Round 9: Colour 4
Round 10: Colour 3
Round 11: Colour 2
Round 12: Colour 3

BOTTOM TRIANGLE

(make 1)

Using G/6 hook and colour 3, 24 ch.

Row 1: Skip 1 ch, 1 sc in each ch to end. (23 sts)

Row 2: 1 ch, turn, sc2tog, 19 sc, sc2tog. (21 sts)

Row 3: 1 ch, turn, 1 sc in each st to end. (21 sts)

Row 4: 1 ch, turn, sc2tog, 17 sc, sc2tog. (19 sts)

Row 5: As Row 3. (19 sts)

Row 6: 1 ch, turn, sc2tog, 15 sc, sc2tog. (17 sts)

Row 7: As Row 3. (17 sts)

Row 8: 1 ch, turn, sc2tog, 13 sc, sc2tog. (15 sts)

Row 9: As Row 3, (15 sts)

Row 10: 1 ch, turn, sc2tog, 11 sc, sc2tog. (13 sts)

Row 11: As Row 3. (13 sts)

Row 12: 1 ch, turn, sc2tog, 9 sc, sc2tog. (11 sts)

Row 13: As Row 3. (11 sts)

Row 14: 1 ch, turn, sc2tog, 7 sc, sc2tog. (9 sts)

Row 15: As Row 3. (9 sts)

Row 16: 1 ch, turn, sc2tog, 5 sc, sc2tog. (7 sts)

Row 17: As Row 3. (7 sts)

Row 18: 1 ch, turn, sc2tog, 3 sc, sc2tog. (5 sts)

Row 19: As Row 3. (5 sts)

Row 20: 1 ch, turn, sc2tog, 1 sc, sc2tog. (3 sts)

Row 21: As Row 3. (3 sts)

Row 22: 1 ch, turn, sc2tog, 1 sc. (2 sts)

Row 23: 1 ch, turn, sc2tog. (1 st)

Fasten off and weave in ends.

JOINING SQUARES

Lay out squares in column. With first two squares WS facing, line up sts on one side of outer round. Using G/6 hook and colour 3 and working through both squares, 2 sc in 1ch-sp at corner of squares, skip 1 st, 1 sc in each st across, 2 sc in next corner 1 ch-sp.

Fasten off and weave in ends.

Rep to join 3rd square.

ADD TRIANGLE BASE

Place triangle with long edge aligned with bottom edge of lowest square. With WS facing, using G/6 hook, skip 1ch-sp corner and join colour 3 in next st along, 23 sc, do not work in next 1ch-sp.

Fasten off colour 3.

Join colour 3 with 1 sc in first skipped 1ch-sp, work 23 sc evenly up triangle side, 3 hdc in triangle tip, 23 sc down other triangle side, 1 sc in 1ch-sp (opposite corner). (49 sts)

Fasten off and weave in ends.

HANGING TABS

FIRST HANGING TAB

With RS of top square facing, using G/6 hook join colour 3 in 1 ch-sp (rightmost corner).

Row 1: 4 hdc. (4 sts)

Row 2: 1 ch, turn, 4 hdc. (4 sts)

Rows 3 to 7: As Row 2.

Fasten off, leaving a tail.

SECOND TAB

Skip 6 sts along top and join colour 3 with standing st.

Row 1: 5 hdc. (5 sts)

Row 2: 1 ch, turn, 5 hdc. (5 sts)

Rows 3 to 7: As Row 2.

Fasten off, leaving a tail.

THIRD TAB

With WS facing, join colour 3 to 1ch-sp (leftmost corner).

Row 1: 4 hdc. (4 sts)

Row 2: 1 ch, turn, 4 hdc. (4 sts)

Rows 3 to 7: As Row 2.

Fasten off, leaving a tail.

Fold each tab in half, toward back of work. Use tail to sew each down to form loops.

TASSEL

Cut a piece of card 6in (15cm) wide. Using colour 3, wind around card 20 to 30 times. Cut another 20in (50cm) strand of colour 3 and slide this under all looped yarn strands at one edge of card. Tie tightly and knot twice to secure, then leave ends free at what will be top of tassel. Gently slide strands from card. Cut another 20in (50cm) strand of colour 1 and wrap it three times tightly around folded strands about one third down from top of tassel. Tie three knots at back of tassel to secure. Cut through strand loops at bottom of tassel and then trim to desired length. Using ends at top, sew tassel onto tip of triangle.

FINISHING

Weave in any remaining ends and block wall panel if required. Insert wooden stick/dowel through tabs to hang.

OFFSET SQUARES POT HOLDER

DESIGNER: CAROL IBBETSON

YARN

Lion Brand 24/7 Cotton (100% cotton), worsted (aran), 100g (186yd/170m), in foll shades:
Colour 1: Black (153); 1 ball
Colour 2: Silver (149); 1 ball
Scheepjes Catona (100% mercerised cotton), fingering (4ply), 10g (27yd/25m), in foll shade:
Colour 3: Vivid Blue (146); 1 ball

HOOK

US size E/4 (3.5mm) hook

OTHER TOOLS AND MATERIALS

8 x 8in (20 x 20cm) thin heat-resistant batting (wadding)
2 buttons, ¾in (20mm) diameter (optional)

GAUGE (TENSION)

16.5 sts and 23 rows measure 4 x 4in (10 x 10cm) over single crochet using a US size E/4 (3.5mm) hook.

FINISHED SIZE

8 x 8in (20 x 20cm) after blocking

POT HOLDER

Work two Offset Squares squares, substituting colours as given.

Block and then place together with RS facing outward, and batting between cut slightly smaller than crochet sides.

EDGING AND HANGING LOOP

Work through both squares to join them together all around.

Using E/4 hook, join colour 3 with a slst through both squares in top right corner.

Round 1: 1 ch, 1 sc through both squares in each st to corner, 3 sc in corner, 1 sc evenly along row ends on left side (approx 42 sc), 3 sc in corner, 1 sc through each st on bottom, 3 sc in corner, 1 sc evenly along row ends on right side (approx 42 sc), 2 sc in corner, 25 ch, 1 sc in 2nd ch from hook and in each ch back to start, slst through other end of this flap to create a hanging loop, 1 sc in corner sp, slst through first st to join.

Fasten off and weave in ends.

STRAP

Using E/4 hook and colour 3, and leaving a long tail, 30 ch.

Row 1: 1 sc in 2nd ch from hook and in each ch to end, turn. (29 sts)

Row 2: 1 ch, 1 sc in each st to end, turn.

Rows 3 and 4: Rep Row 2 twice.

Fasten off leaving a long tail.

JOINING STRAP

Place strap diagonally on holder over your hand and pin each end to holder. Also place pins either side of your hand. Use tails to whip stitch around three sides of strap between pins and back stitch across strap to make a sewn square.

FINISHING

Attach one button on each end of the strap for decoration as shown, if desired.

Weave in all ends.

VICTORIANA BATH MAT

DESIGNER: EMMA POTTER

YARN

Drops Paris (100% cotton), worsted (aran), 50g (82yd/75m), in foll shades:

Colour 1: White (16); 7 balls
Colour 2: Black (15); 7 ball

HOOK

US size H/8 (5mm) hook

GAUGE (TENSION)

A single motif measures approx 4in (10cm) using a US size H/8 (5mm) hook.

FINISHED SIZE

Finished bath mat measures approx 23½ x 39½in (60 x 100cm)

NOTES

Squares are joined using join-as-you-go method. First row and first square of any subsequent row joins on one side, all foll squares will join on two sides.

Slip stitch that joins squares comes from underneath, which means removing loop from hook and pulling loop through from back to front.

FIRST SQUARE

Make one Victoriana square.

JOINING SQUARES

Complete next square to end of Round 3.

Round 4: Join colour 2 in any dc immediately after a 5-ch, 1 ch (counts as first sc), 1 sc in each dc to first 5-ch corner sp, [(3 dc, 3 ch, 3 dc) in skipped st below 5-ch, 5 sc] twice (3 sides of next square completed), to join to prev square work 3 dc in skipped st below 5-ch, 3 ch, slst through 3-ch on corner of first square, 1 dc in skipped st below 5-ch, [slst in next st on first square by removing loop from hook and pulling loop through from back to the front, 1 dc in skipped st below 5-ch] twice (first corner joined), [1 sc, slst in next st on first square by removing loop from hook and pulling loop through from back to the front] 5 times (first side joined), 3 dc in skipped st below 5-ch, slst through 3-ch loop on first square, 3 ch (2nd corner joined), slst in beg 1-ch to join round.

Rep to join one square at a time to make first row.

First square in next row will be joined in same way along one edge. When joining subsequent squares on two sides, complete two sides only of next square before working joining instructions.

BORDER

Round 1: Join colour 2 in first sc after a corner, 1 ch (counts as first sc), [*1 sc in each st of tile to one st before join, (1 sc in st before join, 1 sc in join, 1 sc in st after join); rep from * to corner of rug, (1 sc, 3 ch, 1 sc) in rug corner] 4 times, slst in first st to join.

Round 2: 1 ch, *1 sc in each st to rug corner, (1 sc, 2 ch, 1 sc) in rug corner; rep 3 more times, slst in first st to join.

FINISHING

Fasten off and weave in ends.

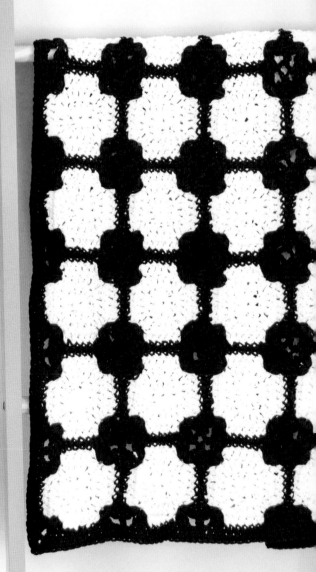

CROCHET TECHNIQUES

This section includes all the stitches and techniques used in the tiles and projects in this book. See How to Use this Book for standard abbreviations and stitch chart symbols.

CHAIN (CH)

Make a loop and pull the yarn through to make the first loop on the hook. *Yarn over and pull up a loop; rep from * to make as many chains as stated.

SLIP STITCH (SLST)

Insert the hook in the stitch, yarn over and pull through both stitch and the loop on the hook.

SINGLE CROCHET (SC)

Insert the hook in the stitch, yarn over and pull through the stitch (2 loops on the hook) (1). Yarn over and pull through both loops on the hook (2).

MAGIC RING

With the yarn tail hanging down, make a loop and hold it between two fingers (3). Insert the hook in the loop and pull the yarn through (4), make a chain to secure, then make stitches into the loop (5). When you have finished pull the tail to tighten the loop. Slip stitch in the first stitch to join.

HALF DOUBLE CROCHET (HDC)

Yarn over and insert the hook in the stitch (6). Yarn over and pull up a loop (3 loops on the hook). Yarn over and pull through all 3 loops (7).

DOUBLE CROCHET (DC)

Yarn over and insert the hook in the stitch (8). Yarn over and pull through the stitch (3 loops on the hook) (9). Yarn over and pull through the first 2 loops on the hook (2 loops left on the hook). Yarn over and pull through the last 2 loops.

TREBLE (TR)

Yarn over twice and insert the hook in the stitch (10). Yarn over and pull through the stitch. Yarn over and pull through the first 2 loops on the hook (3 loops left on the hook) (11). Yarn over and pull through the first 2 loops on the hook (2 loops left on the hook). Yarn over again and pull through the remaining loops.

DOUBLE TREBLE (DTR)

Work as treble crochet, but yarn over 3 times before inserting it in the stitch (12). Yarn over and pull through 2 loops each time, until you have 1 loop left on your hook.

SINGLE CROCHET 2 STITCHES TOGETHER (SC2TOG)

Insert the hook in the first stitch, yarn over and pull a loop through the stitch (2 loops on the hook) (13). Insert the hook in the second stitch, yarn over and pull a loop through the stitch (3 loops on the hook) (14). Yarn over and pull through all 3 loops on the hook.

SINGLE CROCHET 3 STITCHES TOGETHER (SC3TOG)

Follow the instructions for sc2tog until there are 3 loops on the hook (14), insert the hook in the third stitch, yarn over and pull a loop through the stitch (4 loops on the hook). Yarn over and pull through all 4 loops on the hook.

DOUBLE CROCHET 2 STITCHES TOGETHER (DC2TOG)

Yarn over and insert the hook in the first stitch. Yarn over and pull a loop through the stitch (3 loops on the hook) (15). Yarn over and pull through the first 2 loops on the hook (2 loops on the hook) (16). Yarn over and insert the hook in the second stitch). Yarn over and pull through the stitch (4 loops on the hook). Yarn over and pull through the first 2 loops on the hook (3 loops on the hook) (17). Yarn over and pull through all 3 loops on the hook (18).

DOUBLE CROCHET 3 STITCHES TOGETHER (DC3TOG)

Follow the instructions for dc2tog until the final yarn over (17), yarn over and insert the hook in the third stitch, yarn over and pull a loop through the stitch (5 loops on the hook), yarn over and pull through the first 2 loops on the hook (4 loops on the hook), yarn over and pull through all loops on the hook.

DOUBLE CROCHET 4 STITCHES TOGETHER (DC4TOG)

Follow the instructions for dc2tog until the final yarn over (17), *yarn over and insert the hook in the third stitch, yarn over and pull a loop through the stitch (5 loops on the hook), yarn over and pull through the first two loops on the hook (4 loops on hook); rep from * in the fourth stitch (5 loops on hook), yarn over and pull through all loops on the hook.

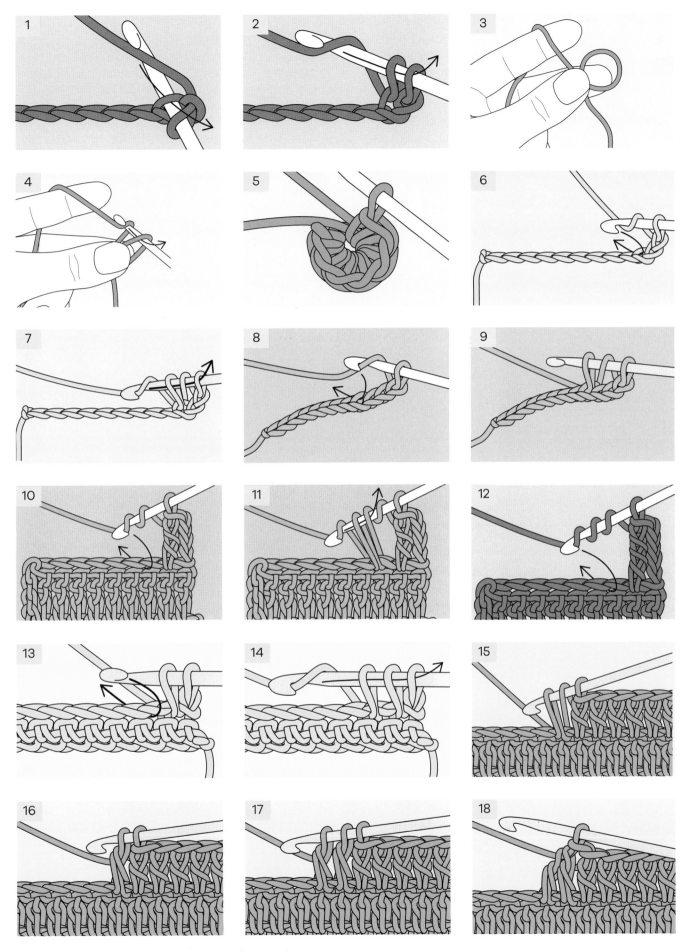

INVISIBLE JOIN

This gives a smooth even edge. Cut the yarn and pull the yarn tail through the last stitch. Thread the yarn tail onto a yarn needle, insert the needle, from front to back, in the next stitch. Now insert the needle back in the same stitch that the yarn tail is coming out of, but in the back loop only, and pull gently (1). Weave the tail end in the wrong side of the fabric and cut the excess (2).

GAUGE (TENSION)

This is not critical on these blocks, but the patterns do give the ideal size of the tile. If your tiles are working up smaller, try a larger size hook than stated. If larger, try a smaller hook.

FRONT LOOP ONLY (FLO)

The front loop of a stitch is the loop closest to you. If the pattern says to work in FLO work your stitches in just this front loop.

BACK LOOP ONLY (BLO)

The back loop is the loop furthest away from you. If the pattern says to work in BLO work your stitches in just this back loop.

FRONT POST STITCHES (FP)

Work the stated stitch as normal, but insert the hook from front to back to front around the post of the stitch instead of in it. The illustrations show FPsc: insert the hook from front to back to front around the post of the stitch (3). Yarn over and pull up a loop, yarn over and pull through 2 loops on the hook (4).

BACK POST STITCHES (BP)

Work the stated stitch as normal, but insert the hook from back to front to back around the post of the stitch instead of in it. The illustrations show BPsc: insert the hook from back to front to back around the post of the stitch (5). Yarn over and pull up a loop, yarn over and pull through 2 loops on the hook (6).

POPCORN (PC)

A popcorn consists of complete stitches worked in the same stitch – so for a 3dc-PC work 3 dc and for a 4dc-PC work 4 dc – and then joined at the top. The illustrations show a 5dc-PC: work 5dc in the stitch (7), remove the hook from the last stitch and insert it, from front to back, in the top of the first stitch of the popcorn, then insert the hook back in the loop from the last stitch again (8), yarn over, pull through both loops on the hook. Some popcorns finish with a chain to secure.

PICOT

Make 3 chain (or the number stated), insert the hook from right to left under the front loop and bottom vertical bar of the chain (9), yarn over and pull through all loops on the hook (10).

CLUSTER (CL)

A cluster is made by partly working a number of stitches in the same stitch or chain space, or sometimes over a few stitches, leaving the last yarn over of each stitch on the hook. Then yarn over hook and pull through all loops. It's often worked in a similar way to a bobble, but the cluster sits flat. The illustrations show a 3dc-cl: yarn over hook, *insert the hook in the stitch or space indicated (11), yarn over, pull up a loop, yarn over, pull through the first 2 loops on the hook; rep from * twice more (4 loops on the hook), yarn over hook and pull through all loops on the hook (12).

PUFF STITCH

This is a series of half double crochet stitches worked in one stitch, similar to a bobble but softer and less defined. The illustrations show a 3hdc-puff st: yarn over and insert the hook in the stitch, yarn over and pull up a long loop to the height of the current round or row (13), [yarn over, insert hook in the same stitch, yarn over and pull up a long loop] twice more (14), yarn over and pull through all 7 loops on the hook (15), yarn over and pull through to close the puff. For a 4hdc-puff st work the section in square brackets 3 times then pull through 9 loops on the hook.

BOBBLE

A bobble is made by partly working a number of stitches in one stitch, leaving the last yarn over of each stitch on the hook. Then yarn over and pull through all loops to form a well-defined bump on the surface. The illustrations show a 5dc-bobble: *yarn over, insert the hook in the stitch, yarn over and pull up a loop, yarn over and pull through the first 2 loops on the hook (16); rep from * 4 more times in the same stitch (6 loops on the hook) (17). Yarn over and pull through all 6 loops on the hook (18).

V STITCH (V-ST)

Work (1 dc, 2 ch, 1 dc) all into the same stitch. Can also be worked with 3 ch between the two dc.

SPIKE STITCH

Work the stated stitch as normal, but into the next stitch the number of rows or rounds below as given in the pattern, pulling up the loops to the height of the working row or round to complete the stitch.

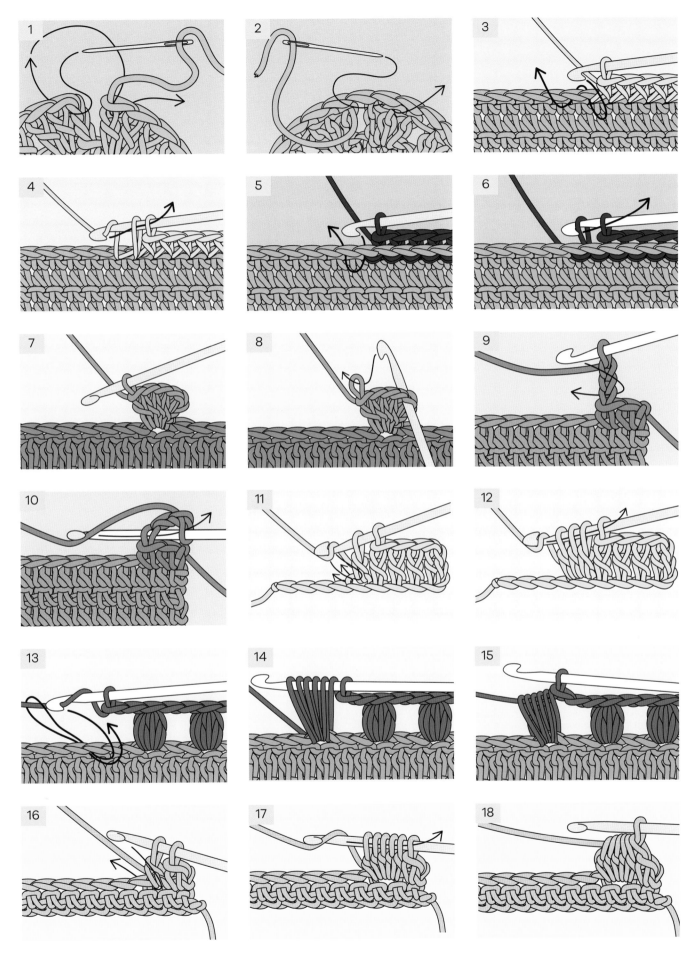

MOSAIC CROCHET OVERLAY METHOD (FLMDC)

With mosaic crochet there are no colour changes within rows/rounds; colours are changed every two rows/rounds. In this version of the technique, the double crochet stitches are worked in the FLO of the corresponding BLO stitch of the same colour 2 rows or rounds below. First make the initial rounds or rows, working in the BLO where instructed. To make the first FLMdc the 2 turquoise stitches are double crochet worked in the FLO of the stitches directly below in a row that's the same colour (1). In the next row, two red stitches are double crochet worked FLO in the BLO stitches 2 rows below, and so on (2). After a few rows or rounds the pattern will be clearer (3). The chart has an X to show which stitches are worked as a FLMdc.

MOSAIC CROCHET INSET METHOD (MDC)

Again there are no colour changes within rows/rounds; colours are changed every two rows/rounds. First make the initial rounds or rows as instructed, always working in both loops of the stitch as normal. In this version of the technique, stitches are skipped in two rows or rounds and chain is worked over them (4 and 5). The double crochet stitches are then worked in front of the chain spaces and into the skipped stitch in the same colour two rounds or rows below (6). After a few rounds the pattern will become clear (7). The chart has an X to show which stitches are worked as a mdc.

TAPESTRY CROCHET

Tapestry crochet is usually worked following a chart, which gives the colour changes. More than one colour is worked in each row or round, with unused yarns carried along and crocheted over to hide them, so they are ready to use when needed (8). The method of making a colour change is the same in a round or row. Begin the colour change in the prev stitch: in the old colour, make the stitch as usual but, before the final yarn over, bring the old colour to the front (to complete the stitch on the reverse side), then pick up and pull through a loop of the new colour (9). Pass the old colour to the back and continue in the new colour, crocheting over the old colour as you go (10).

INTARSIA CROCHET

Intarsia is similar in appearance to tapestry crochet on the right side, but unused colours are dropped at the back and then picked back up on the return row, creating a definite right and wrong side with short floats of yarn between stitches on the back. Intarsia crochet is also usually worked following a chart, which gives the colour changes. As with most colour changes, the switch to a new colour is made on the final yarn over of the stitch directly before (11 and 12). When a colour change is needed on the wrong side, bring the old colour to the front (13) to keep all the floats and yarn ends on the wrong side.

JOIN-AS-YOU-GO

With this technique tiles are joined as they are made, which saves time at the end. The general technique is shown on a granny square, but can be adjusted for any square. First, complete one tile (Square 1) and have the next tile (Square 2) complete up to the two last sides of the final round. Crochet along the third edge and make the corner cluster, then 1 chain (14). Slip stitch in the corner of Square 1 (15) and complete the corner cluster of Square 2 (16), then *slip stitch in the next space between clusters of Square 1. Make the next cluster in Square 2; then rep from * across the side to the corner of Square 2, make the first cluster here, slip stitch in Square 1 as before and complete the corner of Square 2 (17). Continue joining one square at a time. To begin the next row, join the first square as before along one side. Make the next square with one side completed before joining exactly as before, but along two sides (18). The first square of any row only joins on one side. All following squares join on two sides.

BLOCKING

Pin the tile to size using rust-proof pins and steam lightly with an iron. Do not touch the work with the iron but hover over it giving blasts of steam. Leave to dry completely before removing the pins.

SINGLE CROCHET SEAM

Single crochet can be used to create a decorative, sturdy seam on the right side when pieces are placed wrong sides together. Working with right sides together for seaming will make the stitches less obvious. For a single crochet seam, begin at the right-hand edge and join pairs of stitches together through both loops, working single crochet in the usual way (see Single Crochet).

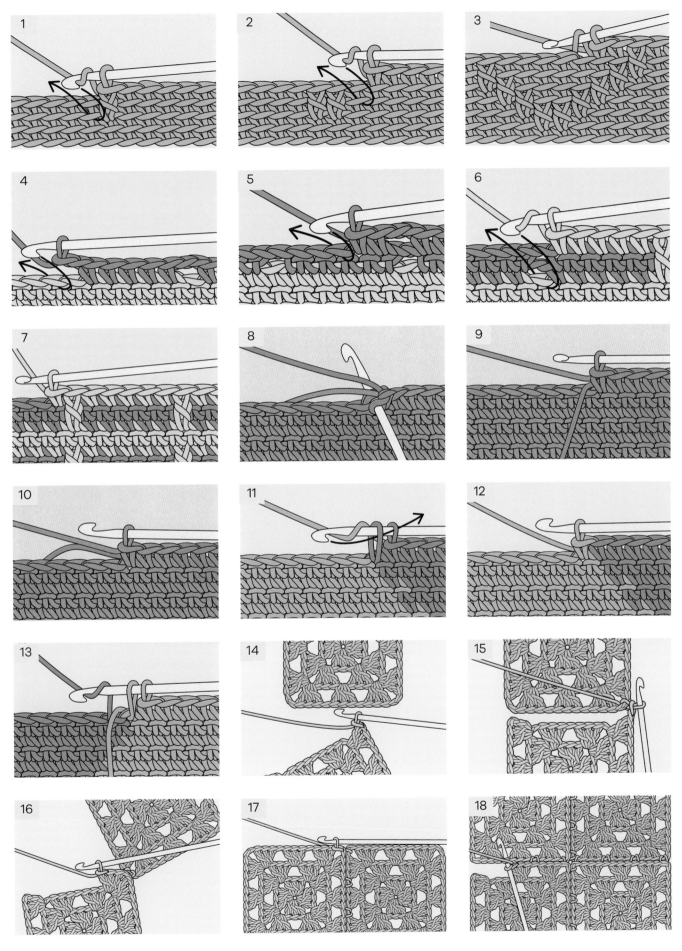

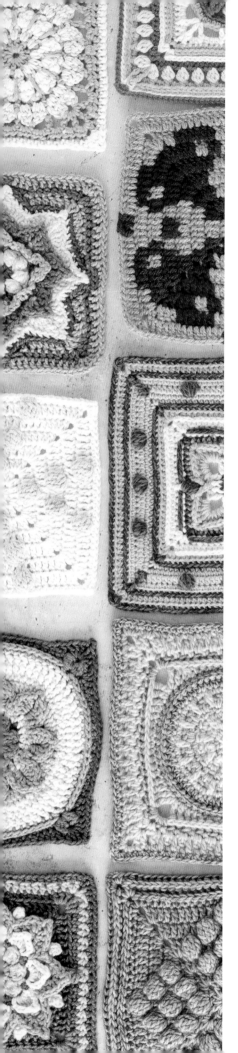

THE DESIGNERS

The publisher would like to thank all of the designers whose patterns and projects appear in this book.

CAITIE MOORE
Instagram: @thoresbycottage
Website: thoresbycottage.com

JULIE YEAGER
Instagram: @julieanny_crochet
Website: julieyeagerdesigns.com

CAROL IBBETSON
Instagram: @coolwooldesign
Website: www.coolwool.net

MEGHAN BALLMER
Instagram: @meghanmakesdo
Website: meghanmakesdo.com

LYNNE ROWE
Instagram: @the_woolnest
Website: knitcrochetcreate.com

JOHANNA LINDAHL
Instagram: @mijocrochet
Website: mijocrochet.se

STEFFI GLAVES
Instagram: @steffi_glaves
Website: steffiglaves.co.uk

ROSINA PLANE
Instagram: @rosinaplane
Website: rosinaplane.com

ANA MORAIS SOARES
Instagram: @oneskeinoflove
Website: oneskeinoflove.com

HATTIE RISDALE
Instagram: @petalshed
Website: thepetalshed.uk

EMMA POTTER
Instagram: @potterandbloom
Website: potterandbloom.com

ANNA NIKIPIROWICZ
Instagram: @annanikipirowicz
Website: moochka.co.uk

RACHELE CARMONA
Instagram: @cypresstextiles
Website: cypresstextiles.net

CATHERINE NORONHA
Instagram: @catherinecrochets
Website: catherinecrochets.com

SARAH SHRIMPTON
Instagram: @annabooshouse
Website: annabooshouse.blogspot.com

INDEX

abbreviations 4
Abstract Daisy 115–16
All of a Cluster 26
Annie 84–5, 160–1
Aphrodite 30
Art Deco Sunset 116–17
Artemis 41
Athena 139–40
Autumn Glow 11–12

Baby Wheels 36–7, 154–5
back loop only 5, 170
back post stitches 5, 170
bag, Petunia 162–3
Ballmer, Meghan 28, 134, 174
bath mat, Victoriana 167
Berry Hearts 132–3
blankets 154–5, 158–9
blocking 172
Blooming Pinwheel 34–5
Blue Bobbles 67
Blue Hygge 24–5
Bobble Burst 65–6
bobble stitch 5, 170

Calypso 37–8
Carmona, Rachele 18, 19, 26, 40, 67, 75, 141, 142, 150, 174
Catalina 53–4
chain stitch 5, 168
charts, using 4, 5
Circe 136–7
Classical Ogee 150–1
Clematis 145
cluster 5, 170
Cobblestone 50–1
Compass Rose 39–40
Concentric Zigzags 96–7
Country Posy 82–3
Crescent Quarter 75–6
Criss-Cross 18
Crystal Ripple 142
cushions 156–7, 160–1

Daisy Girl 31–2
decreasing 5, 168
Deep Space 113–14
Delfina's Square 32–3
Delft Blues 70–1

Dig for Victory 9–10
double crochet stitches 5, 168

Echo 59
equipment 4
Estrella 52–3

Floral Burst 143
Floral Hexagon 141
Flower Power 149–50
Frasera 80–1
front loop only 5, 170
front post stitches 5, 170

gauge 170
Glaves, Steffi 20, 117–33, 135, 174
Grecian 110
Grow Your Garden 63–5

half double crochet 5, 168
Hand Painted 86–8, 156–7
Hebe 14–15, 158–9
Hera 8
Hestia 49–50

Ibbetson, Carol 96–109, 166, 174
Indian Terracotta 77
intarsia crochet 172
invisible join 170
Iridescent 112–13
Iris 137–8

joining squares 155, 159, 167, 172

Kings Cross 120–1

Laceflower 40
Lindahl, Johanna 13, 78, 174
Lotus Blossom 60–1
Love in a Mist 74–5

magic ring 168
Mandalita 55–6, 164–5
Marine Flower 147–8
Medusa 29
Mind the Gap 20

Mindful Mandala 72–3
Moore, Catie 21–5, 55–8, 60, 68–74, 80–3, 164, 174
Morais Soares, Ana 27, 32–7, 43, 61–5, 86–92, 154–7, 163, 174
Moroccan Star 21–3
mosaic crochet technique 172

Nikipirowicz, Anna 9, 11, 50, 65, 147–8, 174
Noronha, Catherine 111–14, 143–5, 174
Northern and Central Lines 123–4

Octaganol Flower 146
Offset Squares 108–9, 166
On a Slant 102–4
Orange Twist 17

Pandora 42–3
Paolozzi 135–6
Pebble Splash 68–9
Persephone 47–8
Petunia 27–8, 162–3
picot 5, 170
Picot Fan 28
Plane, Rosina 64, 93, 160, 174
Playing With Cubes 91–3
Point to Point 19
Popcorn Fantasy 78–9
Popcorn Roundel 148–9
popcorn stitch 5, 170
Port Drops 125–6
Porto Rooftops 124–5
Porto Train Station 127–8
pot holder, Offset Squares 166
Potter, Emma 10, 12, 77, 140, 167, 174
Praça de Ribeira 1 128–9
Praça de Ribeira 2 129–30
puff stitch 5, 170

Rainbows and Rays 15–16
Risdale, Hattie 8, 14, 29–30, 37, 41–2, 47–50, 59, 136–9, 158, 174
Rosemary Clusters 46–7

Rowe, Lynne 17, 115–17, 146, 174
Russell Square 121–2

Samuel 93–5, 160–1
Sao Bento 131–2
Secret Lotus 13–14
Shining Star 100–1
Shrimpton, Sarah 21, 110, 174
single crochet 5, 168, 172
slip stitch 5, 168
Snowflake Sweets 88–90
South-Western Shells 21
spike stitch 5, 170
Spring Garden 43–4
Starburst 144
stitches 4, 5, 168–71
Susana 45–6
symbols 5

Talavera 1 10
Talavera 2 140
tapestry crochet 172
tassels 157, 165
techniques 168–73
tension 170
terminology, US/UK 4
Tessellation 58
Tiled Bricks 104–5
Tottenham Court Road 117–19
treble crochet stitches 5, 168
Tunnel Vision 106–7

V stitch 5, 170
Victoriana 12, 167

Wagon Wheel 46–7
wall panel, Poinsettia 164–5
When Flowers Go Blue 61–3
White and Yellow 134
Wildflower 111–12

Yeager, Julie 15, 31, 39, 45–7, 52–4, 174

Zigzag Swirls 98–9

ISBN-13: 9781446308950 paperback
ISBN-13: 9781446381205 EPUB
ISBN-13: 9781446381199 PDF

This book has been printed on paper from approved suppliers
and made from pulp from sustainable sources.

FSC
www.fsc.org
MIX
Paper from
responsible sources
FSC® C023114

Printed in the UK by Page Bros for:
David and Charles, Ltd
Suite A, Tourism House, Pynes Hill, Exeter, EX2 5WS

10 9 8 7 6 5 4 3 2 1

Senior Commissioning Editor: Sarah Callard
Managing Editor: Jeni Chown
Editor: Jessica Cropper
Project Editor: Marie Clayton
Head of Design: Sam Staddon
Designer: Blanche Williams
Pre-press Designer: Ali Stark
Illustrations: Kuo Kang Chen
Photography: Jason Jenkins
Production Manager: Beverley Richardson

David and Charles publishes high-quality books on
a wide range of subjects. For more information visit
www.davidandcharles.com.

Share your makes with us on social media using #dandcbooks
and follow us on Facebook and Instagram by searching
for @dandcbooks.

Layout of the digital edition of this book may vary depending
on reader hardware and display settings.